ROBERT BOOTH FOWLER is professor of political science at the University of Wisconsin. He is the author of *A New Engagement: Evangelical Political Thought, 1966–1976*, and *Believing Skeptics: American Political Intellectuals, 1945–1964*.

CARRIE CATT

FEMINIST POLITICIAN

Courtesy of the Schlesinger Library, Radcliffe College

CARRIE CATT
FEMINIST POLITICIAN

Robert Booth Fowler

NORTHEASTERN UNIVERSITY PRESS   Boston

Designed by Catherine Dorin

Northeastern University Press

Copyright © 1986 by R. B. Fowler

Library of Congress Cataloging in Publication Data
Fowler, Robert Booth, 1940–
    Carrie Catt : feminist politician.

    Bibliography: p.
    Includes index.
    1. Catt, Carrie Chapman, 1859–1947. 2. Women in politics — United States — Biography. 3. Suffragettes — United States. 4. League of Women Voters (U.S.).
I. Title.
HQ1413.C3F69   1986   324.6′23′0924 [B]   85–21677
ISBN 0–930350–86–3 (alk. paper)
ISBN 1–55553–005–2 (pbk.)

Composed in Baskerville by Eastern Typesetting Company, South Windsor, Connecticut. Printed and bound by Murray Printing Company, Westford, Massachusetts. The paper is Glatfelter Offset, an acid-free sheet.

MANUFACTURED IN THE UNITED STATES OF AMERICA
91   90   89   88   87   86   5   4   3   2   1

for Betsy Booth Fowler
(1907–1976)

Contents

Illustrations

Preface

I first learned about Carrie Chapman Catt (1859–1947) from my mother when I was a child in the 1950s. Catt was a heroine to my mother because she had founded the League of Women Voters and fought for woman suffrage. I did not hear much about Catt again, certainly not in school nor even as I studied and then did research on American political thought well into the 1970s. Even now with the renewed feminist movement Carrie Chapman Catt has attracted scant attention, given her enormous prominence in her time as a self-declared feminist, as president of the National American Woman Suffrage Association in the years when the Anthony amendment campaign was successful (1915–1920), and as creator of the League of Women Voters. This book undertakes to restore to Carrie Catt her central role in the suffragist movement and in the foundation of the League of Women Voters.

This is not in a conventional sense a biography of Carrie Catt. I did not approach Catt with the intention of offering another life of a "notable woman." The first three chapters do report her life, both public and private, but they are basically a foundation for the larger purposes of my study. I am primarily interested in Carrie Catt as a political leader and as a political visionary. As the leader of the suffrage forces, Catt was acknowledged to be a great politician by friend and foe alike. In fact, she was one of the most able politicians in American history in spite of her distinctly ambivalent attitude towards politics and politicians. Catt was nonetheless proud of her skills and her accomplishments as a political leader — and she was sure they contained permanent lessons for feminists. In particular, I am interested in exploring how Catt built her potent suffragist machine (for that was what she created): her organizational theory and practice, her ideas about leadership and her strategic thinking.

At the same time, I would like to examine Carrie Catt's political ideas and her vision for women at whose behest she believed she exercised her political talents. In the process, I intend to show that Catt ultimately sought to encourage the growth of a society in which women (and men) were united as a community of free, equal, and dignified persons, a society in which politics as she knew it (and practiced it) would be no more. It was this vision that influenced her throughout her career. It was for this dream that she favored the enfranchisement of women. And it was with this goal in mind that she established the League of Women Voters.

The result is, I trust, a rich portrait of Carrie Catt, one that I think she would recognize, though not wholly appreciate.

This brings me to the challenges of studying Carrie Catt as a feminist politician. Biography in some sense or not, this book had to explore Catt as a public and a private person as well as politician and feminist. But Catt did not want any of these projects done. Not that she was here, of course, to prevent my work, but her attitude had a direct effect on the research I undertook.

In the 1920s when Catt realized that her friend, Mary G. Peck, proposed to write a biography of her, she objected at once: "We will have no biography, Mary. Let it be said that there was one suffragist who had not discovered herself to be a hero."[1] Earlier she told Peck she wanted no such study and "whoever attempts it while I'm here, will try it over my dead body, and whoever tries it after I'm gone will be haunted by a ghost."[2]

Some of Catt's coolness towards study of her came from personal modesty. Her modesty was surely unusual in a suffrage movement suffused with an abundance of strong-willed and immodest leaders, including Elizabeth Cady Stanton, Anna Howard Shaw, and Alice Paul, who were often eager to tell their life stories. But however unusual Catt's stance was, it was real, if not entirely without limits. She made sure that publications of the National American Woman Suffrage Association did not turn into vehicles for her celebration. She was severely critical of her friends and followers who made the same error: "I do wish you would stop calling me 'great.' I am the commonest old toad the Lord ever made. . . . You just try to arouse my vanity";[3] and she insisted that her story was slight.[4]

Another reason for Catt's lack of enthusiasm for such a study derived from her evolutionary faith, a faith that looked to the future and led Catt to acknowledge her lack of an appreciation for the past. Still another reason came from her reluctance to share her life with others except grudgingly and at her discretion. This strong urge towards privacy is hardly unusual and certainly was not in Catt's Victorian era. Its consequences, however, were real. There are no family letters of Catt's, nor any letters between Catt and her husbands, though many were written. Similarly, there are only a relative few of the vast number of letters Mary Peck, Catt's intimate, sent to Catt. The reason in every case is the same: Catt burned them, apparently to protect her privacy.

It is thus no surprise that Catt did not write an autobiography. She did cooperate with considerable reluctance when one biography of her was written in the early 1940s, though I suspect the reason was that she could count on controlling what it would say — and what it would not.

On the other hand, Catt's attitude towards publishing versions of the suffrage struggle, which necessarily had to include the public Catt, was always more sympathetic. She published her own account with Nettie R. Shuler in 1923 (*Woman Suffrage and Politics: The Inner Story of the Suffrage Movement*), which remains of interest today. By the 1930s and especially the 1940s, Catt increasingly claimed that the significance and the lessons of the women's enfranchisement struggle were being lost to American women. She agreed with Alice Stone Blackwell that interest in the woman suffrage struggle "had so entirely died out,"[5] and she undoubtedly knew the larger meaning of the fact that Blackwell's book on her mother, Lucy Stone, a pioneer for women's rights, sold almost no copies.[6]

Thus, in her later life, eager that progress for women be honored, Catt encouraged people who sought to write about the suffrage movement. She granted it was "only an episode" in women's evolutionary progress,[7] but it was a glorious episode. Modern women took the gains made for granted — "no one thinks [it] has been done by anyone at all"[8] — which was dangerous. Except for *Victory: How Women Won It, 1840–1940*, a joint publication by a number of old suffragists, which an aging Catt oversaw, there was little activity in the direction Catt hoped for. But her mood of concern eventually led her to stop her own policy of gradually destroying her history.

Edna Stantial, the archivist of the N.A.W.S.A., played a major role here, as did others, in obtaining Catt's support for transmitting the Blackwell papers to the Library of Congress and then in convincing Catt to permit her papers to go there upon her death.[9] Catt never did organize her papers. She was just too old for that by the middle 1940s, and the Catt papers, despite the energetic efforts of others, still have numerous fragments of speeches and letters whose origins and dates are permanently lost.

None of this meant that Catt was suddenly convinced she was an important subject, though she was more willing to cooperate with researchers in a modest fashion.[10] Catt wanted the broader story told, and she accepted that she could no longer be treated as hardly part of it. Still, her determination to present only the public Catt affected what she saved and what she burned.

Though Catt's attitude successfully closed off certain avenues for the researcher, even had she continued till death to be opposed to preserving her papers, she would have been defeated. The fact is that, while not all Catt wrote or said in public remains, there is an enormous amount of primary material by and about Carrie Catt. It constitutes both a researcher's dream and a nightmare. Catt was a public figure and much of what she said was in the public record. Moreover, although she may have lacked a sense of history, her associates did not. Throughout her activist life, associates saved her letters in particular, convinced they would be important some day. They were right. For in order to understand Catt's basic values, her private opinions, and her network of relations with other women, which were so important both in her personal and her political life, the several thousand letters from and to Catt are crucial.

While Catt's papers at times seemed to be scattered everywhere, the situation did not turn out to be quite that way. Over the space of the three years that I pursued the research for this book, I drew on three main collections of primary materials, which are close to exhaustive. The first was the collection at the Library of Congress. The Catt collection there is excellent, especially on her later years, and it includes numerous speeches and publications by Catt as well as many letters — the most important of which are letters to Mary G. Peck. The Library of Congress also has the Alice Stone Blackwell papers, which provided some insight on Catt from a peer, and the vast and varied collection on the National American Woman Suffrage Association. In the latter I found a number of more or less hidden treasures, including some of Mary G. Peck's love letters to Catt, as well as much information on the operations of the N.A.W.S.A. under Catt. I read these on microfilm. Then there are the incomparable collections at the Schlesinger Library at Radcliffe College and at the Sophia Smith Library at Smith College. I traveled to both and experienced highly professional assistance as I explored their almost limitless resources.

It is hard to single out particular sources since the Schlesinger Library offers so much, but it was especially helpful in its Maud Wood Park and Anna Howard Shaw materials. The Sophia Smith Library was extremely valuable not only in its letters, which contained surprisingly little duplication with my other sources, but also in its considerable number of Catt speeches and clippings, and in its "Suffrage: U.S." collection, which has a wealth of information on the N.A.W.S.A. in general *and* files on the suffrage movement state-by-state. All of these collections brought on exhaustion in the sheer volume of what they offered, but they were also a joy because folder by folder they inexorably illuminated Catt and her work.

While this book is largely written from primary materials, there are, of course, other sources on Catt. Two earlier efforts to study Catt's speeches by Lola Carolyn Walker and Ima Clevenger were helpful.[11] Also essential was Mary G. Peck's *Carrie Chapman Catt*, the only full-length study of Catt. It is richly detailed and has the advantage of being written by a person who was very close to Catt, but also that disadvantage, which Peck knew herself: "The most difficult thing in the world is to write the life of a person who has been intimately associated with the writer, and the greater the subject is, the harder it is to be impersonal."[12] Ironically, Peck succeeded too well in being impersonal, avoiding Catt's private life, which cannot be done even in an avowedly public biography. Moreover, Peck idealized Catt as a "great person" and was more concerned with explaining Catt's path to greatness and life of greatness than in seriously analyzing, much less probing, her life and work. Nonetheless, it remains an important source, not least because it was written in close collaboration with Catt and thus serves as a sort of official biography.

A second major challenge in studying Carrie Catt was to pursue my goals with a sense of her historical setting. A serious difficulty with what Gerda Lerner has called the "notable woman" approach is that it has often treated its subject in isolation from her times.[13] Because her thought and her politics can be reasonably understood in no other way, a historical context is essential to any portrait of Catt.

This led me in several directions. One was to an appreciation of the conflict in Catt's time among activist women over what to do about women's estate. Of some of the issues Catt was scarcely aware and they did not play an important role in her story. This was particularly true of opinion within the worlds of working class and socialist women. A great many working class women, and not a few of their self-appointed voices, were skeptical of the importance of suffrage (Mother Jones, for example) and sometimes even of feminism, preferring to stress the value of trade unions, socialism, or elevation into the middle classes as better routes for improving the lot of women. Others stressed feminism, including suffrage for women, but joined with all self-declared radicals in faulting the Catt-directed effort as unacceptably middle class and disappointingly averse to striking at the economic roots of women's (and men's) "oppression."[14]

On the other hand, Catt was somewhat aware of the radicals, as they saw themselves, within feminism, especially the so-called Greenwich Village radicals.[15] And she dealt almost daily in the 1915–1920 period with the radicals within the suffrage movement. Alice Paul, Lucy Burns, and what eventually became the Woman's Party could hardly be ignored. They were vigorous and unrelenting in pursuit of their more radical strategy. Catt knew this world and its leading personalities well and she fought a well publicized war against them in the last years of the crusade, trying to eliminate their influence among suffragist women while undertaking to convince the public that most suffragists were not like them. This struggle was a major arena of conflict in the years from 1915 to 1920 (and thereafter). Indeed, the struggle over woman's suffrage — its value, its importance, and the means to achieve it — is a chapter in the diversity among women that is an integral feature of their history. Because it affected so much of what Catt said and did I consider it in chapter 9.

Less crucial was Catt's uneasy relation to the Prohibition movement. Women played a major role in temperance efforts, as such books as Ruth Bordin's *Woman and Temperance* and Barbara Leslie Epstein's *The Politics of Domesticity: Women, Evangelism, and Temperance in Nineteenth-Century America* make clear.[16] But while Catt supported temperance, she insisted that woman suffrage be kept strictly separate from Prohibition (and every other cause). In part this was because Catt judged that her crusade needed as few enemies as possible. But she also disagreed with women temperance advocates who by the twentieth century were in her opinion conservatives on the woman question. For Catt the ultimate answer for women was not defeat of alcohol but transformation of women into citizens of dignity and independence equal to men's.

Another side of the conflict among women in Catt's era was, of course, the determined opposition that woman suffrage faced from organized women antisuffragists. Led by such active figures as Mrs. James Wadsworth and articulated through such periodicals as the *Remonstrance, Woman's Protest,* and *Woman Patriot* as well as numerous books and pamphlets, antisuffragism loomed large in the years before 1920.[17] This opposition was a serious matter and a good deal of Catt's argument and strategy was fashioned with it in mind.

I found the best procedure was to read in primary sources, which I have drawn upon and used extensively in this book. But there are also several able secondary treatments of antisuffragism, especially Jane Jerome Camhi's dissertation, "Women Against Women: American Anti-Suffragism 1880–1920" and Aileen Kraditor's *The Ideas of the Woman Suffrage Movement, 1890–1920*.[18]

The Progressive movement was another important element in Catt's development as a suffragist leader. Throughout this study the connections between Catt and Progressivism receive attention, as they must, though exactly what "Progressivism" implies from the perspective of modern scholarship — if it means anything at all — is murky to say the least. As the monographs have poured forth on Progressive thought and action in almost infinite numbers, predictable skepticism about whether Progressives agreed on anything — even the name — has grown. Indeed, such a view has become fashionable. Contemporary books, such as Robert Crunden's able *Ministers of Reform: The Progressives' Achievement in American Civilization: 1889–1920,* take for granted that "Progressives shared no platform, nor were they members of a single movement."[19] Grand interpretations such as Vernon Louis Parrington's *Main Currents in American Thought,* Eric Goldman's *Rendezvous with Destiny,* or Richard Hofstadter's *Age of Reform: From Bryan to F.D.R.* are distinctly suspect in many interpretive circles. They seem too sweeping in their respective visions of the Progressive Era and too sure of their grasp of a world whose diversity and complexity they systematically underrated.[20]

Yet even a skeptic such as Crunden acknowledges that Progressivism is not a completely empty concept when he concedes of the Progressives: "In general they shared moral values and agreed that America needed a spiritual reformation. . . ."[21] This fact does not deny that there were intense disagreements, and not just about policies or even priorities. But threads of unity were there.

Progressives were, after all, agreed on the need for reform in the United States and saw themselves as actors urgently called to such a mission. In this sense it is wrong to claim the Progressives were mainly conservatives, which is the message of James Weinstein in *The Corporate Ideal in the Liberal State: 1900–1918* and others who share this view.[22] It is equally wrong to confuse the Progressives with genuine radicals, out to reorder the American political, economic, or social order in a fundamental sense, a judgment now rarely made. The better approach is to see Progressives on the whole, as Catt should be seen, as conscious reformers who differed in their concerns but held a common desire for changes in American life and institutions, which they felt would benefit both the individual and the common good.

Neither the view that Progressives were mainly concerned with defensive social control or the view that they were serious, forward-looking reformers quite catches all of the complex truth. This is not to say that the truth lies somewhere in between. It is more accurate to say that there is a good deal of insight in both views. Progressives undoubtedly were reformers, but very often the reforms that Progressives sought had an element of social control in them, always more than middle-class reformers such as Carrie Catt would acknowledge.[23] But this cannot override the fact that the desire for change was a major current in the Progressive world. Progressives were not radicals, in general, but they were not merely social-control conservatives either. In Catt the impulse of social control was real, but it did not travel alone. It was accompanied by a spirit of adventure and an eagerness to enter what she thought was a new and better world.[24]

One characteristic of the reform mood of the Progressives, of course, was a notable diversity in objectives. Hardly an area of American life did not attract attention, but reform of the political order, the economic system, and the moral life were unquestionably the main concerns.

The elements of the reform spirit are, of course, arguable as applied to the movement as a whole, and to Catt. Yet certain features were unmistakable. They provided a basis of common values for Progressives in which Catt eagerly shared. One was distaste for America's corrupt, pluralist politics, a politics involving evil politicians, greedy economic interests, and ignorant immigrant groups, determined to defeat honest, rational, and respectable Americans at every turn. Many Progressives, very much including Catt, also considered blacks as among the enemy. For some Progressives, "the machine" was only the "proximate enemy" and rapacious corporations the ultimate one, while for other Progressives corrupt politicians and their politics were almost the sum and substance of the evil at hand.[25] Either way contempt for American politics pervaded the spirit of Progressivism. To no one was this more true than to Catt whose hostility towards ordinary politics in her era motivated her reformism every day of her life.

A second element was the moralistic mood of Progressive reform. Despite the popularity of Prohibition, or the multiple vice crusades of the time, many, probably most, Progressives did not conceive of moral reform in such a literal sense. Certainly Carrie Catt did not. Rather, the dominant moralistic spirit emphasized the urgent necessity for the growth of social awareness in America. The Progressive stress lay on the necessity of every person, and of society itself, to turn sharply towards society as a whole, towards the nation as a whole, towards others, and away from the self. None of this meant that Progressive moralism repudiated concern with individual independence; on the contrary, perhaps naively, Progressives took for granted that a more social order, composed of more social individuals, would also be a more authentic and freer society.

In order to realize their ambitious objectives, the Progressives were disposed towards, and often obsessed with, organization. In its focus on organization, and in its ardent advocacy of organizing the world, the Progressive Era was, as Samuel P. Hays argued so well in *The Response to Industrialism: 1885–1914*, announcing its marriage to modernity, to a world turned complex, urban, and interdependent. It has several moments or parts, but the characteristic Progressive reform dimension had its roots in what Hofstadter described as the complaint of the unorganized against the upsurge of the organized in economics and in political life, a complaint that led to the unorganized's embrace of organization.[26]

That Carrie Catt was a supreme organizer of the suffrage crusade was acknowledged in her time — and has been since. She was a paradigm for Progressivism's cult of organized reform — "reform" as an act of modernization to be accomplished by organization, bureaucracy, and efficient leadership. She clearly longed for what Wiebe describes as a central Progressive "modernist" dream: "unity upon a perfect meshing of society's parts, a frictionless operation analogous to the factory under a pure scientific management."[27] She longed for it, indeed, for the National American Woman Suffrage Association, for the United States, and for the world.

Finally, no approach to the spirit of Progressivism is possible that does not acknowledge its pervasive and often undifferentiated optimism. As Otis Graham, Jr., remarks, it is true that the optimism proceeded in a mood of perceived crisis (or crises), one in which "foreboding" was a constant refrain.[28] Catt and so many other Progressives fit Graham's analysis in that they were often troubled optimists. But optimists they were. They expected that they (and the United States) could meet the test of the times. Fatalism in any form did not rule. Thus while their analyses sometimes suggested a desperate situation, their spirits were rarely desperate. Without understanding this, we can understand neither Progressive reform nor Carrie Catt, who here as elsewhere was often Progressivism's dutiful daughter.

While I attempt to place Catt in the context of her turbulent times, I do not propose to offer a detailed or novel view of the Progressive Era or of the conflicts among women activists in her era. My effort is a study of Carrie Catt as a feminist politician. My approach has been what one might too grandly call phenomenological.

Ignoring neither her time nor ours, my ultimate aim is to bring Catt alive as a feminist politician, very much in terms of her own self-understanding. What was her life as she saw it? What was she trying to say and to do? We need to see Catt at work not as a one-dimensional figure, but as the angry feminist, the tactical politician, and the Progressive reformer she was. As Evelyn Fox Keller observed Barbara McClintock, so must we observe Carrie Catt: we need to acknowledge Catt for who she was; see how that worked out for her, in this case, in her politics and political thought, and respect her for her human journey on her own terms.[29]

I have been helped in this task by many others, perhaps especially by patient librarians, too numerous to name, at the University of Wisconsin Interlibrary Loan Service, the Sophia Smith Collection at Smith College, the Schlesinger Library at Radcliffe College, and the Library of Congress. I thank these libraries for permission to use their materials. I am also thankful for the use of *Conversations with Alice Paul*, courtesy of the Bancroft Library, and Elinor Lerner's important paper, "Working Class and Immigrant Involvement — the New York Woman Suffrage Movement." I was assisted too by the Women's Studies Research Center of the University of Wisconsin at Madison through their 1984 conference, "Studying Women's Lives." I have been aided by a fair number of people whose conversations with me and reading parts of my work have stimulated me along the way. They know who they are and that I am grateful. I must thank Gerda Lerner, in particular, because she made me ask questions I did not want to ask; Mary C. Reardon, who typed and retyped too many drafts while constantly giving me encouragement along the way; Paula White, Mike Kloman, and Thornton Jacobs, who helped me get the manuscript in shape to publish; Deborah Kops, my editor, who offered me a happy combination of encouragement and firmness; and Ann Twombly, production director, who did so much for the book.

CARRIE CATT

FEMINIST POLITICIAN

Carrie Chapman Catt: The Early Years

The basic facts of Carrie Chapman Catt's early life are well known. Moreover, in her later life she and then some of her admirers often repeated events of her childhood as decisive foreshadowings of the person, especially the feminist, she became. Yet as we shall see, the curious fact about Catt's childhood is how little of it she recalled or shared in her maturity or old age and thus how little we really know of her youth.

Carrie Lane was born January 9, 1859, in Ripon, Wisconsin, then a still-developing area not far from the Wisconsin frontier. Her parents were of Yankee stock whose own families originated in New England. Maria Clinton and Lucius Lane met in Potsdam, New York, where they grew up and went to school. Both of them received a high school education, somewhat unusual for that day. The Clintons were a relatively affluent family, but the Lanes were not well off. Indeed, Lucius joined the California Gold Rush in order to make enough money to be able to marry Maria. He amassed no fortune in California, but in 1855 they were married. The Lanes moved first to the Cleveland area and later to Ripon where Lucius Lane pursued the life of an ordinary farmer. Their first child, a boy, was born in 1856, Carrie followed three years later, in 1859, and the third and final child arrived in 1870. The lure of the West and better opportunity took the Lanes to Charles City, Iowa, in 1866. There they stayed and there Catt spent the years of her youth she most remembered.

Carrie Catt completed high school with considerable success and, determined to go to college, entered Iowa State as a sophomore in 1877. She was duly graduated in 1880, the only woman in a graduating class of seventeen, and began work in a law office pursuant to her college-formed ambition to become a lawyer. In 1881 she was invited to become a teacher in the Mason City, Iowa, schools and she accepted the job. By 1883 she was appointed superintendent of schools in Mason City, an unusual achievement for a woman in her day. In 1885 she resigned the post to marry Leo Chapman, who was editor of the *Mason City Republican*. Marriage did not bring the end of her work outside the home, however. She became her husband's business partner in what turned out to be an impossible enterprise. Leo Chapman hewed to a reform-minded, liberal Republican stance in his paper, generating a good deal of controversy in a world where undeviating support for Republicans and Republicanism, reformed or not, was a way of life.

It is likely that Chapman's reform orientation appealed to his wife and that he in turn was responsive to her own reform urges. Only a month after their marriage a "Woman's World" section edited by Carrie Chapman made an appearance in the *Mason City Republican*. Instead of offering columns on food and fashions, Catt's section focused on serious issues, including woman suffrage.

All went acceptably at the paper until the next year when Chapman (and his wife) rebelled against a Republican candidate for local office, whom they considered particularly obnoxious. The candidate sued Chapman for libel and a local Republican judge obliged him by finding Chapman guilty. Pressure mounted for him to move on and the Chapmans decided to look for more fertile fields. Chapman sold the paper and, leaving his spouse behind temporarily, went to California to seek new opportunities. In less than a year he was dead of typhoid. Catt learned of his death while she was en route from Iowa to assist her ill husband. Like many women before her, she suddenly found herself on her own, without career or substantial financial resources. She was twenty-seven years old.[1]

These are the skeletal facts of Catt's earlier life. The legends of Catt's early years are what illuminate the facts, however. What they reveal at the least is what Catt saw or chose to recount as important about her younger life. As such they are, surely, significant, though what they don't tell us is as important as what they do.

Catt early emerged as a child who was nonconformist in some ways and unusually determined to be independent. And while she gave different dates for her first becoming concerned about equality for women, there is no doubt that it happened when she was still quite young. This development certainly was not the reaffirmation of family

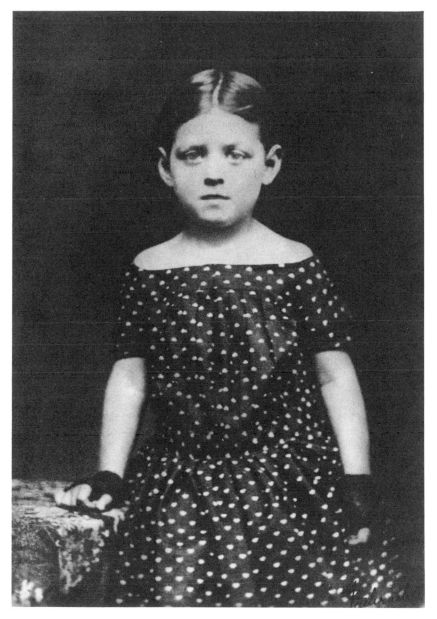

Carrie Lane at the age of six. Courtesy of the Library of Congress.

tradition, nor did it receive sympathetic understanding at home. Neither her father nor her mother approved of women's equality. Yet there is considerable evidence to suggest that her parents were crucial to the process.

On the one hand, Carrie Catt must have been influenced by her father. She does not say so, and indeed in her mature life she almost never mentioned him. Perhaps this is not entirely a surprise since he opposed her choice to enter the world on as equal a footing as possible with men. But there is little doubt that he was the only model at home with which Carrie could have identified. Catt certainly did not identify with her mother, except in a negative sense.

She always maintained contact with her family, and relations remained cordial. But even as a young girl she disapproved of her mother's role in her patriarchal family, of her mother's willing acceptance of that role, and, of course, of her father's position regarding women. Nor did they approve of Catt's choices, particularly when she chose to go to college. In this important sense Carrie was a self-made person, influenced more by her negative reactions to the relations between men and women that she saw as she grew up than by anything else.[2]

A decisive event along the way occurred when she was thirteen and discovered that her mother — and other women — could not vote. She was shocked that voting was a realm for men alone. She was equally shocked that, while both her parents thought this was only right, neither could provide any sensible justification for this inferior status for women. Catt often said no discovery stung her and angered her as much, and none influenced her life more.

By the time Catt was a teenager her independence and nonconformity were well established and revealed themselves in her determination to go to college, despite the fact that she was a woman and despite her father's resistance, which included his refusal to assist her financially. Catt went anyway, teaching school for a year to make enough money to start, and then continuing to support herself through college by working in the Iowa State library and kitchen.

This persistence and willingness to ignore family and social convention was unusual for a woman in her time, and it revealed a part of her independence that she also manifested early, an unusual toughness. Several incidents in her life up to 1881 illustrate this side of Catt. One she often told was how she dealt with the boys with snakes who, trying to frighten her, chased her when she was only seven years old. Carrie decided the only way to deal with them was to beat them at their game, to catch her own snake and to chase after them. Her plan worked perfectly, for as she suspected the boys were actually afraid of snakes too. That ended boys' giving her a bad time. Thus, she learned

early that to beat "forces of evil" you had to be better at their own
game, a tactic she was to master later as a politician. The lesson was
underlined in another elementary school incident. In this instance, a
boy was mercilessly harassing a girl whose skirt was starting to fall off.
The girl was upset and seemingly helpless before this male onslaught.
The bully infuriated Carric, who charged up to him and slapped his
face. Seventy or so years later she could still remark with evident satisfaction: "They had respect for us girls after that!" Later, in college,
after championing the right for women to participate in the college
debating society, Catt began the first talk by a woman by nervously
losing her place in her speech. The college boys present began to laugh
in derision at a "silly" woman. But Catt pulled herself together and
delivered the rest of her talk as if nothing had happened. Once again
she gained respect by proving she too could be tough; and once
again she showed males that nobody was going to overwhelm and
humiliate her.[3]

Invariably Catt remembered these incidents of her growth as the
development of an independent nonconformist and as part of a process in which she became determined to help "dependent" females
break through male domination. Male power and, she might have said,
male oppression were realities that she encountered all along her route
to maturity, and her consistent reaction was to fight back in means she
felt men understood. Thus while Catt then (or later) never expressed
systematic antagonism towards males, clearly she had decided early
that they would not push her around, that she would do what was
necessary to fashion a life in which she would be equal with them and
free from their domination, and, eventually, that she would help other
women to do likewise. To be sure, Catt never summed up her youthful
lessons in quite this fashion. What she did do was tell the stories and
spend most of her life working for woman suffrage, leaving little
doubt as to the unmistakable connections.

Early in her life Catt also manifested what was to be a lifelong
missionary tendency, a drive to serve and change the world. In particular, her infatuation with Robert Ingersoll, a "notorious" religious un-
believer of her age, when she was twelve led her to zealous attempts to
convert both children and adults in her neighborhood to religious
skepticism. This temporary crusade attracted some attention in St.
Charles, Iowa, and the attention was not always favorable. It also reflected, of course, her youthful independence and nonconformity in
a time and place where adult religious skeptics, not to speak of children, were hardly accepted. But it was an early indication of her sense
of mission. Indeed, as a young girl she had a mystical experience con-
firming this notion. She was out walking the family dog and (she

Carrie Lane as a college graduate in 1880. Courtesy of the Library of Congress.

claimed decades later) suddenly heard a voice tell her: "There is important work awaiting you in the future. . . . You have much to learn and you are wasting your time."[4]

These incidents and others suggest that Catt felt from the beginning she was special and that she was to serve her world, a faith she never doubted or relinquished, no matter how sincerely she took note of her limitations.

They also suggest that Catt always had considerable self-confidence. Its origins are hard to trace, but it was supplemented by her discovery in high school of Charles Darwin and Herbert Spencer. They completed a circle by providing her confident personality with a confident philosophy. The first step was a college boy's introduction of Darwin to the teenaged Carrie. That led her to read *The Origin of Species* as a high schooler. It confirmed her skepticism of traditional Christianity. That was followed in college by her enthusiasm for Herbert Spencer. She read him as she had read Darwin as the herald of an optimistic message: a celebration of human evolution and an invitation to people to speed the steady march of the human race to greater glory. As we will see later, Catt remained a committed follower of evolutionary science all her life, basking in its optimistic assessment of human possibilities and happy that it provided her with the philosophic justification for her missionary impulses.[5]

Weaving together these events and discoveries with the bare facts of Catt's life yields a richer view of her as a youth. She was clearly a bright, nonconformist, and resilient child and young adult who was determined to make an independent life for herself by fulfilling some mission in life. She found that men often stood in her way, and yet she was optimistic about life both for her and for "the race." Still, there are a lot of pieces missing. And the portrait is a bit too neat. Despite a few tales suggesting a happy childhood recounted by Catt's biographer, Mary Gray Peck, and the formative incidents Catt recounted, we know too little of Catt's childhood years. We do not know how well her family got along, what its strengths and tensions were, how she saw and felt, even what her daily routines were. There are some hints that her mother was not a happy woman. But Catt insisted that such dissatisfaction as her mother felt simply came from her dislike of farm life and did not affect the family. Indeed, Catt believed her home life was a happy one.[6]

Nor do we really have an adequate grasp on just where her extraordinary independence, ambition, and toughness came from. Why was she the way she was? When did she become so? What were her doubts and confusions about her strong self? Why did she want (or need?) an unshakeable cosmic optimism? What was her first marriage like? How did she react to the death of her first husband? These questions and many more are enclosed in a "private Catt," the person who was determined to keep much of her personal thought and experience to herself.

The Suffrage Movement to 1900

To follow Carrie Chapman Catt's development from her youth to her rapid rise in suffragist circles to the presidency of the National American Woman Suffrage Association, we must have a basic grasp of the history of woman suffrage to 1900. Catt's story is, after all, set against the landscape of a movement that began long before her name was entered on its rolls.

Concern for woman suffrage existed among a tiny group of Americans (women and men) even before the now famous 1848 Declaration of Rights in Seneca Falls, New York. But the "movement" was small then and indeed remained small until the 1880s. Yet small as it was, the movement had connections with the much larger world of pre-Civil War reform and reformers. Its participants were commonly general reformers, involved in such causes as abolition, temperance, and, later, the Civil War. In these years, though, suffragists were not formally organized and, since they were interested in many reforms, it was unclear just how important woman suffrage was to them.[7]

This question was finally — and inevitably — faced in 1868 and 1869 when suffragists split over whether to support black suffrage even at the temporary (it was hoped) delay of votes for women. The division was bitter and the result was two suffrage organizations. One, the American Woman Suffrage Association, led by Lucy Stone, backed the Fifteenth Amendment to the Constitution granting blacks the vote and the other, the National Woman Suffrage Association, directed by Susan B. Anthony and Elizabeth Cady Stanton, broke with most other reformers and the Stone feminists and opposed the Fifteenth Amendment because it did not include women. The dispute had no effect on the larger debate or decision on the Fifteenth Amendment. It has been generally assumed the split greatly damaged the woman suffrage cause for decades. It did drain off much energy into enervating political, organizational, and personal rivalries, but, as Ellen DuBois has argued, there were notable gains: the emergence of an independent women's movement and steps towards its formal political organization, which eventually bore fruit. Moreover, the split did not hurt woman suffrage as much as did the mood of the post–Civil War era, in which reform of all sorts lost its glamor.

For the A.W.S.A., suffrage was part of a broader platform of moral reform, a perspective that reflected the tradition of New England Yankee reform from which Lucy Stone drew. Its leaders insisted that the N.W.S.A. was inclined to focus too exclusively on women's issues, was often too radical on women's questions (for example, too sympathetic to divorce), and did not exercise good tactical judgment (for example, in focusing on a constitutional amendment as the means to suffrage rather than more "realistic" state and local efforts).

Also important was Stone's dislike of the N.W.S.A.'s Anthony. Stone's relationship with Anthony had begun deteriorating even before the Civil War, in 1856 and 1857, when Anthony criticized Stone for getting married and then was displeased when Stone became pregnant. While Stone recognized that behind Anthony's judgments lay a fear that Stone would abandon the cause of women's rights, she considered this criticism ridiculous and she resented Anthony's interference in her life. In time, Stone came to dislike Anthony and to judge her harshly in turn, as an "egotistical" queen bee.[9]

For her part Anthony, Stanton, and their allies saw the A.W.S.A. as a timid organization, not sufficiently devoted either to the cause of women or to the firm measures needed for progress. Their early journal, *Revolution*, signified their mood and, perhaps, their social purpose. Moreover, the N.W.S.A. leaders came to share a great deal of distrust for Lucy Stone and those surrounding her as people who sought to dominate the movement and run it only their way — the mirror image of the criticism by Stone and the A.W.S.A. of Anthony and Stanton and their faction.[10]

The split remained an open wound during the 1870s. It was exacerbated when Susan B. Anthony defended Victoria Woodhull after her controversial defense of free love (though eventually Anthony decided Woodhull was essentially deranged), and later when Anthony attempted to vote and her subsequent trial raised a national storm. The A.W.S.A's *Woman's Journal* expressed silent disapproval of Anthony's militancy, even leaving her off its 1873 list of women who had aided the cause of votes for women. For its part, the N.W.S.A. leaders were disgusted at the timid and narrow reactions of their sisters to Anthony's bold leadership. Despite this legacy of division, though, the woman suffrage movement did unite in 1890 into the National American Woman Suffrage Association. A cooling of the old hostilities during the 1880s as well as a rising determination to concentrate on suffrage as *the* woman's issue, ignoring others and the divisions of the past, paved the path to unity. Agreement at first was fragile and was never monolithic, but it succeeded in large part because Anthony,

Stone, Anna Howard Shaw, and especially Alice Stone Blackwell insisted that it do so in order to promote women's enfranchisement.[11]

The period between 1890 and 1900, when Catt's first presidency began, was a crucial one for the newly fashioned N.A.W.S.A., though not so clearly for the suffrage cause itself. For the N.A.W.S.A. it was an age in which new leadership, under the patronage of Susan B. Anthony, began to emerge and with it a new strategy of serious political organization and pressure. Elizabeth Cady Stanton was the first president of the N.A.W.S.A. (1890–1892). But in the month she was first elected, she left for England, where her daughter and family were. She spent most of her time in England thereafter, making clear that she was losing interest in the woman suffrage movement. She considered herself more radical than the younger leaders entering the N.A.W.S.A. and even Susan B. Anthony in these, her later years. Much of this self-image rested on Stanton's broad feminist concerns, including her hostility to traditional religion and its attitudes towards women as well as her support for liberalized divorce laws.[12]

Also relevant was the fact that Stanton was not attuned to organization politics or a focused, single-goal strategy. As a result, Stanton and Anthony drew somewhat apart, although their mutual affection remained great. Anthony, N.A.W.S.A.'s vice president and then Stanton's successor as president, took over the operation of the campaign for votes for women. Stanton was not enthusiastic about this development, though she accepted it. She openly resented, however, its inevitable fallout, that the younger people Anthony encouraged in the N.A.W.S.A. paid her little heed. As the 1890s unfolded, her advice was solicited less and less frequently, and her pronouncements on a wide variety of subjects were no longer received warmly at national conventions. Anthony noted Stanton's declining status, and she felt ambivalent about it. In the end she chose to try to keep the peace while opening the door more and more for the younger generation. She loved Stanton and the past she represented, but she believed the future would be and should be in hands other than either Stanton's or her own.[13]

Throughout the 1890s Anthony was undoubtedly aware of the inclinations of the second generation towards power. She saw them push against not only Stanton's views, but some of her own cherished ideas as well. An illustration is the contest in the early to mid-1890s, which has subsequently been little noticed, over whether to continue holding the yearly N.A.W.S.A. convention in Washington. Anthony favored following tradition, but most of the new leadership wanted to hold the meetings at different locations around the country. Their aim was to build a national organization with visibility throughout the country. They had the natural support of suffragists from the West, South, and New England who felt their voices did not count enough in the remote, Washington-based N.A.W.S.A. Despite Anthony's pleas the forces of change won out. It was typical of Anthony that she gracefully accepted the decision. She probably also understood its larger meaning. It was not a repudiation of her, but a sign of the new world coming.[14]

The fight over Stanton's *Woman's Bible* in 1896 was even more significant because it was not only a humiliating slap at Stanton, it was, Anthony felt, a direct rejection of Anthony herself. It took on overtones of a confrontation between two generations in the movement, and once again it was a contest Anthony lost. To be sure, she had had the chance to participate in the construction of the *Bible* and turned it down. But the entire dispute was for her a test of loyalty to her friend, Stanton, and their joint stewardship of the woman suffrage movement, and without hesitation she chose to stand by Stanton and the past.

Part I of Stanton's *Woman's Bible* was published in 1895 to an instant uproar of denunciation in the county at large *and also* within the N.A.W.S.A. Part II also generated considerable controversy. Most provocative was the *Bible's* biting critique of the foundation of the Judeo-Christian tradition (more accurately, their version of it). The parts by Stanton were unmistakably hostile to religion in any form, which she compared unfavorably with "rationalism" at every opportunity. She did not, however, directly challenge Christ's divinity, and the only essay that did was discreetly signed "Anon." Moreover, many of the discussions by other contributors went out of their way to defend the Bible as it related to women by offering unorthodox interpretations that attempted to undermine the conventional patriarchal interpretation of its teachings.[15]

In any case, it upset traditional suffragists who thought it was bad politics. Such a view stung Stanton, who charged that such a notion was "but another word for cowardice. How can women's position be changed from that of a subordinate to an equal without the broadest discussion of all the questions involved in her degradation?" she asked.[16] Stanton's critics agreed with her query, but they thought it was silly to attempt to advance on all fronts at once. That would not work, and it only demonstrated to them that Stanton had no political sense. Women's enfranchisement could not, they were sure, be won by a suffrage movement judged to be so radical that it blasphemed religion.

Opponents of Stanton and her *Woman's Bible* came to the 1896 N.A.W.S.A. convention determined to get the organization to disavow the troublesome volumes. Anthony did not like the *Woman's Bible* either, but she had no intention of having this work of her dear friend repudiated by a movement they had founded and nourished together. She worked desperately to block the attempt to disclaim the *Woman's Bible*. But to her probable astonishment, leaders of the younger generation ignored her pleas, pushed ahead, and won.

Stanton was hurt and immediately threatened to resign from the N.A.W.S.A. and urged Anthony to join her. Anthony thought about it, but others counterattacked, trying to persuade Anthony to stay, reaffirming their loyalty to Anthony and their admiration for her leadership. Moreover, as Anthony reflected on the dispute, she became more and more annoyed at Stanton's radical pronouncements. They seemed continually to divert the N.A.W.S.A. The result was that Anthony remained president of the N.A.W.S.A., but she was no longer its unquestioned director, as she must have known.[17]

Whether she ever accepted fully the new state of affairs, we do not know. She remarked in her diary of 1895 that the new women simply did not impress her as much as the old figures, which must have meant Stanton as well as herself. And she worried that for all their skill at organization and effectiveness (for all their Progressive values) perhaps they lacked a broad enough vision of feminism.[18]

When all was said and done, however, Anthony was not an egotistical person. As Kraditor observes, she "saw herself as the prosaic day-to-day worker for the cause." And Anthony appreciated others who were prepared to do the hard, daily work involved in inching towards success.[19] Moreover, on a personal level Anthony grew closer and closer to her coworkers, her "nieces," who were the second generation leaders, while Stanton was far away. Perhaps that personal closeness reassured her. For when she combined it with her own cool analysis of the needs of the future, she was prepared to turn over the movement to the leaders of the second generation.

Catt from 1886 to 1900

With this setting in mind, we can now return to the life of Carrie Lane Chapman and observe her evolution in the fourteen years between 1886 when she became a widow and 1900 when she ascended to the presidency of the N.A.W.S.A. Of this period we know a great deal about the external events in Catt's life, but, if anything, we know less about her private feelings and experiences than we do about her childhood. During these years the private Catt largely disappears in her accounts and in those of her admirers. She becomes almost entirely a public figure: Carrie Chapman Catt, crusader and organizer for woman suffrage.

In need of employment, Carrie Chapman stayed in San Francisco, where her first husband had died, and went to work as an advertising solicitor for a local business paper. It was a painful time for her. She learned to her dismay how lowly the position of most working women was. She also encountered trouble with a man again. While working at her job, one of her male associates grabbed her and repeatedly kissed her until Catt broke free and fled. The experience profoundly upset Catt and though she never talked about it publicly, her intimates knew how important an event it was in her life. It fueled her anger over relations between the sexes and strengthened her determination to help fashion a world in which women were accorded the same dignity and respect as men.[20]

Catt returned to Iowa, to her friends and her family, and began to try to support herself by giving public lectures. We do not know how successful she was in her few ventures. What we do know is that in the years 1887 to 1890 she took two crucial steps that were to influence her life enormously thereafter. First, she fell in love with and married George Catt. Second, she became increasingly interested in the woman suffrage movement and decided to make it her life's work.

Carrie had known George Catt as a fellow student at Iowa State and she renewed her contact with him when she lived in San Francisco. He had become, and was to continue to be, a successful structural engineer. After their renewed acquaintance, George Catt became the ardent wooer of a cautious and resistant Mrs. Chapman. Eventually he won her love. They married in 1890, and if Carrie Catt as well as her friends are to be believed, the Catts' marriage was happy and successful.

It was not, however, greeted with enthusiasm in all quarters. Iowa suffragists had welcomed Carrie Chapman's involvement in the Iowa suffrage movement and some of her newfound coworkers feared the consequences of her marriage, even as they wished her personal happiness. Their worry was that Catt would drop out of the suffrage crusade and become a homemaker and mother. They need not have worried, for this was hardly Catt's (or her husband's) plan. She very much intended to continue her public work. Her husband heartily approved. George Catt was a supporter of woman suffrage and he was clearly as work-oriented as his wife.

Traditional accounts report that Catt insisted, as a precondition for their marriage, that she have free one-third of every year — which soon became most of every year — to promote woman suffrage, and her husband readily agreed. Catt described what happened somewhat differently: "My own Iowa husband said to me: 'I am as earnest a reformer as you are, but we must live. Therefore I will earn the living for two and you will do reform work enough for both.' The result was that I was able to give 365 days work each year for 50 years without a salary."[21]

Either way, it is clear some such arrangement preceded the Catts' marriage and that without it, marriage would not have been acceptable to Carrie Catt. This arrangement, which was highly unusual at that time, occasioned a great deal of comment then and later and rightfully earned Catt something of a reputation as a radical feminist in her conception of women in marriage. But there was, as always, a very practical dimension in her agreement with her husband that was central to her motivation. By 1890 Catt was increasingly sure she wanted to devote herself to the suffrage cause. Her marriage was not exactly to be second in her priorities, but it was not to interfere. Thus her understanding with George Catt was for her as much a practical matter as one of principle.[22]

There does not seem to have been one single moment in which Catt suddenly focused on the suffrage cause and thereafter devoted herself to it without stint. Rather, it seems to have been a matter of her background, her life situation in the mid-1880s, and the beginning of the movement as a serious national entity intersecting. Catt dated her emergence as a full-time activist to the year 1889. But she started before then and worked her way up from the bottom, operating in the state of Iowa. Before going to San Francisco she had organized some friends to convince the state legislature to grant women the vote in local elections. This first venture in organization was resoundingly successful. All but twelve women in her town signed up — an early hint of future organizational skills — but her petition got nowhere with the Iowa legislature. After her return to Iowa from San Francisco, Catt became more and more involved, reaching beyond familiar places and working across the state.[23]

In Iowa efforts to gain votes for women had been underway since the late 1860s. Though the movement had no success, it was active and not unrespectable. Its leaders, such as Mary J. Coggeshall, Narcissa T. Bemis, and Margaret Campbell, always held a special place in Catt's heart: "They were my especial heroes."[24] Coggeshall in particular made a powerful impression on Catt: "She gave her life to this cause and was a noble, high-minded, talented, consecrated woman."[25] To what extent they taught Catt either organizational or leadership skills — or developed her sense of strategy — Catt did not say and we do not know. But it is important to realize that her first loyalties were always to her Iowa models and not to the distant and legendary Susan

B. Anthony or Elizabeth Cady Stanton, about whom she was never as enthusiastic.

It was in 1889 that Catt's efforts (and, no doubt, her availability) were acknowledged when she was elected secretary of the Iowa Woman Suffrage Association and head of field organization. From that base, Catt's ascendency in suffrage circles was rapid. Through her repeated demonstrations of effectiveness as an organizer, she soon became well known and admired. Organization for her was both the route to leadership and the means by which her leadership was exercised, a subject this book will explore at length. Her experience provides a superb example of Robert Wiebe's argument that by the turn of the century organization was the channel to leadership, power, or achievement in America and of Anne Firor Scott's contention that for women the vehicle of women's voluntary organizations was particularly crucial in the process.[26]

While Catt continued to be active in her native and parochial fields of Iowa between 1890 and 1892, she also began to work in a larger arena. The first major step came in 1890 when she took an active role in the campaign for votes for women in South Dakota. Catt was a field worker, trying to get counties and cities organized for electoral victory. While the campaign ended in defeat, it was an invaluable experience for Catt. She got the chance to meet and interact with many of the leaders of the national organization and she displayed an obvious effectiveness which impressed them. Thus it was in South Dakota that she was transformed from "a raw recruit." Of course, she was not yet "a new leader," though 1890 also marked her debut at national conventions of the National American Woman Suffrage Association when she, among many others, gave an address. Her talk was unspectacular and did not attract much attention. Susan B. Anthony's diary of convention events does not even mention it. But for Catt it was a significant step, because it was her debut before the assembled leaders of the N.A.W.S.A.[27]

It was Catt's successful leadership of the Colorado suffrage struggle in 1893 that finally established her as a leader in N.A.W.S.A. circles. Catt received most of the credit for the badly needed Colorado victory and her reputation soared. The triumph in Colorado directly led to her appointment to important tasks within the organization. She was elected as "National Organizer" and her name now appeared in the index to the *Woman's Journal*. In 1895 Catt was promoted to chair of the new National Organization Committee, a post she held till she became N.A.W.S.A. president in 1900. She believed her National Organization Committee post was the most important in the entire N.A.W.S.A. because from it she managed the varied and demanding field campaigns to win the vote in assorted states. By 1895–1896 she was routinely identified as the principal organizer of the movement. In her mind, she was really running it, or at least its most significant aspect.[28]

This view was not shared by the N.A.W.S.A.'s old guard. Yet time was on Catt's side. More and more she cemented her image as the organizer of the cause and more and more her focus on organization drew praise, even though she by no means presided over an unbroken string of victories. By the late 1890s she had won acceptance for the idea that organization and field work were the proper arena for the battle for suffrage. As Alice Stone Blackwell's diaries record, Catt was now an intimate part of the ruling core of the N.A.W.S.A., hosting executive committee meetings and routinely consulted. She became known as the new general, a woman in a hurry, who felt she knew the way.[29]

As an advocate and practitioner of organization, the normally shy Catt was pioneering, frank, and aggressive. Her blunt report to the 1895 convention on the organizational failures of the N.A.W.S.A. made that notoriously clear. So did her determined advocacy and practice of organization that stepped on many (often older) toes. It is in light of this frequently controversial behavior that her ascendancy takes on added meaning. She was nice enough and hardly flamboyant, but she was also, as Anthony and others realized with considerable ambivalence, a hard-driving and skillful proponent of her strategy for suffrage within the N.A.W.S.A. Her election as president in 1900 marked the victory of a new era, an age of organization, and Catt was its prophet.

The Road to Victory,
and Beyond

In 1899, when Catt knew Anthony proposed to resign as president of the N.A.W.S.A., Catt had to consider whether she should run for the office. She protested that "I do not *want* the presidency . . . every feeling I have rebels against it." Yet Catt recognized that "circumstances seem to be forcing me to stand," and she predicted, "I *may* have to stand for election." There was the danger that otherwise it might "fall into hands harmful to the cause . . . particularly the lines of work which seem important."[1] Put more directly, Catt's message was that she wanted the suffrage movement to choose her organizational ethos and goals. And if that required her taking the presidency, she was ready to do so.

As it turned out, Anthony reached the same conclusion and Catt's presidency followed. It was, of course, a milestone in Catt's life which she could hardly have anticipated when she set out years before to promote the suffrage cause. It was not, however, to be as important to her story as her second presidency. In fact, her relatively brief first presidency (1900–1904) was not a glorious period for her, for the N.A.W.S.A., or for the broader suffrage movement. Its importance lay elsewhere. It signaled Catt's arrival as the central leader of the suffrage crusade and the ascension to power of a second generation of activists, a generation committed to the gospel of organization, who were eventually to wrest woman suffrage from a reluctant American polity.

Catt's election was a formality when the actual vote arrived in the 1900 convention. She received 254 of 275 votes cast, with the majority of the rest being cast for Susan B. Anthony. When she stepped forward to accept the mantle of the presidency she was greeted by applause, cheers, and waving handkerchiefs. But silence quickly fell in spontaneous acknowledgment of another significant aspect of the event, Susan B. Anthony's passing from the helm of the formal leadership. With perfect and undoubtedly knowing symbolism, Susan B. Anthony made herself the sole member of Catt's committee of presentation to the convention and she gave Catt her public blessing: "In Mrs. Catt you have my ideal leader. I present to you my successor." Catt accepted the presidency with awe, and as always, touched the important political bases: "Miss Anthony will never have a successor. . . . I shall not be the leader of this cause as Miss Anthony has been, I shall be only an officer of this Association. I will do all that I can, but I cannot do it without the co-operation of each of you."[2]

Catt's first presidency was quite literally a gift from Susan B. Anthony and her acquiescent allies, an offering possible because of Anthony's still dominant control over the N.A.W.S.A. Anthony knew full well that it was she and not any number of N.A.W.S.A. delegates who had selected Catt. In 1900 Anthony was eighty years old. She knew she could no longer handle all the duties of a growing organization. She felt she and Catt were alike in being more rational than emotional and she knew from her extensive interaction with Mrs. Catt over the years that she could be trusted. Above all, though she wasn't a skilled organizer herself, Anthony had long admired what she called Catt's "great genius" as an organizer and administrator and she appreciated the movement's acute need for it by 1900.[3] In short, Anthony selected Catt on the basis of conscious decision that focused on the need of her cause.

Certainly it was not a choice made on the basis of personal feeling, as N.A.W.S.A. insiders knew very well. Anthony had her "nieces," those of the second generation with whom she was especially close, but Catt did not rank high on the list. Anthony did not seem to love her as she loved others surrounding her. It seems likely that she was fond of Catt, but she looked at her coolly, affirming that she should be her successor because she was best for the job, nothing less, but also nothing more.[4]

Moreover, Anthony did not believe she fully understood Catt, who was hardly an open personality. Nor could she have been entirely sure where she stood with Carrie Catt since even in retrospect Catt's assessment of Anthony remains somewhat obscure. Of course, Catt was a protégé of Anthony and, especially on her death, expressed the deepest affection for Anthony as a person. Yet Anthony knew Catt was also implicitly and explicitly critical of the disorganized, unsuccessful suffrage movement Anthony had presided over. Catt could also patronize Anthony behind her back, observing, for instance, that Anthony was unaware of how many people disliked her and her ideas and suggesting that Anthony be left with her illusions since they did no harm any more.[5]

The beauty of Catt's position was that as new president in 1900 she also had the eager (and, in fact, far less ambivalent) support of the other old faction of the suffrage movement, represented by Alice Stone Blackwell. Catt had worked well with the Blackwells and their friends in the 1890s. Alice Blackwell operated from the *Woman's Journal*, now the main organ of the united movement, and she used it to rain praise on Catt, pointing out that, "Not Miss Anthony alone but all the women who have worked for years upon the official board with Mrs. Carrie Chapman Catt are convinced in selecting her for the presidency the Association has made the wisest possible choice."[6]

Both Blackwell and her allies and Anthony agreed that the issue at stake was getting new leadership, free from the conflicts of the past, and committed to a new phase of organizational politics. Their opinion, while decisive in determining the issue without public dispute, did not mean Catt lacked rivals nor that her policies lacked critics.

Some careful work is required to comprehend the situation because Catt and other N.A.W.S.A. leaders liked to keep any controversy far from the public eye. Within the small movement there was a strong norm that harmony was both expected and essential.

Anna Howard Shaw by 1900 was the leading orator of the suffrage movement and her dedicated commitment to the cause undoubtedly entitled her to as large, or even larger, a claim to be Anthony's successor as Catt had. Certainly this was her own view and not hers alone. However, Shaw's connection with the Woman's Christian Temperance Union (she was its Superintendent of the Franchise Department, 1888–1892) bothered activists who did not want to intertwine temperance and suffrage. Others doubted her administrative and organizational skills — perceptively, as the chaotic years of Shaw's N.A.W.S.A. presidency (1904–1915) were to show.

Had the question been a personal one Anthony would have favored Shaw. Anthony loved her deeply as a treasured friend and her "first light." For a considerable time Anthony evaluated Shaw and Catt equally as workers. She tried to maintain this judgment, insisting that each had skills that were a balance for the other. But her appreciation of Catt's organization and leadership skills continued to grow throughout the 1890s until Catt outdistanced Shaw in her mind as her potential successor.[7]

Shaw regretted that Anthony was not to continue on: "I do wish she were not going to resign, I cannot bear to think of it. It seems as if we will be without a head as an organization."[8] At the same time, though, Shaw undertook to become Anthony's heir to the presidency. She was very much engaged in a "tasteful" campaign for the job right up to the 1900 convention when the outcome became clear. Only then did she bow to reality and refuse to allow her supporters to put her up as a formal nominee. It is no wonder that during the year 1900 relations between Shaw and Catt degenerated badly. Catt complained to Alice Blackwell in a most uncharacteristic fashion that Shaw was attacking her not only behind Catt's back, but directly in letters to Catt, letters "filled with hatred." Clearly the stress of the competition for Anthony's nod showed on Shaw's part, and perhaps not on hers alone.[9]

Losing out to Catt hurt Shaw enormously, as she recognized. While she later claimed she had favored Catt, she acknowledged the cost of Catt's success over her in unmistakable terms: "I will admit . . . I made the greatest sacrifice of my life. My greatest ambition had been to succeed Miss Anthony."[10]

Strategic issues separated Catt from another opponent, Lillie Devereux Blake, whose chief booster was Elizabeth Cady Stanton. Blake had often disagreed with Catt over organizational issues, especially in the context of New York operations. Moreover, Blake correctly perceived that Catt was not solidly behind achieving suffrage by working for victory in one state after another, but nourished instead a growing interest in achieving suffrage through a federal constitutional amendment. Blake objected to any suggestion of this centralist approach and found allies among some southern suffragists oriented towards state rights who also feared Catt's focus on Washington.

Stanton had other concerns. Officially she always praised Catt, calling her, for instance, "a good speaker, fine looking and a woman of rare common sense and executive ability." Privately she nourished growing doubts. Stanton did not consider Catt or her allies very radical in their feminism and she did not approve of a single-minded concentration on suffrage. Eventually this division, and related tactical divisions, led to an outright split between Catt and Stanton's daughter, Harriot Stanton Blatch. Yet the person who mattered was not Stanton, but Anthony, and Anthony wanted Catt.[11] More precisely, Anthony wanted what she perceived Catt stood for and might deliver: a "youthful," energized, organizationally active leadership.

Catt inherited a debilitated organization. Maud Wood Park, later to be the effective leader of congressional lobbying, recounts her shocked reaction to the condition of the N.A.W.S.A. at her first convention, the historic 1900 meeting. Park instantly perceived the condition of atrophy into which the organization had fallen under the guidance of the aging Anthony, and she was "appalled." The meeting was held in the basement of a church and attended by only middle-aged and elderly women. The first speaker presented a state report from Missouri in rhyme.[12]

Moreover, Catt had the additional burden of attempting the needed revival in a circumstance where substantial power still rested firmly within the hands of Susan B. Anthony, supported by the influential Shaw. Nothing brought this home more clearly than the bitter fight at the same 1900 convention over the fate of the Organizational Committee. Catt proposed to continue her special committee under the leadership of her close friend and ally, Mary G. Hay. Catt expected it to play a major role in the revitalization process. She was able to obtain convention approval in 1900 for its continuance, but once the N.A.W.S.A. convention elected Catt president, the Executive Committee turned around and eliminated the Organizational Committee, fearing that it would become a vehicle through which Catt would rule the N.A.W.S.A. as a czar. The old guard's ambivalence towards Catt's policies — and her friend — were obviously strong. Despite her landslide election, she was to be on a short leash.

Angry over the repudiation of her friend and the elimination of the very committee that had been her vehicle to success, Catt nevertheless did not quit. She chose to go on, which was an important decision, not because she worked a revolution in the N.A.W.S.A. during her first presidency, but because she gained valuable experience which she was able to use in her second presidency (beginning in 1916). The experience also convinced her that next time she would have to have almost unchecked power within the N.A.W.S.A. to achieve her goals.[13]

Indeed, Catt's first term as president was a quiet time. There was no sense that the organization was hers. She did not figure prominently in Blackwell's sympathetic *Woman's Journal*. She remained very much under the restricting, albeit supportive, gaze of Anthony. Abroad, Stanton was skeptical. Shaw was Catt's vice-president as she had been Anthony's, and she invariably supported Anthony when disagreements arose. The Business Committee, the elite of notables of the N.A.W.S.A., continued to be very influential and within its precincts Catt was only sometimes the first among equals.[14]

Catt turned to her job with zest, though, and did what she could to make the N.A.W.S.A. viable again. She did see its membership and its convention attendance grow into something far more impressive than the skeletal operation of 1900 could boast. Equally important, she relentlessly scrounged for funds and was able to place the N.A.W.S.A. on a sound financial footing. Moreover, Catt repeatedly was on the road, educating women, building membership, finding organizers, and, of course, urging states to adopt woman suffrage. States did not fall into line, however; not one enfranchised women during her first presidency. Nor was there any concrete progress toward adoption of a federal amendment. In fact, Catt experienced much greater progress in her simultaneous work for the international suffrage crusade. She was active, indeed the leader, in the formation of the International Woman Suffrage Alliance during the years 1902 to 1904. She also served as its first president, though it was after 1904 that Catt really poured her energies into the I.W.S.A. Apart from the I.W.S.A., however, Catt's accomplishments were modest from 1901 to 1904, a fact no one contests.[15]

Considering the lack of success for woman suffrage in the early 1900s, and the problems Catt faced in imposing her policies and her leadership on the movement, her retirement from the presidency in 1904 was a stroke of luck for her. She stayed long enough to make a start and obtain experience, but not so long as to be blamed for the scant actual progress toward woman suffrage in the United States. Her successor, Anna Howard Shaw, stayed twelve years and eventually was overwhelmed by mounting criticism over the painful reality that her long regime produced meager results towards victory. Shaw then had to step aside to be replaced by a Carrie Chapman Catt, who was now an experienced veteran, freed of Anthony's checks, ready to make a difference, and whose own record as president could be and was explained away as a factor of short tenure.

Carrie Catt's first presidency was less than four years old when she decided she could go on no longer. She announced her decision in the *Woman's Journal* in February 1904, declaring that "I find a rest . . . has become necessary." The fact was that Catt was not well; she was worn out. But despite her official explanation, one faithfully repeated by most historians of the suffrage movement, it was the badly deteriorating health of her husband and, to a lesser extent, of her mother, that forced her to resign when she did. She wanted to help them in their last years as much as she could.

George Catt died in 1905, his last attack occurring while he and Carrie were sitting together on a park bench. Catt was deeply affected by her husband's death for a long time. Though the reticent, private Catt made few allusions to her feelings, others tell the story, those like Anna Howard Shaw who saw Catt slip into a deep depression. Also complicating the picture was the fact that, while George Catt was a wealthy man, protracted financial complications followed his death. It was not until 1915 that they were fully ironed out, leaving Catt financially secure for the rest of her life.[16]

The Presidency of Anna Howard Shaw

Anna Howard Shaw was in her way a remarkable woman, a doctor and later a totally devoted soldier in the suffrage ranks. We know that, long a close friend and intimate traveling companion of Susan B. Anthony, she was unhappy when Anthony opted for Catt as her successor in 1900. Loyal as she was, however, she supported that decision, understood the practical reasons for it, and continued both her service to the cause and her intimacy with Anthony. When Catt felt she had to leave, both Catt and Anthony turned to Shaw as the logical person to follow as president.

The irony was that by 1904 Shaw was no longer eager for the job. The luster of its appeal had diminished, while the embarrassing but unmistakable problem of her lack of financial resources had not. Nor is it mere speculation to suggest that receiving the presidency as a kind of legacy from Carrie Catt, whose presidency she knew had been "admirable," did not excite her. But she shouldered the responsibility anyway, making a vow to Susan B. Anthony on Anthony's deathbed in 1906 to keep at it as long as her own health permitted. She did not keep that vow, but she served from 1904 to 1915.

Shaw had a reputation as the best orator of the suffrage movement and one of the strengths she brought to her presidency was her willingness to talk and campaign everywhere for suffrage. She was proud of the fact that during her tenure membership rose from 17,000 to 200,000 and the number of suffrage states from four to twelve. Yet woman suffrage did not prosper nearly as rapidly during the later years of her presidency as the expanding and impatient membership sought.

Critics increasingly began to blame Shaw. She was a poor administrator and relations between the national and state associations were often in torpor or turmoil. She was strong willed, which was surely necessary, but not effective at conciliation. Most importantly, perhaps, Shaw could not deal with the conflict that arose over the exceedingly modest pace of the enfranchisement campaign. Indeed, she often was unable to see *issues* that were at stake and she commonly reduced disagreements to personality clashes. Specifically, she did not know how to handle the challenges posed by the emergence of those in the association who sought federal, rather than state-by-state, action and who increasingly called for more militant tactics during 1914 and 1915. When her critics gained widespread support, Shaw's last years as president were marred by board resignations, endless controversy, and the dramatic and painful departure of Alice Paul's Congressional Union (later the Woman's Party) from the N.A.W.S.A. Perhaps the final blow was the election results of 1914 and 1915, which saw defeat after defeat for state suffrage referenda. Five of seven were defeated in 1914. And in 1915 Massachusetts, New Jersey, New York, and Pennsylvania voted "no." The campaigns left an almost bankrupt national treasury and stimulated a widespread judgment that it was time for new leadership.[17]

The fact is that the national suffrage movement fell into a serious and deepening crisis in the years 1910–1915, and the finger of blame pointed to Shaw. By 1915 at the latest, Shaw acknowledged the chaos around her, but she felt she did not deserve to be blamed. She portrayed her detractors as mean-spirited souls who did not like her age (she was 68 in 1915), as incompetents in state associations who shifted fault from themselves (where it belonged) to her, and as destructive people (Alice Paul et al.) who denounced her as a cover for their own desire for power. Nonetheless, Shaw was enough of a realist to accept that her hour was over and she chose to step aside. Her decision was a sad, if necessary, one for the woman who more than any other had hoped she could complete Aunt Susan's crusade.[18]

Once her health and spirits improved, Catt turned her energies outward but mostly to the world scene. She spent a large portion of the years from 1904 to 1915 abroad, working to develop the International Woman Suffrage Alliance, to advance the condition of women all over the globe. It was her goal, Catt declared quite seriously, to "organize the women of the world for suffrage."[19] She certainly tried to fulfill this mission. In the process she acquired an international reputation and a worldwide network of contacts.

In the years before the First World War especially, Catt was a chief voice for woman suffrage in the world. In this as in other respects, America in these years advanced confidently into the larger world and Catt was a noticeable part of that process. During this period she was elected and repeatedly re-elected president of the I.W.S.A. She remained president until 1923, when she was elevated to honorary chair at her request.

Though it was probably not her intention, Catt's activities on the world scene enhanced her standing in the N.A.W.S.A. at home. Her international involvement, including her speeches, was fully reported in the *Woman's Journal*. She received more coverage in the 1904–1915 era than she had during her first presidency. Indeed, her activities often got a good deal more publicity than those of Anna Howard Shaw. Moreover, her frequent absence from the United States freed her from internal N.A.W.S.A. quarrels and from blame for this era of disappointment in the American suffrage movement.

Catt's world tours for suffrage were not entirely her own idea. Anna Howard Shaw, for example, thought Catt should travel for the cause in order to shake her free from what Shaw perceived as her depression. And as Shaw knew, she could not afford to do this sort of thing, while Catt could.[20] Catt's doctor also favored travel for her, literally ordering a two-year world tour from 1909 until 1911. Although given her serious physical illness in 1910 (closely followed by the *Woman's Journal*), it was never particularly clear that travel was the elixir for Catt's physical health that her physicians believed.[21]

In any case, her popularity at home steadily rose. This was well illustrated by the reception she received upon her return from the last of her major trips in 1912. She was now recognized as a world leader of suffragists and feminists. In that light her many admirers welcomed her home before a packed Carnegie Hall audience where they lavished praise on her to a degree to be equaled only eight years later when woman suffrage became the law of the land. She was now a first-class celebrity in the movement and its leader, no matter who was president of the N.A.W.S.A.[22]

What Catt did for the cause of suffrage internationally has not been much investigated. It is not central to our story, though it did embody her typically Progressive assumptions that the principles of reformers were fully universal and properly applicable everywhere in the world and that an American should not hesitate to assume leadership in undertaking their world realization. I am struck in reading her journals, letters, and reports to American suffragists at her serene, unspoken sense of the relative superiority of her world, at her unquestioned confidence that her values would be an indubitable blessing for everyone else, and at her disquiet mixed with fascination at the curious practices and faiths of the rest of humanity.

Catt claimed to know from direct experience what she was talking about. In her journeys she did cover most of the world, traveling slowly in a world before the airplane. On the way she pursued her curiosity about history, culture, and people. It was the same abroad and at home: her interest in detail, in actually inspecting conditions, and in talking with people was without limit.

Catt basically made her visits to encourage existing foreign women's groups and to found others: to organize — as ever, her solution. It inevitably turned out that Catt's wide travels also helped her own cause. Wherever she went, she invariably attracted a great deal of attention as a bustling, energetic American woman trying to change things. The foreign press frequently treated her as a phenomenon, with the consequence that woman suffrage became news all over the world. She fully realized that most of her efforts were modest, in part because in most places that she visited the transformation she sought was almost revolutionary in social terms and only the first steps, if any, were underway. Yet she pressed on and sometimes, especially in European countries or "splinters" of European countries (Australia, for example), she observed dramatic progress, at least toward the enfranchisement of women.

The overwhelming impression one gets from what remains of Carrie Catt's foreign journals and her frequent reports from abroad to the *Woman's Journal* is a sense of banality. Perhaps this is largely because, as Catt herself was aware, she was a poor writer, at least in comparison with her skills as a speaker and as an organizer. A more basic factor may have been Catt's largely unreflective approach to her international work. Reading Catt in the years between her two presidencies, one finds a picture of typically relentless activity emerging, and yet one senses that she was in a fallow phase, perhaps unconsciously restoring her most creative energies, which were to flow out with such great effect after 1915.[23]

While the I.W.S.A. was by far Catt's main project during the interregnum, it was scarcely her only one. At first, when she left the presidency, she stayed on as vice-president-at-large of the N.A.W.S.A., but by 1905 her family troubles had taken their toll and she did not continue this role. Although initially reluctant, by 1909 Catt was at work in New York City, playing a major role in the foundation of the New York City Woman Suffrage Party. It was not until 1914, however, that all her energies were focused on work for women's enfranchisement in the United States. New York was her focus. It had long been her adopted state and Catt was fully aware of its potential as a leader in gaining suffrage not just among Eastern states, where the cause had gained few victories, but also in the country as a whole. After all, in those days New York was by far the largest state in the country and completely unchallenged as the most influential one.

Mary Garrett Hay, a close friend of Catt's, led the New York State campaign, but as early as 1912 Catt accepted the honorary chair of the organized suffrage movement there. In 1915 she completely devoted herself to winning the New York woman suffrage referendum of that year. She became chair of the Empire State Campaign Committee and aggressively toured the state, making numerous appearances and speeches. The same year she founded the New York State Woman

Suffrage Party as an umbrella group to coordinate the increasingly numerous, but not seriously united, suffrage organizations at work in New York, and she was the unanimous choice to lead the organization.[24]

Readers of suffragist publications were kept informed of the New York activities and the real message was that Catt was back. The referendum lost in New York in 1915, but Catt's prestige soared. She was in the midst of the two-year contest for victory in the 1917 referendum when N.A.W.S.A. influentials acknowledged their need for her leadership. In need of direction, they turned to Catt to take the reins of the N.A.W.S.A. again.

From the Presidency to Victory

While by 1915 Catt was busily involved in the New York State campaign and the International Woman Suffrage Alliance (which by now had branches in twenty-six countries), she began to perceive that the national suffrage crusade was not succeeding, a point she saw underlined in the 1915 loss in New York and the defeat of three more referenda on suffrage in 1916 (in Iowa, South Dakota, and West Virginia). Then and thereafter she insisted that she did not want the N.A.W.S.A. presidency. While her public statements did not reveal her actual willingness to serve, her reluctance was not entirely feigned. She was committed to the progress of the I.W.S.A. and was already gearing up for the 1917 suffrage referendum in New York State. She felt a particularly intense allegiance to the cause there and she had made frequent promises to her coworkers to see the fight through to victory. Moreover, Catt suspected that the judgment of the N.A.W.S.A. in turning to her was not entirely healthy. It was her opinion that the movement required younger leadership, which did not mean her at age 56.

When it became obvious that she was the overwhelming choice of the membership and pressure mounted for her to run, Catt resisted. In fact, once at the convention, she held out for several days while supporters offered her sweeteners, forming an informal group to raise money to assist the I.W.S.A., negotiating an agreement with other New York suffrage activists by which they agreed to let Catt go and to urge her to take the presidency, and guaranteeing (very importantly as it was to turn out) that Catt would have a virtually free hand to do her will in the N.A.W.S.A. Also influential in her eventual acceptance was the financial leverage that the Leslie bequest (the almost one million dollars that Mrs. Frank Leslie left to Catt for the suffrage cause) ensured as well as the arrival of war on the European continent, which curtailed the I.W.S.A.'s energies there.[25]

The greatest hoopla at the 1915 convention did not attend Catt's election. It went, instead, to Anna Howard Shaw. In a spirit that undoubtedly had more than a tinge of both guilt and relief, the N.A.W.S.A. convention showered Shaw with praise, roses, and even $30,000.[26] Meanwhile, power shifted to Catt as she was elected president. Mina C. Van Winkle of New Jersey provided a token opposition. She represented what was left of the militants now that Alice Paul and her supporters had abandoned the N.A.W.S.A. and signaled the fact that electing Catt did not at all resolve serious issues about how to conduct the suffrage effort. In accepting its charge, Catt told the convention: "I am an unwilling victim and you all know it." [27] And she left New York for Washington to start her work with regret — "I am off to Washington. O, How I loathe it."[28]

Yet Catt intended to do as good a job as she could. She knew full well that the N.A.W.S.A. was in a sad state, "bankrupt" in every sense of the word. She believed she was not the ideal leader to do something about it, but she had not the slightest doubt that she could do something about it — and the larger cause of women's enfranchisement. She fully expected her service to end with the enactment of the suffrage amendment.[29]

Since so much of this book considers how Catt led a transformed National American Woman Suffrage Association to victory, only a brief overview is appropriate here. While simultaneously struggling to build a truly national organization of unmistakable effectiveness and mobilize what became an army (her word) of two million women, Catt made the strategic decision to concentrate on a constitutional amendment rather than proceeding state by state. At the N.A.W.S.A.'s most famous meeting, the Atlantic City emergency meeting of 1916, Catt energized the association to focus on the national political scene, despite states' rights sentiments, especially from southern suffragists. This was the crucial preliminary battle for Catt, as she knew, and one that she won through the force of her leadership. Yet her attention to the states did not disappear. In particular, Catt remained deeply involved in the struggle to win New York State. Victory came there in 1917 and Catt was well aware of its significance as an example to other states and as a powerful stimulus to Congress. It was with good reason that Catt enthusiastically hailed this triumph "as the very greatest victory this movement has ever had in any country of the world."[30]

Congress did not, however, simply fall into step. Votes for women may have been won in New York in 1917, but a year later east of the Mississippi River only New York and Michigan permitted full participation by women in the electoral process. Nonetheless, Catt maintained political pressure through lobbying and organizing efforts. She kept working until in 1918 the House of Representatives, no longer able to ignore local and state pressures for national suffrage, passed the Anthony amendment.

In the same year the amendment failed in the less responsive Senate. One more year passed before the war was over and in the twilight of the Progressive Era enough senators were found to form the two-thirds majority to ensure passage in the Senate. Even then Catt kept up the pressure. She had long known what later E.R.A. proponents were to discover, that getting congressional approval for a constitutional amendment was one thing, obtaining its approval by three-quarters of the states was something else again. She had planned in detail well in advance for this fight, but still in retrospect it seemed to her her most arduous campaign, particularly in the South and border states.

Victory came in 1920 when Tennessee became the thirty-second state to ratify. Catt's joy knew few bounds then. She was probably never happier than in the glorious hours when victory was secured and she and many of her coworkers paraded through the streets of New York City and, later, when she attended the 1920 victory convention of the N.A.W.S.A. Despite the long, long road, the enfranchisement of women which Catt had pursued for thirty years had come true.[31]

After 1920

With the ratification of the suffrage amendment, Catt's public career had come to a climax. Not surprisingly, her activities seem to fade from the public eye after 1920. And yet, Catt lived on long afterwards, until 1947. She "retired" on several occasions, most notably in 1928 when she bought her last home in New Rochelle, New York. Yet, given her temperament, retirement was not really a possibility for Catt.

She was an active person in her every pore and she understood this about herself very well. She continued her connection with the International Woman Suffrage Alliance and she played some role in the League of Women Voters in its early years. She also continued to disagree with the Woman's Party on virtually every occasion over almost every issue.[32] However, until her death Catt's main public activities were continuing her crusade for world peace, defending the memory of the suffrage movement and her own reputation in particular, and making pronouncements on a wide variety of issues in her role as sage.[33]

Because "war is to me my greatest woe," the peace crusade was closest to Catt's heart.[34] It made demands on her talents that were similar to the suffrage effort. The task obviously was far more formidable than the suffrage struggle, and success eluded Catt's best efforts as it has eluded so many others'. But she did not think this was inevitable. "We may have peace if we will," she declared, with the same optimism that she had regarded the franchise. It was a matter of being willing to make the effort and to pay a price that could hardly be too high for peace. The result would be a dramatic step toward the world of which she dreamt, a world of responsible men and women, who were rational and concerned with mutual respect for each other as they lived a stable common life together — and a world where those who deviated were treated as the "outlaws" they were.[35]

Catt labored very hard for world peace. She spoke all over the country for acceptance of the Versailles Treaty and the League of Nations. She then campaigned for America's participation in the World Court and became a public celebrant of the 1928 Kellogg-Briand Pact "outlawing" war: "it is a mighty stride. . . . He who denies it has a screw loose somewhere."[36] Sometimes, as with her embarrassing praise for the empty Kellogg-Briand Pact or her affection for equally empty pieties ("The introduction of the principles of the Golden Rule into everybody's foreign policy would contribute to a more powerful world"), Catt was an unexpected idealist in foreign affairs, out of touch with the realities of international relations. This was hardly typical of her domestic political analysis where her idealism was equally boundless but disciplined by her more practical political experience. Her idealism was strongest in the 1920s and early 1930s (before Hitler) and led her to oppose any concern with American defense: the answer was at hand in the Kellogg-Briand Pact, the World Court, and the League of Nations. They were the means by which conflicting interests and intemperate furies could be cooled and arbitrated into peace. Arbitration was her solution for international conflict as it was for so many Progressives. Catt believed that in politics reason should be stronger than passion and she took for granted that it actually could be.[37]

At other moments Catt was more characteristically realistic. She appreciated the grim fact that many individuals and countries have gloried in war and that would not be easy to change. She also charged that economic interests — "trade and dollars" — played a painfully large role in the wars that afflicted the world. Indeed, she was often quick to offer an economic explanation of war which would have warmed the heart of Charles A. Beard and fellow skeptics of America's participation in World War I. Ultimately, though, Catt insisted war was rooted in ideas, in people's belief in it. That was its final cause and it was that belief she sought to eradicate.[38]

America and Americans had to join this effort. We had to accept internationalism (the assumption that we were a part of the world) and actively encourage world comity. We could neither withdraw nor expect to dominate. We also had to set an example by abandoning our own "colonial selfishness," which fostered war. In particular, Catt attacked the Monroe Doctrine. It was as selfish as it was dangerous. The answer was international cooperation and disarmament, not colonialism and spheres of influence.[39]

Towards her goals, in 1925 Catt founded the Committee on the Cause and Cure of War. The objective was to lobby Congress and the president and educate the larger public on issues of peace, disarmament, and arbitration. Catt served as the committee's president until 1932. The organization never captured as much of her by then diminished energies as the N.A.W.S.A. had and every means she and its other leaders tried evoked little response from the public. But her efforts went on.[40]

Especially in the 1920s, Catt's peace work involved her in political dissension. Positions differed among women as they had earlier when America entered World War I and that led to competing organizations and ideologies. Two examples illustrate. The Catt-influenced League of Women Voters clashed with the Woman's Party in international peace and women's rights activities on a regular basis, as Susan Becker's research demonstrates.[41] Catt and her brand of Progressive peace activities caused serious divisions with the more radical Women's International League for Peace and Freedom (founded in 1919), as Joan Jensen has shown.[42] And there were other competing ideas, leaders, and groups. Catt was by no means outside these conflicts, somehow serenely above the fray, as her public peace activities might have suggested. But as the 1920s waned, and Catt grew older, she played a more detached role. In fact, her Committee on the Cause and Cure of War was her last political organization, and with its failure she left the field of day-to-day political struggle.

When the Second World War broke out in Europe, Catt reaffirmed her devotion to world order and peace, most notably at the Woman's Centennial Congress in 1940. But like many other Americans of her background and orientation, she proved to be a surprisingly reluctant noninterventionist. Soon she emerged as a public supporter of Britain. She allowed her name to be used by the Committee to Defend America by Aiding the Allies and she vigorously urged all aid (short of America's joining the war) to Great Britain. When the United States entered the war Catt became a dedicated supporter of the Allied cause. Her critics wondered if Catt had reached her dotage. What had happened to her commitment to peace? The explanation was simply that Catt loathed Nazism, indeed so much that she promised herself she would try to outlive Hitler.[43]

Catt had long been aware of the evils of Nazism, particularly in its genocidal policies toward the Jews. Her Hungarian-Jewish friend, Rosika Schwimmer, played an important role in alerting Catt to the intentions of the Nazis towards the Jews. As soon as the Nazis came to power Catt began to help Jewish victims of Nazism. She attempted to get other women to join her in protesting the murderous persecution of Jews by the Nazis, helping to form the Protest Committee of Non-Jewish Women against the Persecution of Jews in Germany as early as 1933. She also served on the Committee of Ten, which in the 1930s lobbied to get the United States to modify its immigration laws so that many more Jews and other refugees from Nazism could escape to America. For these efforts she received the American Hebrew Medal, but the doors remained largely closed.[44]

Peace very much remained on Catt's agenda, though as always her thoughts were for the future, for a world without war. During World War II Catt agreed to serve as honorary chair of the Women's Action Committee for Victory and Lasting Peace, whose internationalist program she thoroughly supported. Although by this time she was unable to do more than lend her name, she did so whenever she could, including endorsing the idea of a Department of Peace in the cabinet and the eventual reality of the United Nations.[45]

It is clear that at the end of her life as all through it she remained convinced that peace was the greatest of all goals for reformers. What did disappear was her hope that somehow woman suffrage would make a significant difference in the pursuit of peace. Things had not worked out that way as, indeed, her dreams for world peace did not bear fruit. In both instances she kept her disappointments private. But she never saw any reason for doubting her ultimate confidence. World community was possible, even destined.

Catt's second realm of activity after 1920 involved protecting and promoting the name of the *mainstream* suffrage movement and its leaders.[46] During its heyday, Catt and the woman suffrage movement had faced a daily barrage of attacks. They often felt (and they often were) embattled. Some of the attacks were whispered but many were very public. Then and later, Catt could live with what she considered more or less rational critiques of the idea of woman suffrage and the movement she led and loved. It was obviously a struggle for her, though, since she refused to consider little that was critical to be rational. Many of these criticisms, however, raised quite crucial points about both women and society and Catt sometimes had to engage her opponents intellectually.

It is true, though, that beginning with the start of World War I in Europe and continuing through America's years of participation some opponents of suffrage engaged in smear campaigns. The most common charge during the war years was that Catt and her movement were somehow both pro-German and pro-socialist (after 1917, pro-Bolshevik). For example, Mrs. James Wadsworth, the leader of antisuffragist forces in the last years of their fight to halt women's enfranchisement, painted the suffrage movement as a dangerous and un-American outbreak intimately connected with "fascism," "socialism," and other aspects of radicalism. Antisuffrage publications, including *Woman's Protest* and *Woman Patriot* made the same point and identified suffragists as "pro-German, pacifists, and socialists." Other critics underlined the theme: "If the Kaiser can get the pacifists, socialists, and suffragists to weaken America . . . the cause of America . . . will be lost."[47] Catt in particular came under fire for her early role in the Woman's Peace Party in 1915 (already long abandoned by 1917) and her friendship with the Hungarian suffragist and peace activist, Rosika Schwimmer. Schwimmer was portrayed as "a Central Powers spy" and readers were left to draw sinister conclusions about Catt.[48]

No doubt Catt hoped that after the war and the victory of woman suffrage she could rest from having to deal with this sort of ludicrous charge. Such was not at all to be the case. Memories were long and the losers in the suffrage battle proved to be determined to exact as much revenge as possible. Some antisuffragists continued to link the victorious suffrage campaign and such figures as Catt and Jane Addams with Lenin, the world communist revolution, and the still evil Germans. They continued to devote their efforts to denunciations of the "Bolshevist-Feminists" and "suffragism, Feminism and Socialism."[49]

Some never gave up. As late as 1946, when yet another Red Scare was gathering steam, Catt came under fire. But her main concern in defending the suffrage cause came from events in the 1920s, which angered her and led her to lash out at critics she saw as dirty and contemptible. In 1924 she was busy replying to elements of the army who constructed and used what became a famous "spider web" to demonstrate the "sinister" connections between assorted women activists and socialists or communists. In 1927 the Daughters of the American Revolution attempted to besmirch Catt and others as part of a list of "doubtful speakers" whose politics were highly suspect. Both attempts involved use of the tactic of guilt by (remote) association later skillfully used by Senator Joseph McCarthy. In another incident the field secretary for the National Association for Constitutional Government published a tract that attacked Catt specifically. "The Strange Case of Mrs. Carrie Chapman Catt" suggested Catt was a communist. Ostensibly, such charges came from those who frankly objected to Catt's work for peace in the 1920s and, to a lesser extent, her enthusiasm for the Children's Bureau, the Child Labor Amendment, and the like.

Catt did not for a moment, however, believe that this was the real story. She felt that the main motivation was continuing anger and bitterness over the adoption of the woman suffrage amendment. It was characteristic of Catt to fight back directly. She had no hesitation in telling off smear-mongers, and she did so. She argued they were wrong to link her abused friends and associates such as Florence Kelley and Jane Addams with communism and wrong to do so in her case too. Moreover, she insisted she was proud to support legislation to assist women and children that offended women reactionaries. In her view, she had nothing to apologize for. Her critics should do the apologizing for their scurrilous and inflammatory charges.[50]

Catt followed the controversies very closely, keeping reams of press clippings and letters about them, and she devoted enormous energy to her full participation in these tempests. What is less obvious is why Catt reacted so strongly to smear attempts. It was surprising, given how coolly she had reacted (at least in public) to this sort of thing before 1920. The explanation probably lay neither in her relatively less crowded schedule in the 1920s nor in a newly thin skin (in private Catt had always been as thin-skinned as anybody else is). Rather, it lay in her intimation that her own (and her friends') life's work was at stake. Her critics were trying to take away what she and others had done, not by legislation, but by rewriting history.

It was partly in this context that Catt began rethinking her previous doctrinaire opposition to suffrage histories, at least insofar as they accented her. She felt uncomfortable about the hagiographic urges of many of her followers, but all along she had collected numerous publications and letters that addressed the history of women in general and woman suffrage in particular, always recognizing, as she wrote Alice Blackwell in 1908, that "the story will be an important one." Her impulse to have preserved what she considered the truth increased in the 1930s when she became alarmed that no one with the knowledge or authority was telling the suffrage story, and she determined to do something about it. She joined other veterans of the movement in putting together *Victory: How Women Won It*, which eventually found a publisher. She contended that "such a book has been very much needed for everyday use," and insisted that even if this was not true for very many besides her, "it will stand the test of time." It would be a true story.[51]

Catt's anxiety increased, if anything, in the 1940s as the suffrage era became increasingly remote. By then smears of her and suffrage were largely ancient history. Yet her need to keep alive the vision and the facts of the suffrage battles was even more acute. She worried: "How can we expect the coming world, not yet born[,] to ever know the truth about it?" And she suspected that "if we do not look after our own history, it will be left in the same condition I found the history of man suffrage," that is, there would be no history there at all.[52] After *Victory*, Catt did not propose to write the story herself. She knew she was too old for that by the 1940s. She had done all that she could to preserve and thus protect the chapter of the history of women that meant so much to her. She could only hope others would fill the gap.

In spite of her embroilments, Catt often played the role of the retired and honored sage after 1920. In the early and middle 1920s Catt was a favorite of some popular magazines, even making the cover of *Time* magazine in 1926. *Good Housekeeping* and *Woman's Home Companion* published her thoughts on all sorts of topics. Undoubtedly such treatment kept her name before the literate public. After a few years this sort of public exposure declined in frequency, but for a smaller public Catt continued to play the role of a political elder.[53]

After she purchased her large, stately home in New Rochelle, New York, in 1928, she strove to create something of a quiet country world, one where she had room to raise all the flowers she so loved. She created a small society around herself there, but even from her semi-retirement her voice was heard. She issued statements on women, on politics, and on presidents.

Her last major foray into the world of political activism was her involvement with the Woman's Centennial Congress of 1940. While by then an old woman, Catt nonetheless was busy in formulating and overseeing this gathering of women, a meeting that attracted a fair amount of national attention. Josephine Schain, chair of the executive committee of the congress, and Edna Stantial clearly ran the event, but Catt was at the center. It was her swan song and everyone there knew it. Her address, the main event of the congress, contained familiar Progressive echoes as she urged women to get involved in the world around them and especially to join the struggle against the international forces of war and despotism.[54]

Mostly, though, Catt stayed in New Rochelle in her last years. From there she was the subject of numerous, but increasingly retrospective, newspaper interviews as she moved toward and then beyond her eightieth birthday. From there she also received numerous honors and awards. The one that mattered the most to her was the Chi Omega Achievement Award, in 1941, honoring her contribution to women. In the form of a gold medal, it was presented at a formal dinner in the White House attended by a parade of notables and presided over by Eleanor Roosevelt. Her appearance to accept the Chi Omega Award was her last on the public stage. Then eighty-two years old and feeling her age, Catt's retirement began in earnest thereafter.[55]

By 1947, Catt was infirm and all but forgotten. Her heart failed after a gallstone operation and her friends were happy that death came quickly to Catt before she was mentally or physically a shadow of her former self. Her death did draw considerable notice, but in the spirit of a period added to complete a sentence written long ago. She was already the past.[56]

The Private Catt

The public Catt was well known in her time and as a result much of her public life can be reconstructed today. But the private, more personal Carrie Catt eluded many of the people who knew and admired her. Statements from her contemporaries evoking a one-dimensional figure are easy to unearth. Catt, it was said, "has no other life. She is not a religious leader . . . a political lawyer, . . . a speculative Shelleyite . . . nor a philanthropic aristocrat. . . . She is a plain woman."[1] Others bathed Catt, especially in her later years, in such adoration that the human Catt slips away from us as perhaps it did from them. It is striking how few hints of any inner life there are in memoirs of Catt or those that touch on Catt. She is always the public person and often the perfect public person.

Of course, Catt's Victorian upbringing and late Victorian adulthood, and those of her closest friends and allies, made a tremendous difference. Openness about one's inner life was not in fashion, at least among people of their class background. However, she was, even beyond the norm of the time, an extraordinarily private person.

We have seen how the glimpses Catt permitted of her childhood throw light on her motivations as a suffrage reformer and on her struggle against women's humiliation in general. Similar insight is available regarding Catt as an adult, but one has to work to get behind her finely meshed screen of privacy.

In exploring aspects of the private Catt I proceed with a sense that this is only one part of the story I am telling. Catt's political history is more than her psychology and I do not propose to reduce it to psychology. Nor have I pretended to a knowledge of psychological interpretation I lack. Yet I have looked below the public surface, to catch her basic concerns and tensions as revealed in her letters especially to close friends. When one does look at Catt through this lens we see a basically successful person, an integrated and effective personality. But we also see one whose considerable personal strengths were matched by quite human tensions and ambivalences that touched every dimension of her life.

One of the dilemmas Catt faced was the reconciliation of her intense idealism with an overwhelming pragmatism. She was a remarkable example of the practical politician; her practical approach to life dominated her suffrage work and permeated her strategic and tactical decisions, often to brilliant, if controversial, effect. Her practicality also guided her political aspirations. She wanted to be known as a competent, effective leader.

Indeed, as Catt knew very well, her soul was often just not practical; it was often downright mundane. She was remarkably ordinary, not in what she did or how she did it, but in how she was as a person. A reader of her letters and her travel journals rapidly discovered this (perhaps distressing) fact as the hours and days pass by and Catt rambles on about food or financial dilemmas, the routine circumstances of the Iowa campaign or luggage problems in Java, her flowers (a particularly favorite subject), or the sights in India.

True enough, Catt cultivated this self-portrait, fashioned from a disciplined life and an impatience with those whose romantic idealism did not touch earth. But one does not get the sense that her practical, even mundane, self-image was in the slightest a pose. As far as she was concerned, she was an ordinary, practical person. As she said to her close friend, Mary Peck, in admitting her dislike for poetry, "the savage emotion and lofty dreams of most great poets are beyond me." Who could doubt such a self-assessment from a person whose literary tastes ran to tales about Buffalo Bill and detective stories and who felt no resonance in poetry, the plays of Shakespeare, or even the stories of Kipling.[2]

Yet this cannot possibly be the entire story of Carrie Catt. Catt had to have had an incredibly powerful idealism driving her extraordinary life of service. In fact, her idealism did run deeply. There is no other explanation of her life. Her followers appreciated this trait; while they respected her practicality, it was Catt's idealism they loved. And Catt too recognized and affirmed this overwhelming idealism.

Part of Catt's self-image was as the pioneer: "all my heroes and heroines are pioneers." Her pioneer was above all an idealist, someone "big enough" and prepared "to step out of the beaten path" to do "a good thing." Such idealism was essential to her existence. It was a matter of what a properly ethical life should be: "To the right that needs assistance . . . Give yourselves." It was also, she took it for granted, the formula for her own (and she thought others') personal happiness: "There is a royal road to happiness; it lies in consecration — and conscience."[3] Her adventures in politics flowed from the wells of this idealism, of course, wells that as Mary Peck recognized implied a spiritual dimension to the ordinary Catt, which was rarely on public display. Peck put it rather too grandly for Catt's taste when she told Catt, "the same elemental instinct lies behind your life that lay behind Lincoln's. One senses something spiritual. . . ."[4] But Catt knew what Peck was talking about. Beneath the cool, practical exterior lay a passionately idealistic Catt.

Conjoined to her idealism was another powerful dimension of the private Catt, her anger. Catt had a reputation as something of an impatient activist as a younger woman in the suffrage movement. Although as a mature activist her reputation was that of an efficient, pleasant person, even tempered and controlled, there was a level at which she was angry, and that anger motivated her, just as her idealism did. Directed at the condition of women, the anger, as we have seen, had been there since she was a child. Unlike her idealism, it almost never surfaced in the public Catt, but, once again, its existence was no secret to Catt's intimates.

Only when one appreciates the force of idealism and anger in Catt's personality can one obtain any insight into her intensely passionate center. In her public personality she may have seemed rather bland, and she did even to herself, but this was only one side of Carrie Catt.

One of the more puzzling aspects of an image of Catt as an ordinary, practical person is how inadequately it helps us explain her frequent and sometimes lengthy illnesses. Catt had numerous physical troubles. Some of Catt's periods of illness, which invariably forced her to withdraw from her battles, had specific medical causes. This was the case, for instance, when she caught typhoid after her all-out effort in the South Dakota campaign of 1890. Some were just plain bad luck, such as her broken leg in 1931. Others were unmistakably connected with her reaction to deaths in her family. But most were obviously related to personal exhaustion which appears to have come from her frantic overwork under extreme tension. This was the situation following her first presidency of the National American Woman Suffrage

Association in 1904. In this instance, her exhaustion compounded by
the subsequent deaths of her husband and her mother, Catt had to
take a long rest cruise before she emerged a recovered person. Her
good friend Clara Hyde suggested that there was a suspicious pattern
in which Catt became ill when progress on women's enfranchisement
seemed to slow. But long after women won enfranchisement extensive
health problems continued to haunt Carrie Catt.[5]

It is clear that at times Catt had trouble remaining on an even
keel. Despite her affection for a rational, disciplined life, her own existence revolved around a recurring pattern of too intense involvement
followed by physical collapse and requisite periods of recovery. There
never were any conventional mental breakdowns, though where one
draws the line between Catt's bouts of nervous exhaustion and mental
collapse is a legitimate question. The larger point, however, is that the
record of Carrie Catt's life suggests a good deal of intense, even over-
intense, living and surprisingly little of the calm serenity that was her
public face.

Catt sought to keep her inner intensity and her emotional side
below the surface. She did not want to dwell on this aspect of her
nature, in part because she was so determined to demonstrate that a
woman could be as "rational" as any man could claim to be. Also important, though, was her recognition that she had difficulties expressing her feelings and emotions, a fact for which she was well known
and not entirely admired.

Catt was a shy and unusually reserved individual, which led Susan
B. Anthony in the early 1890s to view her as an unimpressive woman.[6]
In time that public Catt faded away, but her reputation for reticence
and for maintaining personal self-control under all circumstances remained and became a legend among her coworkers. While she could
be warm, even they felt compelled to acknowledge that she "was sometimes thought cold."[7] Anna Howard Shaw underlined the point when
she wrote to Lucy Anthony once of her amazement when after helping
Catt on a minor matter, Catt suddenly exclaimed "Heaven bless you"
and then "threw her arms about my neck and kissed me. I never saw
her make such a demonstration before."[8] Or, did she see her do so
again. Even her close friend, Mary Peck, observed the same Catt, only
she complained about it directly to her idol. She told Catt that she
could be like "cold boiled halibut" and more than once rebuked her
because "you never said anything about your feelings."[9]

Catt had her moments, maybe many moments, when she regretted her repressed self and wished she were more open with her emotions. As she wrote to Anna Howard Shaw, "I wish daily that I could
express in words my feelings but I have never been able to do so. . . ."

And she added, significantly, "it is now hopeless."[10] She had, however, more moments in which she felt no such regrets, for she lived most of her life otherwise — and with few evident doubts. And while she rarely faulted other people, she made an exception when they were in her judgment not in control of their feelings and passions. She had little patience with Elizabeth Cady Stanton on just such grounds. Stanton was often out of control, Catt believed, and Catt's condemnation followed. Her dislike for such people, or for outbursts of "irrational" emotionalism, was so intense that one has to wonder if Catt's condemnations were not mostly against the restless and powerful inner feelings of her own nature.

This possibility makes some sense in light of Catt's devotion to the idea of discipline. For her it was an unquestioned virtue and she was frequently its eager prophet. She believed in its suitability in her life in the most conventional senses. She was, as she said, "awfully old fashioned. . . . I neither drink smoke, play cards nor gamble." She could live with persons less virtuous, since "All my party do . . . these things except smoke." But there was no doubt in her mind that they were weak in falling prey to such follies. They lacked her personal discipline. "I *do feel superior.*"[11]

It is more interesting that Catt perceived the suffrage movement sometimes as an exercise in discipline. In social and political terms she would have agreed, at least in part, with later observers who viewed it in just this fashion. After all, she was a Progressive reformer, and many of her specific reforms were part of an overall attempt to discipline "immoral" forces — corrupt politicians, "ignorant" immigrants, and the like — to the benefit of the disciplined as well as the rest of the society.

What is remarkable, though, is that she felt increased personal discipline was as important a result of the suffrage crusade as any other both for her and, she claimed, for all suffragists. Of course, the struggle for votes for women was important as a "noble cause" to "establish a new and good thing." But Catt celebrated it also because it encouraged a personal "discipline not otherwise obtainable." Indeed, "As I look back over the years, . . . I realize that the greatest thing in the long campaign for us was not its crowning victory but the discipline it gave us all."[12]

This affirmation of the suffrage crusade because it increased her personal discipline must seem strange unless we accept that it derived from an individual whose need for discipline must have been overwhelming and whose own discipline was a hard-won act of the will. Catt suspected her passionate, emotional side, clearly, and her concern with discipline was frequently the result. Catt's idealism, her pain, her anger, her passionate drive, these among other parts of her life were in fact not easy for her to discipline. Mary Peck got it right in part when she observed of her heroine, Catt: "The only way for you to live was to fill your life so full of work you could not think of unhappy things. Your idea of hell probably is a place where there is nothing to do but think."[13]

How much or how often Catt was unhappy, especially as she dealt with the tension between her public face and her much more passionate private side, we do not know. There were times when Catt privately gave vent to negative feelings about herself, once remarking, for instance, "at the present I do not like myself."[14] These times were almost always, however, when Catt was ill. There is no reason to think they were expressions of anything other than the normal discouragement most of us feel when sick.

But this dimension of the private Catt should not be exaggerated; she could be quite lively and did sometimes give vent (in private) to her emotions. Anger, warmth, and a sense of humor often appeared. Her reserve was far from crippling or somehow pathological in its effects. Thus it was with good reason that Catt scoffed at the idea that she was the model of calm self-discipline.[15]

Moreover, while it is not easy to measure this sort of thing, Carrie Catt had a fairly rich life of emotional relationships with other people. She was in no way the lonely spinster who fit the antisuffragists' stereotype of N.A.W.S.A. crusaders. She had many friends. She maintained contact with her immediate family and other relatives throughout her life. She married twice, and all observers agree with her own pictures of her marriages as successful and loving relationships. The depth of her emotional closeness with her family and her husbands is, however, hard to gauge. They left no testimony and Catt's own reflections on her emotions towards them are meager, as Catt's characteristic privacy ensured. Moreover, even in these relationships there is at least a hint that Catt's reserve continued to operate. Catt and her second husband, for instance, consciously chose not to share much of their work challenges and problems with each other.[16]

Catt did not have any children by either of her two husbands. Neither Catt nor her correspondents refer to the subject. It is possible that sexual or fertility problems were the explanation. More probable is the fact that Catt at least in her longer second marriage was so intensely devoted to women's enfranchisement that she did not want children. We do know that Catt claimed to like "little Folks," believed that they mattered enormously in life, and held dear the debatable idea that happiness in life was normally and rightly associated with having children. Perhaps these sentiments suggest that there were times when she regretted not having children. But she never said so.[17]

We are on much firmer ground in Carrie Catt's unquestioned capacity for friendship with other women. Catt had numerous friends throughout her long life, including several who were genuinely intimate personal friends. As an old woman, she looked back to her decades of struggle for women's enfranchisement with nostalgia for her many friendships: "The old days will always be the best to us . . . what made them great was the fast friendships we made, the trust and confidence we felt for our comrades."[18] These friendships are the best testimony there could be that Catt was quite effective in building enduring emotional bonds, bonds that helped her immensely in her work as suffragist.

Catt did not really forge such relationships with any of the three women who were fellow leaders in the women's movement, namely, Susan B. Anthony, Alice Stone Blackwell, and Anna Howard Shaw. Anthony was Catt's patron, as we know. But Anthony sponsored Catt less out of affection than out of frank recognition that Catt was the best organizer among the second generation of suffragist leaders, someone whom the movement needed by 1900. Catt's feeling for Anthony is difficult to assess. She admired Anthony for her service to women, though it is significant that Catt did not grant her the "pioneer" status she so respected in people, a status latter-day enthusiasts awarded Anthony as a matter of course. Yes, Catt said, Anthony was the most important early contributor to the liberation of women in America, but she was hardly the first. Anthony's contribution in Catt's eyes derived from her determined, unyielding, driving role as a crusader for women's rights. When plans to honor Anthony's memory first began to gain currency in the 1930s, Catt was unenthusiastic. Anthony was great, Catt cheerfully conceded, but no memorial was necessary. After World War II, Catt reversed herself, however, and actively solicited funds for a memorial (insofar as this was possible for a person in her late eighties). Catt's words unfailingly and warmly honored Anthony's contribution. Yet a sense of distance is always present; they are not the expressions of someone who deeply cared for Anthony or for whom Anthony was a close friend.[19]

The explanation for the obvious lack of a close relationship with Alice Stone Blackwell is simpler. Blackwell was another patron of Catt's, one who was quite unambiguous in her enthusiastic support of Catt and her work throughout the decades of the suffrage struggle. However, Blackwell, like Anthony, was of an older generation. While they met at conventions and suffrage association executive meetings often enough, Blackwell and Catt never worked together for any time in the way Catt and Anthony did. Blackwell's base was always the Boston area and there was too little contact between the two women for a close friendship to flourish.[20]

This was hardly the case regarding Catt and Anna Howard Shaw. Until Shaw's death in 1919, Catt and Shaw spent an enormous amount of time, decades in fact, in almost daily contact. They knew each other very, very well. And they were, most of the time, friends, despite their occasional leadership rivalry. Still, it is doubtful there were close bonds of friendship between these two women.

The story of this relationship is interesting and complex, and it tells us a good deal about Catt. It is easier to chart than Catt's interactions with Anthony or Blackwell because an enormous number of letters, especially from Shaw, exist. To understand the relations between the two major leaders of the "second" generation of suffrage leaders, Shaw and Catt, one must start with the realization that for the unmarried Shaw, Susan B. Anthony was the central figure of her adult emotional life. And after her death in 1906, Anthony's real nieces, especially Lucy Anthony, came to fill this role. "Aunt Susan" was, as Shaw said, "the one great passion of my life."[21] Shaw saw her career as a suffrage worker as a conscious service to Anthony and, after Anthony's death, to her memory. In this world of Anthony-worship and association with those of her family, others came a distant second.[22]

Between Catt and Shaw there does seem to have been a good relationship in the 1890s when they were both associates of "Aunt Susan." Catt showered tributes on Shaw in those days, reporting how much others in the cause admired her and, again and again, celebrating Shaw's greatest ability, her oratory. Letters of this sort, in fact, may be found — from Catt to Shaw anyway — as late as 1916. But over time their frequency diminished and their breathless quality disappeared. Moreover, Catt's continued emphasis on Shaw as the great orator had a perhaps not entirely unintended double meaning which Shaw could not have missed. Shaw was the great orator, the letters said, but in later years that is all they said. They certainly did not say Shaw was the great leader or the appropriate successor to Anthony. They could not, since Shaw wasn't an effective leader and because Catt judged that Shaw was much inferior to herself in that role. Catt made all this explicit after she took over from Shaw in 1916. "I have always thought it was a cruel mistake that you had to be National President . . . the burden and responsibility of administration takes spontaneity and emotion and joy out of one. All these are qualities an orator must have. . . . You may not regret those eleven years . . . but I do for you."[23]

Overall, though, except for the period of direct competition between the two women in 1900, Catt and Shaw were friends. They worked together for thirty years. At various points in their long collaboration they expressed affection for each other which they undoubtedly felt. Most of their letters, however, especially in Shaw's last years, are strictly businesslike in tone, written by two colleagues in a common course, not two close friends.[24]

Shaw's death in 1919 was unexpected and Catt was genuinely upset. Life went right on for Catt, however, without much further mention of Shaw. In Catt's last years her basic affection for the long-dead Shaw was reawakened when others arranged to have a World War II ship named the *Anna Howard Shaw*. Catt was glad because she knew that Shaw would be happy to have any instrument of liberty named for her. She hoped it would be a ship like Shaw, a strong, fighting ship. Perhaps she missed Shaw more by then. Certainly she knew and admired Shaw's contribution to their joint cause. But she also knew she and Shaw had had a complicated and less than intimate friendship.[25]

Most of Catt's friendships were much less troubled than that with Anna Howard Shaw. Some were founded during the first two decades of the twentieth century, when Catt gradually formed around her a circle of adoring younger friends to whom she was "Mother Catt," as Anthony had earlier gathered her "nieces." Others came after 1920 when Catt had "retired." In almost every case these friendships too were born from mutual association in one cause or another. They amply demonstrate Catt's extensive capacity to make friends. Especially those of the 1930s and 1940s reveal a Catt who grew increasingly affectionate towards her friends, who signed letters to a host of friends "lovingly" and wrote in a friendly, warm tone.[26] There are many examples.

One warm friendship was with Catt's onetime secretary, Clara Hyde (Catt called her "Steady") with whom Catt carried on an extensive and affectionate correspondence in the teens and 1920s. Some of their letters discuss personal subjects, albeit cautiously.[27] Another was with Josephine Schain, a fellow suffragist, administrator of the Committee on the Cause and Cure of War, and chair of the Executive Committee of Catt's 1940 Woman's Centennial Congress. Most of their extensive correspondence details a business relationship, but in time Catt's letters shifted from "Dear Mrs. Schain" to "Dear Josephine" and their letters become those between friends who were also colleagues.[28] A third was with Edna Stantial, active in the W.C.C. and archivist of the National American Woman Suffrage Association, who was widely respected for her loving concern for her friends, including Catt.[29] Still another was with an old New York suffrage ally, Harriet

Laidlaw, of whom Catt spoke as warmly as of anyone. She was "my dear precious lady" who made "the world radiant wherever you go."[30] And there were others, such as Mrs. Ben Hooper, as she wished to be known, one-time president of the General Federation of Women's Clubs.[31]

There were other women who were closer to Catt in her mature life and who provide us with the best glimpse of Catt's success in forming emotional bonds of some intensity. Some of these women worked with Catt on political issues and were in awe of her at least initially. Others enjoyed a more equal and open exchange. Finally, there was one friend who tried to break Catt's bounds and become Catt's lover.

Maud Wood Park was a close friend whose affection for Catt was at first akin to hero-worship. Park became associated with Catt in the suffragist struggle, eventually becoming her most important associate in the last years, serving as head of the congressional lobbying effort. Later Park became the head of Catt's League of Women Voters. There are hundreds of letters remaining between Catt and Maud Wood Park. While these letters from the teens right up to Catt's death in 1947 often concern mutual work, they also demonstrate that these two women became close friends by any standard. Especially over time the letters betray in their salutations and closings great warmth, an indication not to be ignored when one considers that Catt almost always addressed her correspondents as Mrs. or Miss and signed her letters equally formally — with her full name. Park frequently saluted Catt as the "Great Chief" or "Beloved Chief." Over and over she celebrated Catt as leader and as a friend; and on a number of occasions she wrote poems of affection and devotion to Catt. Much more unusual was the warmth, if not the intimacy, of Catt's responses. Maud Wood Park became "Maud" and "My dearest Maud" and Catt repeatedly signed her letters "lovingly, C.C.C." Especially as the years went by, both women shared their daily lives and in Park's case at least a good many personal feelings. Moreover, there was at times a kind of relaxed and informal attitude on Catt's part that was extremely rare, illustrated, for instance, by the following passage in a letter of commiseration Catt wrote to Park when Park had a toe amputated: "I have seriously thought about having both my legs off, but I must hear first how you feel after having one toe off, poor old Maudie. . . . I love you just as much with nine toes as when you had ten."[32] Only someone who has read thousands of Catt's letters can appreciate how different the tone of the Catt–Park correspondence is from the usual formal and distant Catt style.[33]

Rosika Schwimmer was another friend whose connection with Catt began with a political alliance and a personal admiration for Catt. Schwimmer was a zealous Hungarian feminist and pacifist. Catt and

Schwimmer first became acquainted through Catt's International Woman Suffrage Alliance, probably sometime after 1904. In succeeding years they became cordial friends and allies in the often discouraging struggle for the enfranchisement of women in the world at large. Indeed, it appears that Schwimmer became the best friend Catt had among the numerous women throughout the world with whom she dealt, particularly in the period between 1905 and 1914 when she was most active as president of the I.W.S.A. Catt and Schwimmer's friendship suffered tremendously, however, after World War I broke out and the United States entered the war. Schwimmer clashed with popular opinion in Europe and eventually America in her unyielding (and courageous) pacificism. Her stance provided the enemies of the American suffrage cause (well into the 1920s) with good material to assault the patriotism of Catt and the National American Woman Suffrage Association. They sought to paint Schwimmer not only as she was, a pacifist, but also as pro-German, which she was not, and to link Catt and the N.A.W.S.A. as tightly as they could with those causes through Schwimmer. The situation was complicated in the 1920s by the presence of Schwimmer in the United States and her unsuccessful but intensely controversial effort to gain United States citizenship.

Catt, for her part, undertook to separate the American suffrage cause from the controversial Schwimmer while at the same time defending her, an approach that satisfied no one. It infuriated Schwimmer, whose letters to Catt on Catt's maneuvers and on what she took to be Catt's less than energetic endeavors to obtain citizenship for her are among the most personal and poignant (and sometimes bitter) that Catt ever received. Catt's replies reflected her own anguish and illuminated how much Schwimmer's friendship meant to her. Eventually in the 1930s tensions eased and the two women resumed their lively and apparently rich friendship. And Catt resumed work on what was a decades-long struggle for Schwimmer to obtain status as an American citizen.[34]

Carrie Catt's closeness to Alda Wilson illustrates Catt's need for and success at building friendships based on companionship. Wilson became Catt's companion during the "retirement" decades in New Rochelle. She lived in the Catt home and in Catt's last years was, in effect, her nurse. More than anyone else's, including Catt's two husbands, Wilson's life was woven into Catt's on a daily, indeed an hourly, basis — and for a much longer time.

While Wilson had played a modest role in the suffrage movement, in her later decades as Catt's companion in private life, Wilson shared with Catt not just the routine, everyday matters, but also the special things that meant so much to Catt at home: the quiet evenings by the

Catt's home in New Rochelle, New York. Courtesy of the Library of Congress.

fire, the hours spent working with flowers, and the rest. How much of her inner self Catt shared with Wilson is not known, but their emotional closeness was evident to Catt's other friends. They appreciated Wilson a great deal because she took such good care of Catt — who in her seventies and eighties needed the loving help Wilson provided. They were deeply dependent on each other.[35]

The even more obvious, and clearly more significant, friendship of this sort was with Mary Garrett Hay, known to Catt as Mollie. Hay was Catt's closest coworker and then companion during her suffrage decades.[36]

The two women were hardly identical. Hay's background was affluent and she had the support of a father with whom she had strongly identified when she was a child. Hay never married and instead spent all her adult life as an activist. Yet the two women also had a lot in common. They were both intensely dedicated to the cause of the enfranchisement of women. They were of about the same age and were in the same generation of the suffrage movement. Both came from the Midwest and both eventually transferred their lives to New York City and its environs. Both came up through the suffrage ranks though, unlike Catt, Hay had been active in the Woman's Christian Temperance Union. Hay served first in local and then state Indiana suffrage circles, as Catt had in Iowa. Both came into the national scene through the organizational wing of the N.A.W.S.A. and both were known as tough and practical advocates of success through organization.

By the late 1890s the Catt–Hay friendship was already close, forged in numerous joint efforts to win their twin battle: the battle for woman suffrage and for the gospel of organization within the N.A.W.S.A. By the turn of the century they were a team and they continued to be for the twenty-five years they worked together for votes for women. Even though Catt went on to leadership of the N.A.W.S.A. and Hay rarely occupied high position in the organization, she continued to watch out for Catt and to be her closest advisor and friend, as everyone who knew them recognized. After 1900 Hay gradually turned her attention to the fight for suffrage in New York State. Here too she and Catt worked closely in the middle teens. Hay became the campaign leader and acquired the respected reputation in New York as the "Big Boss," and she attained considerable popularity with the press and with politicians (who, no doubt, recognized one of their own).

Throughout the years of the Catt–Hay working partnership, others among the suffragist elite acknowledged the pair's closeness and equally respected their organizational talents. But they did not respect Catt and Hay equally; far from it. Critics objected to Hay's tendency to issue orders and to her allegedly rigid bureaucratic and hierarchical approach to organization. Moreover, because Hay was so close to Catt and yet below her in the suffrage hierarchy, critics of Catt's decisions found it convenient to make their complaints by faulting Hay. Indeed, Hay proved to be a lightening rod for Catt time and again, most famously when the N.A.W.S.A. elite selected Catt as president in 1900 and immediately turned around and abolished her Organizational Committee, which was scheduled to be headed by Hay.

Hay was an independent factor in her own right in the continuing controversy that surrounded her, however. She had a reputation for imperiousness; she could be tactless, and she did not hesitate to point out the failures of others. No one disliked her more than Anna Howard Shaw, who conceded that part of her antipathy was class-oriented. Shaw spent much of her life struggling for enough money to survive. This was never a problem for the wealthy Hay and only briefly for Catt. Shaw's feelings were clear: "I loathe exclusiveness and snobbery and old families and the first people and all that sort of vulgarity. They seem like Mrs. Hay."[37]

But the problem for Shaw — and others — more often went directly to the issue of Hay's hard-driving authoritarianism. To Shaw, Hay was a perpetual "disrupting force" given to "attacking every woman whom she thinks stands in her way whom she cannot control."[38] It also annoyed Shaw that Hay was so close to Catt. It was "a great pity that Mrs. Catt forces us either to accept Miss Hay or else fail to enlist herself personally."[39]

The victory for woman suffrage in New York State in 1917 was a glorious moment in Hay's life. But it was the end of neither her activism nor her close association with Catt. Hay went on to become extremely prominent in Republican Party affairs in the 1920s and served as a national proponent of the maintenance and enforcement of Prohibition. Catt's interests, as we know, lay elsewhere in this period, but it is safe to assume that the two women consulted with each other frequently.

In fact, they had been living together since the death of Catt's second husband in 1905. All together, they lived under the same roof for two decades. This fact, of course, is dramatic evidence of the closeness of the Catt–Hay friendship, especially when we keep in mind that neither woman needed financial support. The most conclusive testimony came from Catt's own behavior. When Hay died of a cerebral hemorrhage in 1928, Catt was devastated. It was, as Mary Peck put it, "the great blow" of the last third of Catt's life. She decided later that she wished to be buried next to Hay — not either of her husbands — which was as eloquent a statement of her feelings as there could be.[40]

The nature of Catt's relation with Mollie Hay, however, is much less clear. We have really only the letters between them to shed any light on it. The fact that Catt and Hay lived together so long only complicates the matter, since both the number of letters they wrote to each other and the periods in which they wrote them are limited (which was also the case between Alda Wilson and Catt).

Some of the Catt–Hay letters that remain depart from the usual pattern of Catt's letters, business as usual in the suffrage cause, the travel reports, accounts of the latest flowers that characterize all of Catt's letters. As always, it was when Catt or Hay was sick that the reserve broke down and Catt, with a frankness all the more credible because of its rarity, said such things as: "Dear, precious Mollie, take best care of yourself, for I cannot get on without you. By and by I shall come home and look after you."[41] Catt almost always addressed her letters to Hay "Mollie," frequently with such affectionate salutations

"My dear Old Maid, Mollie," "Blessed Mollie," or "My beloved." Even in the 1920s, when Catt's letters to Hay seemed less enthusiastic, Hay was still "My dear." Similarly, Catt almost always signed her letters to Hay "lovingly" and, a good deal more unusually, signed them "C.C.C." rather than her almost invariable "Carrie Chapman Catt."[42]

Under a tombstone that says, "Here lie two friends, united in friendship . . . in service to a great cause," Catt is buried next to Hay, as she wished.

Catt's friendship with Mary G. Peck reveals a capacity for a quite different kind and depth of friendship.

Mary Peck abandoned her career as an English teacher at the University of Minnesota to work both for the New York State suffrage effort and for the N.A.W.S.A. She wrote on behalf of suffrage, including a short book, *The Rise of the Woman Suffrage Party,* and did such things as chair the Speakers Bureau of the Empire State Campaign Committee in 1915.[43] Peck was a small figure in the overall movement, however, and her relationship with Catt was almost entirely a personal one.

Peck first met Catt in 1909, much later than Hay had, but once their friendship started it flowered quickly. It was a relationship of unique intimacy for both women. The friendship is also unique for Catt in that it is the best recorded, in the hundreds of letters they exchanged, of which many still exist. The letters trail off in the late 1920s when Catt asked Peck to come to live in New Rochelle and she did so. Reports from others confirm that they continued to be very close until Catt's death, though Peck, unlike Hay, never lived in Catt's house (Alda Wilson was living with Catt during most of those later years). Peck's own tribute to Catt in her later years came in her biography, *Carrie Chapman Catt,* the only one that exists.

The Catt–Peck letters not only give us the best insight into an intimate friendship of Catt's, but are the best source for an exploration of the private Catt that we have. The reason is that Peck refused to accept Catt's usual businesslike and distant approach to letter writing — and to human relationships. She wrote very personal letters to Catt, letters that are often impressive as letters. Catt considered "Mary Gray Peck . . . the most wonderful letter writer that I have ever known,"[44] and she was repeatedly confronted in them by a Peck who insisted that Catt reply in equally personal fashion (if not equal style). Clearly, Peck sought a deeply personal relationship with Catt and to a considerable extent she succeeded.

The Catt–Peck friendship deserves to be described as a romantic attachment. This was most obvious in regard to Peck. Peck was in love with Catt for decades and everything one can discover about Peck's feelings and behavior suggests that she was in love with Catt in an erotic sense as well as in others.

Peck missed few opportunities to show her love for Catt. She sent her, for instance, an almost unending stream of gifts. At times "flood" would be the better word, since in one letter Catt thanks Peck for sending her what was the twenty-seventh gift from Peck during that spring alone.[45] Besides the gifts, there were the words: "What wouldn't I give to have lived like you. . . . For many years you have been to me the embodiment of human charm and loveliness and nobility, and this will be true to my dying day. So sharp is the feeling that I hesitate to put it into clumsy words."[46] "If you only knew how often I think of you, you'd wonder how I ever think of anything else!"[47] "Good night, darling, beautiful, glorious, priceless, peerless, unutterably precious Pandora."[48] "Good night, Pandora . . . I love you ardently, beloved Pandora."[49]

Peck also drew attention to the praise Catt got from others (with Peck's evident approval): "Much has been said about the quality of your mind, your genius for arousing great forces, your concentration on practical ends, your power to attract personal devotion, your passion for turning everything and everybody to practical account, your unparalleled genius for organization, in the drive of your energy." But she always went on to claim a more intimate appreciation of Catt; for example: "It has seemed to me there was a peculiar understanding between us. . . . I could see in you as perhaps the deepest spring of action, pity," and "I understand your need of land, gardens, animals, space."[50] And why not, since Peck felt she knew Catt most intimately. They had experienced together "long midsummer nights when the sun hardly set, the longing, the heartbreak, the passionate adoration, the grief at parting." Her love was forever: "Life cures most of us, but some of us are incurable."[51]

No doubt Peck's letters reflect a spirit that is similar to other women lovers of the past, about whom Faderman argues that the women opened "their souls to each other" and spoke in "a language that was in no way different from the language of heterosexual love."[52] While Catt's replies do not match this spirit, in time her love for Mary became unmistakable. In a number of ways, Catt signaled Peck quite directly as to how important Peck had become to her. She often wrote to her — and only her — "I love you."[53] She wrote her in 1929: "I am never going to give you up for another. I like you the best."[54] And, particularly in 1928, when Catt thought her heart problems would prove fatal, Catt let down her guard, conceding, "It has been one of the joys of my life when I had you for my friend." While "two people

Carrie Catt, seated, far right, in 1932. The other women are, left to right, Esther Ogden, Mary G. Peck, Alda Wilson, and Miss Ogden. Courtesy of the Library of Congress.

rarely can talk closely to each other," Catt had found a special, "understanding sympathy" in Peck.[55]

Another sign of their intimacy was Catt's acceptance of Peck's criticisms of her. Peck did criticize occasionally, something that almost never happened to Catt, perhaps because the kind of friendship that includes loving criticism usually eluded her. Peck, unlike most of Catt's other friends, obviously did not intend to be only a worshiper. She insisted on the full rights of an equal, close relationship. Her criticisms of Catt almost always focused on Catt's occasional attempts to avoid such a relationship. Yet Catt liked Peck's admonitions or jibes — a typical Catt reply begins, "I have your letter calling me a liar."[56] And Catt answered in kind, especially whenever Peck fell into one of her more adoring rhapsodies: "No one but you ever discovered I had any charms and of course you are an ass";[57] or, "You wrote another letter concerning the charm of my lower lip! I took a day off and went cavorting from mirror to mirror and grinning like a Cheshire cat in hope of catching that 'haunting smile.' . . . Stop that," Catt urged.[58] Peck did not follow this advice and on at least one occasion Catt wrote her that her latest letters were just too personal and effusive and had to be tossed "to the flames."[59]

Peck never married, and there are no indications of romantic or sexual involvements with men. Her letters never mention men and, rarely, for that matter, other women. She had some other friends, but her devotion to Catt was obviously intense — and exclusive. There can be no question that the center of Peck's adult emotional life was Catt.

The intensity of Peck's feeling for Catt, however, was not entirely reciprocated by Catt. Though it could be said of their friendship that it was a member of the species of "romantic friendships" that "were love relationships in every sense except perhaps genital,"[60] Catt was also attracted to men, having married twice. Moreover, she had many other friends and, in Hay at least, one other who was very close to her.

And yet it is obvious that Catt and Peck had a deep love for one another, which meant a great deal to both of them. Catt chose to protest when it seemed to become too personal in Peck's hands, while Peck, if she knew of the implicit erotic aspect of her feelings, kept that from Catt. If they were lovers, they were so only as far as Catt's traditional and unquestioned acceptance of heterosexuality permitted.

The larger point, best illustrated by her experience with Peck but reinforced by her friendship with other women, her ties to coworkers and family, and her two successful marriages, is that the private Catt was quite able to create emotional relationships with others. She was shy and even repressed to a degree, but she was capable of great warmth.

Evolutionary Optimism

Catt was, in private and in public, more than anything else an optimist. She had a faith in personal and historical possibility that was integral to her thought and action, her very being. Nothing was more important to her as a person. Nothing sustained her more often. Nothing occasioned more liturgies of celebration from her privately or publicly.

It was quite literally a wrap with which she warmed herself constantly in a world that she found politically and, perhaps personally, inhospitable. For her, as for the Emerson she does not mention, her optimism was her practical religion.

Optimism for Catt meant "faith in God's eternal law for the evolution of the race" (which, she said, was the "chief control of my life") and confidence that this evolution would bring great good.[61] Acquired at Iowa State in the Gilded Age, this evolutionary faith was a fashionable replacement for Christianity. Usually derived from the thought of Herbert Spencer, such views were much less popular by the Progressive Era, though Lester Ward's version, which stressed the openness of evolution to the efforts of human manipulation, attracted some Progressive reformers. By the end of World War I all forms of evolutionary optimism went out of fashion, but Catt's faith lasted until her death. Her attitudes in this as in other areas had long before been formed and they were not subject to changing fashions.[62]

Catt's cosmic optimism was not typical among suffragists of her era. But it was not unique. Charlotte Perkins Gilman, the leading theorist of feminism in Catt's era, was very much a fellow evolutionist. Gilman's version was notable for its sharp antagonism toward those she felt were inferior in evolutionary development. Indeed, she eventually moved from New York City to get away from foreigners (Jews). She also developed a distinct sense of skepticism towards traditional religion and its claims. Catt was hardly enthusiastic about immigrants in the United States, but she preferred to emphasize that evolution was equally guaranteed to all peoples, at whatever stage they were at the moment. Moreover, her evolutionary optimism always contained the belief that God ordained and oversaw the entire process. It was, ultimately, God's process and God's universe.

When Catt wrote of particular religions, however, she was usually very critical. To her they were so permeated by "false beliefs" and "superstition" that they disgusted her. Especially regarding women, their teachings were repugnant: "the sacred word of the four great religious systems of the world command obedience and subjection"; and the social practices towards women which these teachings often encouraged were appalling.[63]

About Christianity Catt was rather circumspect, as we might expect from one who was such a sensitive, practical politician. There was, of course, a long tradition of discussion about Christianity among women in the United States interested in altering the status of women. Throughout the nineteenth century women had investigated, and sometimes criticized, the implications of the Bible, the practices of the Christian churches, and Christian theology as they affected women.

There were many opinions and numerous controversies over the role of Christianity in this context, some women bitterly assailing the religion, others defending it, and still others seeking to change or pare away parts of the religion or its operations that seemed to oppress women. Catt was well aware of these disputes. She was equally aware of the almost endless numbers of clergy who earnestly opposed woman suffrage because of their patriarchal understanding of the teaching of Christianity and of the similar arguments of the antisuffragist movement.[64]

Yet Catt did not join those who proposed a full-scale attack on Christianity. Before she was a major leader of the woman's movement, she indicated how ridiculous she thought St. Paul's patriarchal ideas about women were and she insisted that the Bible in general could hardly be a moral guide to the modern world in all aspects. After all, she wrote, the Bible appeared to sanction evils such as slavery, the rigid subordination of women, and the like. At the same time, however, Catt was quick to affirm the Bible as a proper source of ethical truth — though she was vague as to what she meant. And when Elizabeth Cady Stanton's revisionist *Woman's Bible* appeared to threaten the popularity of the women's movement, Catt not only resisted the temptation to work on it, but aggressively disassociated the N.A.W.S.A. from it — and Stanton.[65]

It is significant, though, that Catt cannot be found explicitly declaring how she stood on Christianity as a religion and its ultimate claims, an omission all the more significant given how often she proclaimed her faith in evolution. Her followers are equally vague when it comes to the question of Catt and Christianity. The reason probably is that they knew that their leader was not a Christian in any conventional sense. Nowhere in her papers does Catt declare a faith in Christ (or even mention him). Nor did Catt ever join a Christian church in an age in which this was routinely expected of one of her class.[66]

She did write for several Christian publications after 1920, generally on international relations and peace concerns. She wrote for them, clearly, as part of her effort to rally all possible forces to her cause. Yet, even in these articles there were some rather explicit statements critical of Christian *practice* in human history. She boldly insisted that Christians and Christian nations had engaged in many horrible and inexcusable wars throughout human history. They had a lot to apologize for, and their enlistment in a campaign for peace was, Catt implied, exactly the way for them to achieve expiation of their sins.[67]

Although not really a Christian, Catt wasn't an atheist or an agnostic, nor is there any sign that reform for her, as with many of Arthur Mann's Yankee reformers, was a public substitute for the loss of a private god.[68] Nor was her strong sense of discipline and duty a substitute road to personal happiness. She was a reasonably dutiful and responsible adult, to be sure, but she did not see herself driven in these ways and there is no reason to see her that way. Duty was not central to her emotional life, not the means to personal satisfaction, not a substitute for God. Idealism was much more important, and God was hardly eclipsed in her universe. In Catt's world God was very much present as a support for her belief in a benevolent evolution, which was the justification for her optimism.

Her main concern was not God or religion, however, but applying her optimistic faith to life. It dominated her approach to the struggle for women's enfranchisement and her quest for world peace in both her private and public pronouncements. Thus Catt always expected her causes to gain ultimate victory because she knew evolution was at work and on her side. No matter what, she said over and over in different ways, we were to have faith: "Evolution may seem to move slowly, but never forget that it does move, and always onward."[69] Defeats (of which there were so many) did not seem to faze her because of her faith in destiny's final blessing. One might wonder if she were really protesting too much, but this does not seem to have been the case. The faith was real, total, and rock-like. Maud Wood Park summed up Carrie Catt's outlook nicely: "She looks on the world with a kind of ironic recognition of its weaknesses and its futility, yet she is able to keep aflame an invincible faith that 'all things work together for good.' "[70]

While her evolutionary confidence, obviously, undergirded these unending announcements, so did Catt's typically practical insight that believing things could turn out well — that, for instance, suffrage would triumph — could and did drive her and others to make it happen. She told a story of two frogs, one a pessimist, another an optimist, who fell in a pail of milk; the pessimist gave up, but the optimist turned it into butter and escaped. Hers was a practical optimism and Catt could hardly have had any other kind.[71]

Her insight into the pragmatic advantage of such an optimistic evolutionary faith was complemented by her belief that while evolution was sovereign and inevitable, still "evolvers" or "evolutors" were essential to help the process unfold. Like Lester Ward, she was sure that "evolution would move faster and avoid pit falls if there were plenty of 'evolutors' who would try and think straight and act accordingly."[72] Catt's image of herself, of course, was as one of those people. When she was called to sum up her life's project it was normal for her to speak in these terms: "I have spent my life in a sincere endeavor to help God's law of Evolution evolve."[73]

The implication of Catt's evolutionary optimism for her as a person and as an activist was surely enormous. It covered all pain — the pain of deaths, the pain of shyness and lack of confidence, the pain of defeats in action. At the same time it was a faith that called for and spurred her on to action. It was a reformer's faith and one that provided concrete assistance for the reformer in her daily struggles. Surely the origins of her evolutionary optimism were partly intellectual, but they also lay elsewhere, deep in the private Catt, in her need for strength as a woman to affirm herself, to act in the world, and, perhaps, to address the pain this shy and somewhat repressed farm girl felt from her earliest years. We do not know its deepest springs, nor can we be sure if she knew. What we do know is that this faith was a living one for her and all that she did was built from its foundation. It allowed her to face outward from the private Catt to the public world.

The Case for Suffrage:
Catt's Ideal for Women

Carrie Catt was not a great political philosopher or even an important contributor to political theory within the modest tradition of American political thought. She neither claimed to be nor wanted to be. Yet, outside her ideas, Catt cannot really be understood as a feminist politician. While they may not have soared much beyond her time and place, her ideas were integral to her definition of what she was doing and to how she was doing it.

Aileen Kraditor argues that the "woman suffrage movement had no official ideology," and Kraditor is undoubtedly correct.[1] This was true not only because there were many different strands in the arguments made for suffrage, but also because it was a Progressive Era movement, not inclined to think in abstract or philosophical terms. Nor did leaders such as Catt attempt to impose a single ideological unity on their movement. They took any allies they could find and did not ask for the reasons behind their support. Moreover, Catt herself was disposed to be eclectic in arguing for woman suffrage. She was not sure how to approach suffrage for women: as a right, as a duty, or as a privilege. What mattered to her was its achievement.

Yet Catt's arguments over time do have a unity that consists of much more than the eclectic grab bag that she sometimes suggested they were. She articulated certain approaches and themes faithfully that provide insight into her basic political values and goals beyond suffrage.

61

Aileen Kraditor and Janet Zollinger Giele pioneered in the study of the thought of the suffragists.[2] Kraditor's analysis stresses that suffragists supported the enfranchisement of women on two pillars, one drawing from natural-right arguments, the other emphasizing the social benefits that suffragists contended voting women would produce for society. Kraditor terms the latter arguments "expediency" claims, suggesting they were proposed in good part as a means for building support by whatever means worked. Giele notes in particular that the social-benefit approach made suffrage more attractive to men — and to women — because it appeared more "feminine."[3]

Undoubtedly this strategic consideration was important in the partial shift of suffragist arguments during the Progressive Era toward an "expediency" or public-welfare emphasis. But accenting expediency over social benefit can be misleading. Most suffragists were deeply convinced that wide-ranging public benefits would come from the Anthony amendment and sincerely sought most of these gains as public goods. In the Progressive Era most suffragist leaders naturally justified reforms in terms of their larger good.

Kraditor's general analysis does apply to Catt. She consistently invoked both general-benefit and natural-rights arguments for woman suffrage. At the same time, however, Catt employed another argument. Over and over she argued for suffrage as a means to end the *humiliation* of women, to restore their dignity as human beings equal to men. Though this view did not conflict with the standard arguments, it was not the same. And it mattered more to Catt than any other.

Public Benefit

The language of social benefit did routinely suffuse Catt's argument for woman suffrage. Even though women opponents insisted that where suffrage for women existed there were no discernible social gains, Catt thought differently. And she took for granted that woman suffrage could be and should be justified in this fashion, and that it represented an effective argument to do so. For her the vote was "a tool with which to build a better nation," and suffrage therefore could pass the supreme test for public policy — "to provide for the common welfare" — and the one test for Catt's personal morality — "To help humanity upward."[4] Her arguments here are familiar ones to those who know anything about the popular prosuffrage case of her day. In particular, suffrage would aid society, Catt thought, because it would assist the weak, curtail vice, improve the home, and, especially, improve the chances for peace abroad and for democratic government at home.

She was never very clear why votes for women would help the weak, though she seems to have thought women, or "the best women," would want to and could do so if they had the vote. Mostly she was content to affirm in vague terms that woman suffrage would benefit "all the weak and erring . . . all the homeless and unloved."[5] Or she would make a denunciation of "men who draw vast dividends from very underpaid labor" or proclaim that "posterity assuredly will pronounce child labor in our generation a disgrace."[6] But she never really made clear why woman suffrage could or would do much about these things.

Catt was specifically concerned with the possibility that women's enfranchisement would help socially vulnerable women — divorced and single women and those who had to work for a living — and their children. Catt expected that voting women would make a difference because women were sensitive to the plight of the vulnerable, children especially. She believed that developments in the 1920s, after women's enfranchisement, showed her to be right. The passage of the Sheppard-Towner Act and the success of the Child Labor Amendment in Congress suggested to her that voting women could make politicians assist the vulnerable, though much more needed to be done. The result, she was sure, would be a better nation.[7]

Ironically, her antisuffragist critics both disagreed and agreed with her. Before the adoption of the Anthony amendment they insisted that all it would produce was a formal equality which would not help the weak at all in the real world. Amendments and laws would change little and instead they would open the door to a covert exploitation that would be worse.[8] After 1920 and the appearance of the first protective legislation, especially for children, they turned around and charged that women's enfranchisement was producing dangerous social experiments that threatened the basic economic and social order of the United States.[9]

Fighting "vice" appealed to Catt at least as a reason for woman suffrage. She had in mind particularly the vice of alcohol, but the exploitation of women through prostitution was another topic she frequently addressed. For her to attack "vice" was really to strike back at the opponents of a proper democracy (and woman suffrage — since to her they were intimately linked) rather than to satisfy her personal puritanical urges. For example, she felt alcohol's political effects every day she campaigned for women's enfranchisement. Alcohol and those in the liquor business constantly corrupted American democracy by "buying" voters and politicians in an effort to defeat woman suffrage, which they feared would lead to Prohibition. So did all the forces of vice. "Have you ever known of a white slaver, a professional gambler, a political briber . . . who was not an anti-suffragist? I never have."[10]

When the public benefit that suffrage could bring was to promote a better home, Catt had somewhat less to say. Her perspective was different from Jane Addams's, who believed that every woman's heart was in the home. For Addams this meant that public action by women was a natural extension of the home into society, the addressing of family problems in public life.[11] Catt did at times affirm that "home means more to a woman than it ever can to a man," but she was not exactly family-oriented. She was only rarely a homemaker and she had no children. Nor did Catt think about women primarily as guardians of home and family. According to her analysis, things were rapidly changing. By then, many women worked and technological developments no longer required women to be in the home all the time even if they did not have to work. If Catt had any favorite unifying image of women it was as citizens rather than homemakers. Addams was very much a Progressive in her similar devotion to public citizenship, but she fused the role of homemaker and citizen for women in a way that Catt did not.[12]

There was, however, one dimension of the gain that Catt thought could come to the home after women voted that she deeply believed in and advocated. This was her belief that it could end ("destroy" was her word) "obedience of women in the home."[13] Indeed, she held the radical view that this was what the women's movement was all about "at home." She did not doubt that this change would enhance the life of the country as a whole, but that was *not* the context in which she presented it. It was, rather, part (an explosive part) of her argument for enfranchisement to abolish women's humiliation — regardless of its social costs.

Catt recognized that her views on family relations were too radical to advance as a popular argument — with men *or* women. She addressed the issue when critics pushed her to, but mostly she did not discuss family life.

Again and again antisuffragists asserted that women belonged in the home, where they served so well. They feared for home and motherhood itself. They worried that the "sanctity of . . . womanhood and her home" would disappear in a suffrage-stimulated social revolution that would involve "easy" divorce and "free love" and the death of monogomy and of love itself.[14]

There is no question that this charge was the core of the antisuffragist anxiety over women's enfranchisement. For them suffrage challenged "the link of woman to the home that underlay the entire ideology" of opposition to votes for women. To put it another way, what was at issue was different images of women, and the idea that women in particular were the defenders of a family-oriented society.[15]

Catt did not take lightly the charge that the enfranchisement of women would undermine the home and through it all society. Its potential to hurt her cause, especially with traditional women, was much too great for her to ignore the charge. Her responses were revealing. She deftly sidestepped her own goals and chose instead to insist that votes for women would not promote "free love" or "easy divorce." She did not see how they could and she hoped, in fact, that they would not. She also denied that such notions were attractive to most of her fellow workers: "Free love is not and never has been a tenet of suffragists."[16] There were a few public opponents of "family" and marriage within the women's movement, but Catt knew and insisted they were a tiny minority. And in a famous clash with the head of the Man Suffrage Association in 1915, she identified "red light district(s)" as places where defenseless and voteless women were exploited, and as more significant strongholds of those in favor of divorce and permissive sexual behavior than was the suffragist movement.[17]

Such statements can naturally lead one to the mistaken belief that Catt fits in nicely with Ellen DuBois's perceptive suggestion that suffragists of Catt's generation were not at all radical in their conceptions of women in the home.[18] As we know, this was hardly the case for Catt, who thought "destroying obedience" was a real goal of the feminism she endorsed, and whose own marriages were far from traditional. But the public Catt did not go out of her way to let her larger audience know that her sexual conservatism was not a good guide to how much, in fact, she hoped that antisuffragist fears for the fate of patriarchal family would come true.

She was inclined simply to laugh at a related argument of the antisuffragists that suggested that women could not handle any life except the secure life of patriarchal domesticity. Opponents' contentions that a larger life for women would create too much stress, exhaust their limited psychological resources, and even promote the spread of "insanity" among women were not uncommon.[19] But Catt thought it was obvious that this was a myth propagated by rich Eastern women who knew little about most women in American life, and even less of history. "The objection that the 'nervous system' of women is not sufficiently stable to endure the strain of political responsibility, an objection heard disgustingly often in the East, is naturally not heard [in the West]. A 'Nervous System' which has sufficient caliber to face rattlesnakes . . . cyclones, and to 'Prove us' a claim, will hardly be charged here with too much delicacy."[20]

Perhaps it was her own experience as a woman married to two men who were from all accounts emotionally healthy and independent that explains why Catt did not rise to antisuffragist suggestions that proper, homebody women would lose contact with "real" men as the result of the revolution suffrage would instigate. Men would become effeminate, it was said, and there were public calls for "men" to stand up and be men and repulse the suffragists' attempt to destroy them.[21]

But another, greater reason was that Catt did not think primarily in family or gender terms. Always she searched for equal citizens united to serve the public good. It was in this spirit that she argued most strongly for the potential social gains of women's enfranchisement in terms of advancing democracy and world peace. Indeed, it was with these specific social benefits in mind that she spoke and wrote for woman suffrage with heart and soul.

I will discuss Catt's conceptions of democracy in some detail later. Here it is sufficient to note that Catt thought American democracy needed to be cleaned up and directed toward social rather than selfish ends. She was sure women could make a difference by eliminating corrupt officials, promoting honest elections, and negating selfish interest groups. Women could apply the only remedy available: "The remedy . . . lies in the integrity and courage of American citizens to rise . . . and declare that the time must speedily come when we shall have purity in government."[22]

But, the antisuffragists' question was, Why would voting women make such a difference? Why were they so special? They thought Catt and her legion of reformers were blinded by their enthusiasm. No one could alter the dirty and enduring realm of politics. Moreover, they thought women were innocent of politics, on the whole, and therefore particularly ill equipped to accomplish this unlikely mission.[23]

But Catt thought — or hoped — that women could improve American democracy. She never claimed that women were purer or nobler than men and thus would naturally defeat evil; Catt never celebrated women over men. Nor did she contend that women were more politically astute than men. Her view, rather, was that women *could* do the job *if* they entered politics and brought to bear their *potential* as human beings because they, unlike men, were free of the history, culture, and current practice of modern politics. The nature of women provided no guarantee, but their very innocence from the ways of politics and their relatively "pure" values because of this innocence provided the opportunity — *if* they were properly trained and led.[24]

Catt also took it for granted that democracy improved as more citizens gained incorporation into the political system. It became more alive and more authentic, and elite rule suffered. "With the enfranchisement of women the ruling class will disappear forever. Popular government, with no privileged class based on religion, wealth, race or sex . . . will become an established fact."[25] It was in light of this faith that she unhesitatingly affirmed that "The enfranchisement of women will be the crowning glory of democratic government."[26]

Such uplifting sentiments did not sit well, however with Catt's opponents. While Catt celebrated women's enfranchisement and democracy together, they insisted Catt and the N.A.W.S.A. were hypocrites. How, they demanded, could the leader of the suffragists and the "small but noisy" minority of women aligned with her claim to be serious democrats? Antisuffragists charged that suffragists were actually trying to "impose upon the majority of women . . . what they do not want and have never asked for": woman suffrage. Suffragists were flagrantly undertaking "to override the fundamental principle of democracy — the rule of the majority."[27]

For antisuffragists the proof of this hypocrisy lay in suffrage crusaders' affinity for pressing their cause through state legislatures and Congress rather than by using referenda or even initiatives in the many states when they were available. Antisuffragists urged that women be allowed to vote on women's enfranchisement (a proposal that had its own irony, of course). Short of that, even letting all men vote would have demonstrated some commitment to democracy by suffragists who, these critics often suspected, rejected the idea because they liked operating in the dark corridors with political machines and hidden elites whom they so ostentatiously denounced in public. They were not democrats but machine politicians par excellance.[28]

There was a good deal of truth to these charges where Catt is concerned. She was akin to a *machine* politician, at least insofar as she was prepared to match her opponents with all the skills of organization and wiles of strategy that she felt were so necessary to thread one's way through the American political process. And along the way Catt did not, in fact, show any enthusiasm for pursuing means that her critics believed to be more democratic, such as referenda by men — or women. Catt simply knew the facts, that suffrage referenda often lost as a majority of male voters voted "no," while referenda by women in nonsuffrage states simply were not going to happen. To be sure, Catt and her allies sometimes used existent referenda procedures and, in time, often won. But her decision by 1916 to push for a constitutional amendment rather than fighting only state-by-state and often referenda-by-referenda did represent a choice to reach for a victory in national legislative halls. Of course, even a constitutional amendment required three-quarters of the states to approve it. But Catt realized that the issue would be decided in state legislatures, not by public referenda. More to the point, perhaps, Catt's strategic choice to work for passage of the Nineteenth Amendment did not seem to her a denial of her commitment to democracy. It was only a practical calculation to advance her cause, not a significant statement of her philosophy of ideal government. Ideal government would be an inclusive, politically egalitarian, and uncorrupted democracy, which Catt was convinced woman suffrage would facilitate as nothing else could. This ideal was proof of Catt's commitment to democracy, she believed, and she was more than content to let the matter rest there.

However, she did rely on her limited faith in democracy when she thought it would serve her immediate goal of suffrage for women, during World War I in particular. It was then that she pounded home her conviction that a commitment to democracy in principle required the granting of suffrage to women. After all, was not America involved in the war to defend and promote democracy? If so, then how could Congress avoid making democracy real at home, especially in light of the fact that women could vote in Germany? Congress had no choice. It had to vote a constitutional amendment for woman suffrage to avoid rendering America's participation in the war a fraud.[29]

Catt's strategic purpose here was, obviously, not subtle. In part she was merely mobilizing proclaimed American war objectives to her advantage. Yet there was another, quite authentic side to her appeal. War could make sense to her only if it was fought for a cause, even a cause such as democracy. Granting women suffrage could make the war truly legitimate; U.S. war aims would be less hollow and no American woman would need be skeptical about the war.

As important in the long run for Catt was the potential enfranchising women had for her almost sacred goal: world peace. "For thousands of years," Catt argued, "men have begun all the wars," and their attempts to clean up the mess left behind merely led on to the next war.[30] While in later, postsuffrage years, Catt appreciated that in light of this sad record it would "take a long time to get the fighting habit out of them,"[31] her hopes were higher before 1920. To be sure, she granted that both sexes had great capacity for what she called hysterical, nonrational behavior. The difference was that men expressed theirs by fighting. Women did so in other ways and therefore voting women would inevitably check men's affinity for war. Catt was less clear as to why men expressed their "hysteria" in war and women did not. The explanation she usually favored was cultural. Catt also thought women's role in society placed them in a position to favor life and reject war, which was too often over matters such as "oil or coal or trade." She always claimed that, had women been able to be active citizens before World War I, there would have been no war.[32]

While her confidence here was in those days real, its plausibility was tissue-thin. Opponents ridiculed the idea that women could end war. They did not see women as quite the peace lovers Catt thought them to be. And the pacifists tended to encourage the warlike, as pacifists always did, even if unintentionally. While Catt thought differently both before and after the Great War, she implicitly agreed with her critics during the war. After all, her claim then was that enfranchised women would be strongly committed to the war and to the fighting patriotism of that day. Then votes for women, were in Catt's phrase, "an imperative war measure." This was not merely Catt the strategist at work; she was perfectly sincere. And it never seems to have occurred to her that she could not have it both ways; if woman suffrage was socially beneficial because it would advance peace, how could it also be good because it would help win wars?[33]

Natural Rights

The first language of the women's movement in the United States was the language of rights. The Declaration of Rights and Sentiments spoke in these terms. So did the pioneers of the movement, such as Elizabeth Cady Stanton.[34] So did Catt, even though her arguments were complicated by her simultaneous claims for the social benefits of suffrage.

Her often repeated view was straightforward: Women had a right to vote as human beings who could not be governed without their consent and their participation. Catt often called on this tenet of Western liberalism with a special American twist, stressing the issue of taxation without representation. But mostly she — with others — invoked the familiar right of consent of the governed to press her suffrage claims and left it at that. For she knew that the language of rights, especially the right of consent, was so pervasive in American experience and culture that her appeal could not be ignored.[35]

Catt was unlike most others who invoked such a rights claim for women in that she did have at least some sense of what she meant when she made this kind of claim. While the ordinary "arguments" on this score consisted of little more than assertions that women had a vague thing known as equal right and thus should be allowed to vote, Catt spoke from her Spencerian naturalism, grounding her notion of rights in a view of human nature in which all people had an equal right to liberty and consent. However, Catt normally followed the popular path of announcing this right rather than developing its ontological, analytical, and epistemological meanings and implications.[36]

It is no surprise that most of Catt's attention went to stressing equality regarding the right to vote. She agreed with John Stuart Mill that the right was universal and, unlike Mill, she really meant it. That led her to an angry set of comparisons, time and again, with women's status as citizens vis-à-vis the males who had the right to vote in the United States and in some cases had no trouble obtaining it, despite the absence of any demonstrated record of merit. To her this was obviously absurd. Her message was that women and everyone else should have the equal right.

This was the kind of argument of which she was a master because it allowed her to bring rights down from an abstract philosophical realm in which she was neither comfortable nor particularly competent to show what was at stake in practical life. And by exposing in concrete terms what she took to be laughable inconsistencies in the application of human rights, she assumed people would be left with no choice. They would have to agree with her that women should receive the vote.[37]

The serious problem with Catt's rights argument was that she never explored how it fit or didn't fit with her social-benefit argument. She had no interest in examining questions such as how compatible the individualism of a rights approach was with the implicit social utilitarianism of her social-benefit claims or, in more practical terms, how likely a woman focused on her rights would be to care intensely about social evils and vice versa. The two arguments were lumped together, and that was that.

Only in one instance, carefully brought up after the Anthony suffrage amendment was law, did Catt suggest there might be a difficulty, specifically regarding mothers and their children. In the 1920s she thought she saw signs that some "liberated" women were pursuing lifestyles opened up by acknowledgment of their rights as persons that occasionally damaged the social good. She worried that some women were ignoring their children (as men also could and did), which no society could tolerate. It is significant, though, that Catt tried to have it both ways. Her complaint spoke in unmistakable terms of concern with social benefit, but she phrased it in the language of rights. What was at dispute, she thought, was a clash between the rights of children and those of their parents.[38]

Her inability to address the inevitable tension between social-benefit arguments and rights claims brings us to the interesting fact that Catt's (and others') natural-rights case for votes for women drew relatively little blood. It created only modest controversy among opponents of woman suffrage. Instead, antisuffragists engaged her taxation without representation theme, suggesting that the point was irrelevant. Taxation and representation were not linked in the United States in the first place. Moreover, for a democratic country suffrage should not be tied to taxation.[39]

On the whole, however, Catt received little response when she called for equal rights. The reason was that the antisuffragists did not propose to enter this realm. Catt spoke of the rights of women, while they spoke of the duty of women. Catt tried to balance rights and social-benefit arguments, or at least spoke in terms of both, while the antisuffragists consistently argued exclusively in terms of social benefit (disagreeing with Catt, of course, on what its nature was).

Kraditor suggests that we may conclude that Catt and her friends had a very different idea of women from that of the antisuffragists. Catt's image was of a free, independent, rights-bearing person. Theirs was of a duty-oriented, family-oriented, serving person.[40] This is a crucial point. But it is an incomplete one unless one also notes Catt's optimistic assumption that women could simultaneously be rights-oriented individuals concerned with their self-development *and* devoted to the service of the larger community.

Catt's characteristically American faith that enhanced individualism and expanded liberty would work for the betterment of all depended on her unspoken assumption that people could also be good Progressives. Her opponents thought this was naive and proposed simply to escape the danger of the triumph of selfishness among women (at least) by denying them any individual rights whatsoever. They refused to honor women as individuals, just as Catt refused to recognize that encouraging both individualism and community at the same time could not be accomplished merely by invoking Progressive optimism.[41]

Dignity

Much more than traditional accounts of Catt's arguments for woman suffrage suggest, anger motivated her. She was angry at the way women were treated and her anger went beyond arguments that held such treatment was wrong because it denied their rights or did not contribute to the communal good. Catt was furious because she thought women were daily humiliated and thus denied human dignity. She was insistent that they should rise up and refuse ever again to be "slave, or servant, or dependent, or plaything."[42] This would, she appreciated, require an enormous change in society and in many women. But it was what she wanted. And it was why, above all, she wanted suffrage. It was to be a means of leverage to force men to give ground, whether as a right or as a means to improve society overall. Here is what we may call the unknown Catt.

Catt tended to discuss the suffrage issue in a cool, rational fashion, a style we know she greatly admired in others and consciously strove to follow herself. Yet Catt could abandon that practice on occasion and her talk could turn fiery. This almost always happened when she reviewed the condition of women. More than any other topic and more than any other aspect of the suffrage question, the condition of women angered her and drove her to express her anger. Then she stopped being moderate and started attacking her country's record on women, deploring its "ghastly and inexcusable failures." Then she bitterly deplored the "hideous wrongs" women had experienced over time and the reality of their practical "martyrdom" in the United States.[43] Her anger was even greater when she looked at the experiences of women in other parts of the world. South America was a particular subject for her rage. There, as far as she was concerned, women had "a role little better than that of sexual slaves."[44]

We know that this anger was something that developed in Catt in her youth and her young adulthood. But her adult experiences in the American and international suffrage campaigns continued to fire and expand her feelings. In this she followed the pattern of the pioneers of the women's rights effort. For her as for them it was something intensely personal, developed not just from intellectual sentiments but from very real personal experience.[45]

When Catt did express her anger, she followed it up with ominous warnings that sex wars would develop if something were not done, usually if women did not get their opportunity through the vote. Of course, she always added that she was not threatening anybody, just stating a basic fact of psychology: keeping women down was bound to have disastrous consequences for the relations among the sexes. And one senses that Carrie Catt thought this was only reasonable. For from her perspective anger was entirely appropriate given the way women were treated in the United States (and in the world). She did not feel she could be expected to be "moderate" about the situation any longer.

Her frustration was that so many people just did not understand. "The humiliation which proud spirited American women feel . . . is deeper than I believe any man living can understand."[46] Catt meant that and she also meant her outrage at those who dared to say that most women liked the old, patriarchal order. "We are told these subjected earlier women were content. No doubt, content like the imprisoned bird which sings in its cage in forgetfulness of the freedom which is its birthright. But how quickly these imprisoned ones learn to lift their wings and to fly when the bars are no longer there!"[47]

Nothing made the appalling humiliation clearer to Catt than men's resistance to woman suffrage, their resistance denying women their legitimate dignity as equal citizens. "The truth is," she said, during the suffrage campaign and afterwards, "there never was but one objection to women suffrage on the part of men, and that was the 'superiority complex of the male.' There never was but one objection to their own enfranchisement on the part of women, and that was the 'inferiority complex of the female.' " At its heart Catt's suffrage work was an attempt to challenge such patriarchal ideas among men and, she thought sadly, among some women too. The "struggle for the vote was not what it appeared on the surface. Rather, it was an effort to bring men to feel less superior and women to feel less inferior."[48]

Thus while some suffragists may be criticized for not really challenging the image of women in their time as passive, weak, and unable to be independent, Catt may not. Her goal was to destroy not only the image, but the far too prevalent reality from which the image was formed.[49] Her opponents understood Catt's purposes very well. Again and again they attacked Catt and the suffrage movement on just these grounds, fearful of what the consequences would be in terms of women. They said that true womanhood would be destroyed and women would become like men and in the process acquire all the bad traits and habits of men. They would be "besmirched" by political activity; they would become competitive and antagonistic (especially towards men); they would no longer trust men — their fathers, brothers, husbands, and sons. They would lose their special "spiritual" side, as the obviously "nerve sick" suffragist women proved.[50]

Catt did not share these anxieties. Women would not lose all their positive traits, she thought, above all their concern for others. But they might well lose traits that Catt believed were unfortunate. They might become less naively trusting of men, or anyone, and this was all to the good. Trusting to others to decide one's fate was foolish, not admirable. Shrinking from competition was often a handicap in life, and women needed no additional handicaps. And a "spiritual" side of women, when it meant a fluttery dependence on men, would hardly be a loss.

Nor did Catt think exercising power was beyond women: they could and should exercise it. Indeed, she was bent on creating organizations that would allow them to do just that. As for the possible dangers to women in the dimension of politics involving force, Catt did not deny the dangers, whoever employed it. But if the antisuffragists feared the effects of force they should look first at men's behavior and condemn male use of force at home, in society, and among nations. To reduce its sway women should work to train women to discard this sad male record and adopt the political tools, such as suffrage, that would speed the end of this pernicious reality. Women would have to do it themselves, but they could. The outcome could not be guaranteed, but Catt was typically optimistic: "If these women have the power to put their hopes into the ballot they are going to mold a better future."[51]

To obtain a fitting, self-governing dignity, of course, women would have to be free. No one without extensive choice in life had dignity. The road to freedom involved rebelling at "the idea that obedience is necessary to women" so that they would obtain "such self-respect that they would not grant obedience."[52] Suffrage was, once again, crucial in the process. It would provide objective freedom in politics and could give them the means to expand liberty in other realms. Women who had the vote, in short, had the chance to become free individuals. As she said when the last state had ratified the suffrage amendment: "Let us remember we are no longer petitioners. We are not wards of the nation, but free and equal citizens. Let us practice the dignity of sovereigns." Or, as she put it on another occasion, "The woman with a vote can stand straight and look Godward. She is no longer a part of life's furniture established in this place or in that at the will of another."[53]

Yet we should not overemphasize Catt as a proponent of freedom as an end in itself. It was important to her, and certainly she believed women's enfranchisement would be a major step forward, but she was seeking something that to her was ultimately greater. She was after self-respect and the respect of others for women — she was after dignity. And she was convinced that choice was integral to this goal: it enabled women to control their lives.[54] In the voting booth and elsewhere freedom would propel women towards becoming masters of their fate. She wanted women to join men and obtain human dignity in a world without slaves — and for that end above all Catt fought for women suffrage.[55]

Perhaps Catt's stress on mastery was a bit unrealistic in her age of growing organization in America. But she contended it simply was not true that organization need limit human mastery. Indeed, she was confident, perhaps too confident, that efficient organization could only increase mastery. All her years and work in the N.A.W.S.A. were predicated on this assumption. Women had scant dignity and scant mastery in part because they were unorganized and faced enemies who knew and practiced the mysteries of organization. She sought to beat their enemies at their own game, and she was supremely confident that there was no other way to do so.

We can see Catt's commitment to self-mastery for women in a concrete fashion in her attitude towards the problem of "white slavery." The abuse of young women by men who forced them across state lines and into prostitution, and the male state's failure to eliminate the practice, deeply upset her. From her wide international experience, Catt knew that white slavery was a horrible reality that existed all over the world, wherever women lacked independence and the power to maintain it. White slavery was an ugly symbol of women's status, whether women were white, yellow, brown, or whatever. It existed because women were dependent, not by nature but by social condition. Unable to control their own lives, they were prey for others. They would inevitably remain so until they acquired a rebellious consciousness and the political resources to alter their condition. Suffrage for women would give them the leverage to assert their natural dignity and defeat its antithesis, in this case, white slavery.

To be sure, here as elsewhere Catt did not contend that enfranchisement of women was a magic solution. It would not eliminate white slavery, but it would provide the circumstances under which it could be gravely wounded. White slavery's ultimate extinction would require a change in the economic situation of poor women, better pay, more economic opportunity. All of which were also necessary for women if they were to obtain self-mastery. The broader point is, however, that for Catt white slavery was not unlike sexual assault for Brownmiller and other current feminists. It was the extreme example that revealed the ultimate reality of women's place in the patriarchal social order.[56]

The new, dignified woman that Catt sought, a person who was an independent citizen, free and equal with all other citizens, would escape such treatment. Humiliation would not be her fate. Nor should men expect that or any other negative consequences. The truth was that "every right gained has made women freer, more self-reliant, more respected by men. Every one of them has made women happier and far better comrades to men."[57]

Catt felt that time would work to her advantage. Again and again she invoked the inevitability of change for women, their enfranchisement in particular, and asserted it as a powerful reason for adopting votes for women. The basis for Catt's faith here was her evolutionary naturalism. Somehow the world was progressing and in her mind that ensured victory for woman suffrage. Conservatives, "the flotsam and jetsam of civilization," could not stop it: "They do not know the meaning of the word "progress," they have never heard of evolution."[58] They did not see the signs that were unmistakable. Women had demonstrated they were ready for suffrage. They were increasingly educated. They eagerly voted where they had the opportunity. Society was progressing in its natural way. Women were ready to take an equal part in American politics. Who were venal politicians and the masses of men to waste time denying what was good — and inevitable?[59]

Exactly why Catt thought inevitability was such a powerful argument for the enfranchisement of women is not always self-evident. But she was on to something, as evidenced by her opponents' equal insistence that woman suffrage was no certainty at all and should not be treated as such. Catt used the arguments as a morale builder for the faithful, often exhorting her followers forward with promises of victories to come. Mostly, though, her objective seems to have been different. Her aim was to express what she took to be a fact — the inevitability of suffrage — and thereby disarm her opponents' will. Why bother to fight us, she seemed to say. We are going to win and so you might as well give in now and, as she put it, we can go back to being friends again.[60]

Reassured by the direction of natural evolution, confident of women's natural rights, hopeful of the social benefits of women's enfranchisement, Catt spent half a lifetime promoting woman suffrage. The heart of her case, though, remained her belief in the ideal of women's self-mastery, that suffrage would be a step toward their self-realization as dignified, free beings in command (as much as possible) of their own lives. This is why Catt could and did *demand* suffrage and encouraged other women to do the same. For in demanding it they were affirming themselves as real people and acquiring a means to continue their march forward. "WOMEN ARISE: DEMAND THE VOTE . . . Demand to vote. Women, ARISE." In the end, that was Catt's goal and dream. It was what she was all about: "Women arise."[61]

CHAPTER 5
Democracy and Politics

In her work as a reformer Catt repeatedly had to face both the question of democracy and the issue of democratic institutions in the United States. She was ambivalent about democracy as an ideal and unmistakably hostile to what she saw as the central features of democracy in America. About both matters she had a great deal to say, for as she struggled to enact the enfranchisement of women she thought she learned a great deal about democracy in theory and in practice.

Carrie Catt always insisted she was very much a democrat. She believed that government's legitimacy must rest with popular consent, that the popular will (or majority) must ultimately rule, that the means for citizen participation and free expression in political life must be numerous. But Catt also recognized her ambivalence. "I am a *good* democrat in theory but my faith weakens when it meets bad air . . . and horrid smells." She admitted she was "an aristocrat with democratic leanings."[1]

Of course, her ambivalence was nothing unusual for a thoughtful American, certainly not in the Progressive Era, when ambivalence about democracy was the common feeling of reformers and intellectuals. Yet her ambivalence was something Catt sought to keep private even though she was not sure it ultimately mattered. After all, democracy of sorts had arrived in the modern world, obviously in the United States, and there could be no turning back. As a dedicated believer in evolution, she felt she had no choice but to accept the larger outlines of human development, and democracy was one of them for now. She did not want to align herself, for example, with those she termed "the pessimists," those who "wish they could roll it back." "They are the 'left-overs', the 'back number.' . . . They are like the man who recently wrote a book on the subject that the earth is flat."[2]

Of course, Catt appreciated that her ambivalence did matter in one way. She was struggling to get women the vote to make a democracy more democratic. This was the reason she gave most often in public as she argued for woman suffrage. The irony of her actual ambivalence about democracy would have been rich fodder for her antisuffragist enemies who could have painted her as a hypocrite. Catt kept them ignorant of her ambivalence, but they suspected the truth about Catt and the leadership elite of the N.A.W.S.A. anyway and accused them of being phony democrats. Real democrats would not try to push suffrage through Congress; real democrats would go to the people in the states and ask them — men and women — for their opinion on woman suffrage. In public Catt repudiated this definition of a real democrat, of course.[3] And in private her reason was clear: "We propose to get the vote for the women of the nation without submitting them to the humiliation of making them appeal to every 'Tom, Dick and Harry.' "[4]

Catt's doubts about democracy in general were grounded in her estimation of the citizenry — just as one might expect from one whose principal goal met defeat after defeat at the polls. The problem was, always, "the immense proportion of ignorance and irresponsibility among the voters."[5] When good causes lost, the fault was people and their stupidity: "Let us lay the blame where it belongs — upon that stupidity."[6]

The issue was *not* just men or men voters either, despite some suggestion to the contrary. Yes, Catt favored woman suffrage as a means to improve democracy and politics, but she generally denied improvement would automatically come just because women obtained the vote. Women would not necessarily be better than men unless they were educated, a fact that explained her commitment to education for women as a necessary accompaniment to enfranchisement. Even then educated women would be better citizens than men not because they were women but because men were so often poorly educated — already so often corrupted by politicians and political "leaders." This is why Catt's expressions of distaste for the "stupid" who were the "great masses of people" included both sexes and why she bemoaned "the unquestioned discovery that a startlingly large proportion of the population are not men and women at all, but children in grown-up bodies."[7]

Catt oscillated between locating the problem in people's education (something that could be corrected) and judging much more pessimistically that inherently limited intelligence and psychological strength were at issue. Certainly she judged that most people had exceedingly modest intellectual capacity. She also contended that people were largely selfish. She frequently claimed that people were too easily manipulated psychologically, and she believed that no area of study would bear more fruit than investigation of the often unfortunate political effects of mass psychology. She was interested in the new field of psychology. And she insisted that the suffrage movement take due notice of its lessons about psychological dimensions and vulnerabilities, since knowledge of the human mind was the best way to understand politics.[8]

It was in light of these doubts that Catt was an enthusiast for political leadership. At times she talked just as her fellow Progressives W. E. B. DuBois or Herbert Croly did of the responsibilities of the educated elite, sometimes of the leading 10 percent, at other points the best 30 percent. They had the responsibility to lead ordinary people in politics and to educate them to do better on their own. "It is the duty of those who are intelligent to uplift the ignorant." Here was Catt's Progressive sense of noblesse oblige in full flower.

Yet Catt reflected not only the era's suspicions about the masses and its taste for leadership. She was equally given to enthusiasm about people, their abilities, and their judgment. She needed some of this faith, one supposes, in order to keep on campaigning for woman suffrage, since it required popular approval. In the euphoria of victory in 1920 Catt felt warmly towards popular judgment. However, she had some of that faith in her always. Its roots lay in her commitment to evolution and what she always believed to be its inevitable gift of progress. For Catt it had to be true that basically people could be rational, and sometime were, though they had a long way to go before they were fully rational.[9]

Overall, her democratic loyalty remained tepid. Victory in the suffrage battle eventually strengthened it, but her sense of caution remained strong. Her lack of confidence in the consistent wisdom of people never disappeared. She had lost too many elections for that to happen.

On the other hand, Catt's attitudes towards American democracy were hardly ambivalent. There she had no hesitation in delivering the most stinging rebukes. Much of Catt's life was a series of "battles against social institutions"[10] in a very American tradition and this was never truer than in her dissent from American politics, a dissent that included much more than her disgust over the exclusion of women.

Catt was modern in her perception that American democracy was not mainly about the Constitution or our formal institutions of government. She denied neither their importance nor their worth. Yet democracy in the United States was most fundamentally about politics and politicians, the way public decisions were made and those who made them. For both she had neither respect nor patience. They were a disgrace. No one who knew or heard Carrie Catt could doubt her judgment. The irony here, of course, was that Catt was herself a gifted politician, as later chapters will demonstrate. She denied it in public and in private — "I am not [a] politician" — and she did not see how she could be, since "politics is no place for a reformer."[11] To be sure, she was not a corrupt politician, but in every other way she played the game of American politics, as her close associates, and her enemies, understood so very well. It was only naive, outside admirers who claimed she was "decidedly not a politician,"[12] a judgment as pleasing to Catt as she surveyed the politics and politicians of her day as it was laughably off the mark.

As far as Catt was concerned, however, politics was a disease from which little good could come, a disease that was pervasive and that was getting worse. It encouraged hypocrisy and corruption; it operated through a selfish pluralism which was appalling, and it involved an electorate who were often shameful. Above all, it produced that most wretched of creatures, the politician, of whom she said that she could not write, lest what she said "be barred from the mails."[13] She had seen them in action for decades, and experience was a teacher she followed.

It was, for example, no wonder that, after suffrage lost in 1918 in the Senate, Catt never came back to watch those politicians in action. It was a symbolic withdrawal that expressed her lifelong disgust. She completely agreed with Anna Shaw's view: "When I sit in the gallery of the Senate and look down on the senators . . . and I don't have to sit in the gallery to look down on them."[14] Catt didn't denounce most senators in public. She was far too smart to make that mistake, but in her inner circle of workers she often repeated her judgment about those men, supposedly the most exalted of politicians. She was serious in her antagonism towards them and all politicians. What else would one expect from someone who suspected that her defeats by politicians were lessons from God to teach woman suffragists about contact with sin?[15]

The hypocrisy of politicians never ceased to astound her, especially the incredible gap between the principles they endorsed and the behavior they manifested. As bad was their ability to live comfortably with their hypocrisy. They had no understanding of an honest answer or a firm commitment. The irony was, she protested, that while hypocritical, untrustworthy, and corrupt politicians pulled their tricks, the party system held millions in the absolute thrall of the god of party loyalty. This loyalty allowed the whole system to go on its rotten way untouched, and it implicated most male Americans (later she would add women) in the corrupt system.[16]

The worst part of American politics, though, was the corruption of the electoral process itself. This sickened Catt. Again and again she indignantly reported blatant vote stealing that went on with the connivance of boss-appointed corrupt election officials who in many states were able to manipulate the appalling vagueness of the election laws with impunity. At other times she denounced similar immorality engineered by elected public officials. "I have seen with my own eyes, money paid to delegates in both Democratic and Republican conventions and I have also seen money paid to illiterate foreign voters in woman suffrage referendum elections."[17]

Wherever politics operated in America, at the polling place or in legislatures, corruption of one form or another seemed to her to flourish in a shocking manner. On and on went "the trading and trickery, the buying and selling." It cost woman suffrage victories in numerous legislatures, she believed, and it cost it victory in such referenda as Michigan's in 1912 and Iowa's in 1916, among others. Catt found it frustrating and nauseating and she could not and would not come to terms with this situation. Nor would she entertain the idea that it was not as much a reality as she believed. Like so many other Progressives, she could not easily accept defeat except as the result of political chicanery. The "good" could not lose because people did not always agree that it was good; it could only lose because of dishonesty at worst or lack of education at best.[18]

Robert Wiebe offers a somewhat different explanation for the Progressives' obsession with all-powerful "abstractions" such as Trusts and Political Machines or, as Catt would say, Political Corruption. He suggests that it was a way of unconsciously affirming the smaller and, they felt, more attractive worlds from which they came. "Political Corruption" did not appear to play this role for Catt. She used it more as a convenient explanation for her defeats, an explanation that did not challenge her confidence in ultimate victory.[19]

On the other hand, Catt was not imagining corruption. It abounded in her America. Stolen elections were not uncommon. Neither were bought legislators. But the larger point is that such corruption, however great or small, could not be reconciled by Catt with her ideal of a decent political order. It stood in the way not just of woman suffrage, but of a proper democracy itself. Catt summed up her view in a letter about a setback her cause received in the 1919 New Hampshire legislature. "I am not so much depressed over the result . . . as I am by the conviction it was obtained in the ever-recurring criminal way." "Many a night . . . I walked the floor in mental agony aroused by the fact that we did not have representative institutions, but that the money of the corrupt interest could make laws, make and break men, write constitutions, and build our civilization."[20]

Catt's "mental agony" was the product of her earnest belief in "clean democracy" and her anger at how often corruption violated her dream. Yet Catt was not entirely straightforward with her public, and perhaps with herself, in her complaints about corruption. She spoke of how corruption flouted the majority again and again. Yet she was herself at best an ambivalent supporter of majority rule. Moreover, she had trouble distinguishing between corruption and the politics of pressure groups. She tended to denounce both as if they were the same force for evil.

In fact, one of the things Catt disliked most about politics was its pluralist reality. That politics was, and has always been, largely about different groups and different interests "trading" (and, sometimes, "selling") to get what they want was a fact Catt could not bear. Politics should be noble, she thought, concerned with high principles and the common good. Those who thought otherwise, or acted otherwise, were corrupt, as was the American political system as a whole. She never had any tolerance for the idea that group interest — and politicians who served one or another group interest — was integral to a representative democracy. Nor, of course, did she suspect for a moment what an outsider might have said of her N.A.W.S.A.: that it was just another interest group, pushing and shoving for what it wanted, whatever its high-flown rhetoric. For Catt the struggle was always clear; it was ever a matter of virtue versus corruption, principle versus selfishness, truth versus evil bosses and interest groups. This was a surprisingly naive — if very Progressive — analysis from so able a practitioner in the realm of politics.

The evil interests that lay behind corrupt politics were everywhere, according to Catt. Interests such as "the Vice Trust" or the brewers were "vampires." They drank from the cup of human weakness for sex, drink, gambling, and money, and their victims were legion. They were hard to defeat not just because they were so corrupt; they were also well organized in effective divisions, each determined to block woman suffrage, which could drive a stake through their evil hearts. Taken together, they were what Catt described as our "invisible government."[21]

While Catt's conviction that these "spoilers . . . are our real opponents" is challenged by those who believe she took her women opponents too lightly,[22] the notion that American government was in the hands of corrupt politicians and an "invisible government" had long been standard fare for other suffragists, including Anna Howard Shaw. For Catt that notion was a master explanation for defeat and for the troubling deficiency of the American political system, and she was outraged. Her report on "their" activities in Tennessee is typical: "In the five weeks . . . I have been called more names, been more maligned, more lied about. . . . They appropriated our telegrams, tapped our telephones, listened outside our windows and transoms."[23]

Since Catt fervently believed that the brewers and all the "liquor-interests" were integral to corruption in American politics and the "invisible government," she hated them in particular. She blamed them for defeating women's enfranchisement time and again. Certainly beer and liquor interests did fight woman suffrage, calculating that its victory would greatly assist the forces of Prohibition. And they often did not fight in ways Catt held to be honest, much less honorable. Catt knew what she was doing when she singled them out as enemies.

At the same time, however, Catt was careful to keep the suffrage movement separate from the temperance and then the Prohibition movements as much as she could and even claimed she was not a Prohibitionist.[24] The drinking interests opposed her, so it would not seem to matter, but she did not want to antagonize them. Nor did she want to invite the enmity for woman suffrage of any possible citizen who might favor both votes for women and drinking. Of course she knew that some women in temperance groups had supported woman suffrage, but she doubted they had really done much good for the cause, while combining causes could do unmistakable harm.[25]

By the 1920s when both the Anthony and the Prohibition amendments were part of the Constitution, Catt felt it was safe to reveal her true feelings and she emerged as a public defender of "the great experiment." She conceded at times that drinking was "probably" not immoral and suspected that a less drastic approach than absolute prohibition might have been acceptable. Most of the time, however, she defended Prohibition with grim determination through the 1920s and early 1930s. She even served on the last-ditch Committee of Fifteen in 1931, which attempted to re-energize the failing effort to enforce Prohibition. The reasons were always the same. She was convinced that alcohol's social costs were too high and she remembered too well its corrupting effects on the crusade for women's enfranchisement.[26]

There was still another aspect of American politics that troubled Catt — the social, racial and ethnic mix of the American citizenry. As we know, she had a good many doubts about her fellow citizens' capacity for democratic politics in general. But she felt matters were made much worse in particular by "the others," those within the electorate who were uneducated, immigrant, or black. Catt felt that they polluted American democracy in conjunction with the politicians and special interests who so easily manipulated them. She insisted they were enemies of a proper American democracy.

The awkward truth is that many in the suffrage movement were distinctly hostile to immigrants, blacks, and other minorities and, indeed, sometimes sought woman suffrage partly to increase the numbers of those who shared their conclusion that minorities were threats to the basic American cultural and political order.[27] Actually, the suffrage and feminist movements of this era were overwhelmingly middle-class and WASP and well aware that support for their Progressive "reform" agenda was distinctly modest among blacks and immigrants. But vague fears and emotionalism were the main reasons for that hostility, despite the suffrage reformers' ordinarily relentless moralism and invocations to reason.

Ironically, opponents of woman suffrage were as much and, often, more hostile to "the others" than Catt and the suffrage movement were. They charged that the enfranchisement of women would put "the others" in charge of the United States. Antisuffrage publications often sounded this theme, expressing concern about immigrants, "vicious" women, and the like. They particularly appealed to southern white women by dredging up fears regarding blacks voting and were not at all above running stories about black rapists and "the white woman's peril."[28]

Catt's uneasiness about "the others" had several bases. The first was her conviction that they were allied with the corruptors of honest, democratic politics. The second, often related, was that her ever-political eye diagnosed the "others" as posing a problem of crisis dimensions in the campaign for women's voting rights. Again and again she denounced "the others" because she believed they were against her sacred cause: "the illiterate is universally an anti-women suffragist"; or, the "only classes of American society which are undivided in their support of the anti-suffrage side . . . are the illiterate and vicious elements."[29] Her experience in numerous suffrage campaigns produced this belief, and Catt was unforgiving.

The facts, to the extent we know them, were more complicated than Catt thought. Overall, there is no doubt that there was a class tinge to the forces arrayed in the battle. Especially by the latter years of the suffrage campaign, however, there was signficant working-class and immigrant support for woman suffrage. The situation in New York City has received careful attention and it has been established that a number of unions and other working-class groups backed women's enfranchisement as did some ethnic groups, especially Jews.[30]

Less often cited, but lurking in the background, was a third basis for Catt's unease, her perception of the status of women in immigrant and black cultures. Once again, although the actual picture was more mixed than they realized, many suffragists had reason to doubt whether the commonplace patriarchal attitudes and practices among "new Americans" were models they wanted encouraged. What is not so clear is why Catt and others thought they were qualitatively different from the patriarchy firmly dominant among "old Americans."

A long list of "others" aroused Catt's ire as irresponsible citizens (a list that was not defined at all by sex). Catt hoped voting women could combat their evil effects and quite freely argued for suffrage on just such grounds. At the head of the list without doubt were the immigrants. Catt's tirades against them fully demonstrate her deep antipathy toward "the others" as well as her unsettling willingness to employ demagoguery to advance her ends.

Catt first discovered the role of immigrants in politics when she campaigned in South Dakota in the 1890s and encountered the German-Russians. She was not impressed with what she saw. There were many other experiences that followed over the course of three decades. They brought home to Catt the great number of immigrants (and their offspring) in the United States — as well as their almost infinitely diverse cultures. Yet what mainly struck her was their similarities, especially in politics. They were united in ignorance of American culture and politics, while they (if males) could vote and "American" women could not.

> Many an American woman with revolutionary blood in her veins, born on American soil, educated in American schools, familiar with American history and ideals, has seen the process by which the votes of men born in other lands, unable to speak our language, unable to read their ballots, but automatically enfranchised when the Nation extends its certificate of naturalization.[31]

The process made no sense to her just because these people were so "exceedingly ignorant" of the American system of government and politics. For the short-run she proposed to get tough with immigrant citizens. She eagerly supported imposing a minimum educational standard for all voters, with explicit provision that knowledge of English be required. She favored increasing the period required before foreigners could become citizens as another means to reduce their impact on the political process. Another idea was to insist on compulsory voting for native Americans so that they would have the maximum influence on elections.[32] Meanwhile, Catt felt everyone should be warned and warned again of the dangers of the "others." Americans needed to face the practical fact that our immigrants were part of a process that "dipped deeper and deeper into the slum life of Europe . . . every ship brings us illiteracy, poverty and irresponsibility."[33]

Catt did not believe she was a nativist. The evidence, though, suggests she was. The distinction she made was that the problem she saw had its origins in neither nature nor ancestry. It was a lack of knowledge and "the vast amount of illiteracy" that made "the task imposed on us" of fashioning a better world "appalling" in its difficulty. Yet since the problem was a cultural one, it could be addressed by proper education. Time would solve it.[34]

There is no doubt that most Progressives did not demonstrate much sensitivity toward the cultures and values of those they opposed.[35] Catt clearly did not, nor did the antisuffragists and many socialists.[36] Particularly during suffrage years, Catt did not favor a broad, pluralist national community. She was not interested in multiculturalism, much less a rainbow America. Far from it.

Her reason was a practical one. It was not that she hated "the others," but rather that she thought they were a force blocking the changes she wanted. However, in her mind there was nothing permanent about their opposition or their liabilities that engendered it. Catt's judgment was that America could and should accept "the others" only when it "educated" and transformed them. Their origins might be varied, but their culture and basic values would then be uniform. This was her ideal, and until that ideal was reached they were enemies.

Such a view accorded surprisingly well with the Catt who was the longtime leader of the International Woman Suffrage Alliance, a woman who frequently traveled over the world and lived in assorted foreign places for considerable periods of time. This seemingly worldly-wise Catt must be kept in mind when reflecting on her sometimes heated denunciations of "the others," since sophistication seems contradictory with such obvious prejudice. What Catt felt she learned from her world travels and international friends was that people were fundamentally the same, just as the sexes were. What kept people apart so often were cultural chasms. Such differences were at best a bother and at worst a menace, but not fundamental. People could and should learn from each other, and strive constantly towards what they had in common as human beings. Cultural difference was something to be overcome at home and abroad, and education could accomplish this goal.

That Catt at the same time seemed to believe in culturally specific *values* does not negate her belief that the world was one. But it certainly explains why she rejected the idea that cultural differences were basic while at the same time she was a cultural nationalist. Quite unconsciously Catt rejected cultural pluralism because people were one and because she assumed that, if they were properly educated, they would agree with her about what was really important in life. Thus for her, internationalism and cultural nationalism went together, happily united in her mind, if only there.[37]

The question of black Americans was even more sensitive for Catt and the suffragist movement. Many black women leaders and organizations enthusiastically supported woman suffrage. As Rosalyn Terborg-Penn's scholarship has shown, however, they were never welcomed by the mainstream suffragist movement (nor later by the National Woman's Party).[38] Indeed, racism was as pervasive in the N.A.W.S.A. as it was among white Progressives in general, and the black was rarely on any white's Progressive agenda.

Catt was no exception. There was no doubt that blacks were among "the others" she saw as the enemy. Though her views require careful treatment, no gloss can be given to her routine discussion of blacks in generic and highly unflattering terms. Moreover, Catt felt just as negatively about others she saw as nonwhites. Intense Hispanic opposition to suffrage did not surprise her, for example, because "the lower the civilization, the more bitter and vindictive the opposition." Nor did she have much enthusiasm for American Indians, as she said in her famous "Comparisons are Odious" oration (which the *Woman's Journal* labeled "brilliant"). Given their scant progress on the ladder of civilization, it was literally incredible to her that male Indians could vote while white women could not.[39]

Most of Catt's complaints, though, were directed towards blacks. She frequently objected to the fact that some blacks still had the vote, despite the efforts of many white southerners, including Progressives, to impose voting tests that eventually disenfranchised blacks in the South until the 1960s. She bemoaned the "existence in our body politic of nearly a million illiterate Negroes . . . and the problems of poverty, insanity and criminality arising out of these conditions."[40] Furthermore, her critics fairly direct us to her faithful support for "states' rights" in racial matters. She never proposed for a minute repudiating "the policy of allowing local attitudes on race . . . to determine local policy." And it is true enough that Catt "condoned avowed racism and encouraged it by holding conventions in southern cities and support-ing known racists for national N.A.W.S.A. offices."[41]

One could also point out her hypocrisy in telling the few blacks who made contact with the N.A.W.S.A. that all doors were open to them there, when in fact the truth was very much the opposite.[42] And in 1920 in Tennessee, when she sought to wrest approval of the An-thony amendment from Tennessee's reluctant legislature, and oppo-nents tried to label her an integrationist and an advocate of interracial marriage, Catt rushed out a statement of reassurance, characterizing legal miscegenation as an "absolute crime against nature."[43]

Intermarriage was the exception, though, in that only on that sub-ject did Catt speak in terms of nature and race. That blacks were in-ferior she took for granted; she was surely a racist in this sense. But her assumption was that blacks' inferiority was grounded in culture, not nature, and therefore would not be permanent. Moreover, her rather amazing support of southern white mores — which drew praise from other leaders such as Alice Stone Blackwell[44] — had nothing to do with race in her view. She saw herself merely assessing realities and making practical calculations about how to win votes — and states — for suffrage. Catt did not think she could succeed without a *national* movement and eventual legislative approval of the amendment from at least a few states in the South where women's rights were intensely unpopular. Her task was incomparably harder than that faced in the 1970s by E.R.A. advocates in a South much more a part of the national culture (only one southern state legislature ratified the E.R.A.). Thus, it is not surprising that Catt, very much the single-issue politician, made the racist decision to cooperate with what southern white allies she could find.

Even then she thought it would be hard going for woman suffrage in the South, though at least her generation of suffragists was not burdened with the old anti-South reform tradition. As Catt wrote in 1900, the problem with a suffragist like Susan B. Anthony in the South was that she was known as an outspoken enemy of the entire southern way of life and had "little idea how those old 'Confeds' hate her."[45] Catt did not intend to assume that burden. Suffrage had enough ene-mies without automatically writing off the thirteen states of the former Confederacy and their sensitive border state allies.

That Catt was accepting racism did not particularly concern her. She did not want to think about the issue, nor, indeed, did she want to think about black Americans. It was Mary Peck's view that "she instinc-tively . . . wishes there were no Negoes in the country."[46] Yet it was also Catt's belief that racial barriers should fall in the United States. She was eager for black women to have the vote and claimed they belonged in the N.A.W.S.A. Yet when such issues came to a head in the 1903 N.A.W.S.A. Convention Catt decided the odds against fighting the southern perspective were too great and she quickly agreed not to demand the vote for black women. Her remarks even on that occasion, however, could not have been reassuring to confirmed racists. First she affirmed the Progressive gospel that the answer in the end would be cooperation — in this case for all races to work together for progress. Second, Catt went out of her way to challenge the idea that there was a superior race. She reminded her listeners that the Anglo-Saxons were once a pretty insignificant "race" in world terms. And she saw no reason why their subsequent history provided any particular basis for self-congratulation.[47]

In fact, as Catt's correspondence shows unmistakably, she had no use for overt racism, which appealed to the ugly side of people. As she lamented to Mary Peck in a letter on the Tennessee fight in 1920: "Women . . . are here appealing to Negro phobia and every other cave man's prejudice."[48] To black audiences she made clear that rights must apply to all, writing, for example, in the N.A.A.C.P.'s *Crisis* in 1917 that "suffrage democracy knows no bias of race, color, creed or sex."[49] And once she had her suffrage amendment safely in the Constitution she joined those bucking northern as well as southern popular opinion in calling for an immediate end to racial discrimination.[50]

Still, there is no denying her dismal public record during the suffrage crusade. She wanted white southern support and she correctly knew she would obtain none, in her time, without pandering to racism. She made what she felt was a necessary politician's choice. But it is rather sad to observe that she had not a moment of doubt about the choice she made. Even if one can sympathize with her distaste for moral purists who accomplished little and, she suspected, actually liked to lose, her lack of ambivalence in acquiescing so quickly to racism is impossible to condone.

Immigrants, illiterates, and blacks were her adversaries, but they were not the exclusive list of Catt's opponents, of "the others" she feared so much. They were constant worries, but Catt also occasionally singled out others, underlining the constant preoccupation of this sometime democrat with the failings of so many of her fellow citizens. Catt fretted about the "morally unfit," for instance, though exactly who or what they were was sometimes murky — except that they tended to be against what she favored.[51]

Much less often did Catt identify "the others" in class terms. Her 1900 speech accepting her first presidency was one such instance: "There are whole precincts of voters in this country whose united intelligence does not equal that of one representative American woman.

Yet to such classes as these we are asked to take our cause as the court of final resort."[52] But she meant groups, not economic classes. Catt saw the world in group terms and the unintelligent were a group as were immigrants, blacks, and the illiterate.

Like most Progressives, Catt resisted class analysis and language. Class categories were too foreign, too conflict producing, and too abstract (though her group analysis encouraged a similar tendency to speak in broad categories). Moreover, she just did not believe the problem was one of economic condition. The real divisions that mattered were cultural, which in turn derived from education and background.

Thus when Catt did speak of class, economics was not on her mind. She could denounce the lower classes occasionally or praise her favorite, the middle class ("the most coherent, tightest-welded, farthest searching section of society"), but her words did not touch economic status. She simply would not acknowledge that class in this sense played a role in any of the struggles she faced. Of course, she knew that her suffrage cause primarily attracted what the *Woman's Journal* called the "bourgeois," but that did not mean its aspirations or its motivations were in the slightest connected with an economic class. Truth transcended class, as she hoped it would groups.[53] Moreover, she certainly did not see how someone like herself, who opposed "conservatism" and attacked the elite interests of politicians, brewers, the railroads, and other economic forces that resisted woman suffrage and exploited working women and children, could be considered a class apologist.[54]

She did not think this way. She was an idealist, in her view, loyal to truth, not to a class by any definition. And she was a reformer, convinced that class, nature, or culture need not stand in the way of a proper democracy. There was nothing in all that besmirched American political democracy that we, aided by evolving nature, could not reform. This was her Progressive faith.

A Reformed Democracy

At times Carrie Catt seemed almost to glory in her part in the Progressive chorus of complaint about American democracy. Certainly she had a list of grievances that was endless and a tendency to repeat it at tiring length. This was, however, only part of the story. She also had definite ideas about the shape an ideal democracy would take and a great deal of confidence that the policies that would help achieve that goal were known, if not yet implemented. Indeed, Catt endorsed an array of reform schemes over the years: primaries to undercut political parties and their bosses; longer terms for elected officials that would free them from the unrelenting and corrupting influence of daily politics; restrictions on the role of money in campaigns and elsewhere in political life.[1]

These proposals are only examples, a few of the many reforms that caught her attention at one time or another. Some of them would have increased popular rule, others reduced it. But, as we know, Catt's basic concern was not necessarily the maximization of democracy in this sense. A "reformed" democracy was her goal and it involved several interrelated objectives. The first, of course, was the enfranchisement of women. It would make American democracy much more authentic simply by including the excluded female half of its population. She also hoped it would send a vast army of women into public life who might serve to advance the common good.

The second objective was fashioning the right kind of citizen, one who was independent, self-confident, and rational. What she wanted for all citizens exactly paralleled what she wanted for women in particular. They must become free and dignified beings, able to serve the public good with a tough and thoughtful independence.

The kind of independence she loved was the independence of the nonconformist who is prepared for the fact that the "world may howl at you; it may jeer at you; it may even mob you." But the truly independent citizen would not mind. He or she would be confident, Catt reassured, that in "the end the world will surrender to you if you are right."[2] At the same time, of course, Catt's ideal assumed that the good citizen would not slip into the pursuit of self-interest. Her individualism was fierce, but it was a special kind of individualism, one devoted to serving the larger good. We were to be as free as possible, but our freedom would have meaning only if we served the community. Her goal was very similar to Jane Addams's or Herbert Croly's: a social individualism. Her ideal was a democracy composed of independent people who knew how to struggle together and who genuinely cared about their mutual growth.

Such a people would constitute a true democracy in contrast to the "democracy" Catt so often felt she confronted, the democracy of false individualism. False individualism was the gospel of personhood defined in terms of selfishness, of the pursuit of merely personal and private interests. This motivated the politicians, the evil interests, and, yes, their clients — the ignorant, the immigrants, and "the others." It was a corruption of the American dream of individualism and democracy into individual cupidity and collective corruption.

It followed that Catt had no use for individualism defined as anarchism, at least as Catt perceived that doctrine. She did not want the individual to be sovereign if that meant somehow being free of service to the larger whole. Moreover, she could not take the anarchism she knew seriously. It was dogmatic and not practical and Catt was too committed to the American political system (despite everything) and too fascinated with political power to warm towards anarchism.

Yet her own anarchist sympathies were there in her relentless attacks on politics and political institutions and in her undiluted celebration of the pioneering individual against the claims of all institutions. In our own age these sentiments might have led her to an anarchist stance, but as a Progressive Catt preferred to deliver incantations on the practical solutions available: we must visualize the democratic process as it should be; "Men ought to regard Election Day and the vote they cast as the holiest and most religious service they ever perform." She hoped that the day would come when women could "too look upon the ballot as a holy thing, a right; a duty."[3] That she thought it would come probably explains why she never really opened the door to her anarchist inclinations. As always, her optimism overrode all else.

Beyond Catt's sanguine faith that nature was leading the human race towards her values, she also grounded her optimism in her belief that education could create the social individual. The answer was education and not, despite her other suggestions and the assumption of some of her fellow Progressives, reform of the "defective political machinery."[4] Indeed, most of Catt's reform package for American government consisted of education and more education. Democracy required education to build sturdy citizens and to defeat its enemy, selfish politics.[5]

Its first task was to provide basic literacy, literacy in reading and writing English *and* literacy in how American politics worked. But its broader goal was to inculcate her ideal of the good citizen. Though her conservative critics correctly perceived what was afoot,[6] Catt did not put it this way. She thought that she was as disinterested as the model citizen. She was not pushing values, she believed, but urging education in truth, a truth that would encourage a tough-minded individualism, not indoctrination or conformity.

Of course, Catt's devotion to education was hardly atypical for a Progressive. It was routine in the age of Jane Addams, John Dewey, and many others, some of whose faith in public education as the means to realize their particular goals knew few bounds.[7] But while Progressives ritualistically bowed before education, their conceptions of this deity were by no means uniform.[8] Carrie Catt had no interest in Progressive educational ideas that made a cult of the child, nor in schemes to provide skilled workers for the new industrial age, nor even in the fearful promotion of "Americanization." She was, to be sure, ardent in her insistence on education for immigrants and others whom she saw as "foreigners." But her goal was not particularly to make them American citizens, since she had no high estimate of American citizens. What she wanted from them was something very different, their transformation into Catt's vision for all citizens, imperfectly realized in the United States.

The one exception, however, occurred during America's participation in World War I. When she served as chair of the education committee for the Women's Committee of the Council of National Defense, Catt frankly worked to instill patriotism in children, women, and immigrants. Yet even Catt's notion of patriotic education had its twists. She was all for patriotism as long as it was her version, one that taught the value of peace and the importance of the eradication of militarism.[9]

How to realize her dream of the social individual was an interesting question that she did not ignore. She did not pretend to know anything about the means of education. Perhaps if she had had that knowledge, she would have been less naive in her faith in education. But she did have definite policies in mind as the means to her end. There should be at the top a cabinet-level Department of Education to recognize education's essential importance to a flourishing democracy and to provide leadership.[10] After that, Catt judged, it was up to concerned citizens to create the institutions and curricula that could make a difference. Certainly, she contended, education could not be a matter for children only — especially education for citizenship. Adult education was needed for citizenship as well as basic literacy.[11]

Her own efforts to promote proper education were extensive and revealing. They came not just in her lifelong role as public speaker, but more particularly in her eager support for what became known as "Suffrage Schools" and, later, "Citizenship Schools." First established to train N.A.W.S.A. workers, they lingered on in the 1920s serving a broader function. Still in existence are the entire curricula of these schools — which were formed both as what we would today call workshops and as a nine-month correspondence course through the *Woman Citizen*. They tell us a great deal about Catt's version of proper education.[12]

From one perspective, the lessons are somewhat surprising. They are usually turgid, no matter who the author. They are often boring in their bland affection for description over analysis. And they concentrate to a numbing degree on one federal cabinet department or agency after another. On the other hand, a real effort was made to provide insight into how government, including federal agencies, actually worked and there was a good deal of blunt talk about how politics was exercised in the United States. Overall, the content was a rather unexciting civics lesson (rather, at least thirty lessons), but the spirit was rarely pious and sometimes quite "realistic."

The assumptions of Catt's course were several, if unstated. It reflected her judgment that a heavy dose of conventional civic education was necessary to effective citizenship, but it had to be supplemented by practical advice for political success. The model assumed a rational, disinterested citizen who really cared about politics and government. What was missing, however, in Catt's curriculum as well as in her general faith in education as a means to citizenship is motivation. Why would people want this kind of education unless they just happened, for whatever reasons, to seek it? Also missing is why this education would make people the kind of citizens she sought. Catt never seriously addressed either point. She took for granted that educated people would want to be good citizens, just as she took for granted the value her educational ideas had for good citizenship. These are curious assumptions today, but their popularity in the Progressive Era made them self-evident, needing no defense to Catt.

The third objective of Catt's trinity toward a genuine democracy was social. The first involved legal change: women's enfranchisement. The second involved creation of a good citizen through education. The third involved finding an institutional mechanism through which ideal citizens, women especially, could transform American political life.

At this third objective Catt faced a dilemma. Practical as she was, she appreciated all too well that politics in her America proceeded through political parties. She was herself, as her critics said, "a professional woman politican."[13] She considered it obvious that people had to deal with realities to gain political effectiveness and political reform. Education had to include practical facts because at that moment "an Irish bartender rather outclasses the scholar" when it came to knowledge about politics in America.[14] Catt's dilemma was that the politics and parties of her era seemed so contemptible. Her pragmatic spirit urged independent citizens into them anyway, but her idealistic side sought an alternative, a new institution for new citizens. Eventually she decided she would have to create one; thus was born the League of Women Voters.

Urging enfranchised women and citizens of either sex to enter ordinary politics was usually hard for Catt. Her heart was just not in it, but she did it anyway because it was the main path to influence. She did hope that people could come to appreciate politics' other advantages for them, its tremendous educational value, its inherent interest as an exposure to "the complete drama of life," and its opportunities for enjoyment.[15]

But Catt's eagerness for politics as usual was very modest. She revealed her deepest sentiments in her inability to follow her own advice. She was simply too bitter over how the parties and their minions had behaved during the suffrage fight. And as a reformer, even a "half-politician" reformer, she could not stomach the established parties, no matter how often she urged others to do so.[16]

And yet, even as she stood outside the parties, Catt could not resist involving herself in electoral politics. She did contain herself during her years as a suffrage crusader and she later advocated a similar restraint for her League of Women Voters. But it was not natural to her inclinations. Perhaps her favorite politician was fellow-reformer Woodrow Wilson. She would have liked to have endorsed Wilson in

1916, but she held off because she wanted to adhere to nonpartisanship until suffrage achieved victory. She would have endorsed him had he run again in 1920. Catt saw Wilson as an ally of reform at home, including (eventually) woman suffrage, and abroad, in the struggle for world peace. In her private correspondence she praised him lavishly. She thought his excellence was obvious in comparison with the alternatives in both parties who were "the merest shrimps." Indeed, at the time of his death Catt rated Woodrow Wilson with Washington and Lincoln, confident that he "was a great man; history will not deny him that status and no enemy can."[17]

Her first political endorsement came in the last moments of the 1920 presidential campaign when Catt reversed her public stance of neutrality and came out for Democrat James Cox over Republican Warren G. Harding. Cox's mild support of the League of Nations was decisive. Catt was widely denounced both for speaking out and for her choice. Her action appears to have had no impact towards reducing Harding's massive victory, though it did cause her newly independent League of Women Voters considerable trouble and led to many resignations by Republican members. Ironically, Catt soon came to respect Harding as a president who (she erroneously thought) cared about the World Court and wished to assist women. Indeed, on his death she eulogized Harding as "an exceptionally clean and high-minded character," one "that mothers like to point out as an example for their sons."[18]

Embarrassment as a result of her public support of Cox in 1920 kept Catt out of the business of endorsing presidential candidates for a time. Yet she did enter electoral politics in the 1920s: first in 1920 and then in 1926, to oppose the candidacy of Republican James J. Wadsworth for re-election to the United States Senate from New York. There was probably no person in political life whom Catt detested more than Wadsworth. He had fought suffrage with all his energies and his wife had for a time been the national leader for the antisuffrage forces. Moreover, Catt found him as unacceptable in the 1920s as she had when he fought women's enfranchisement. Wadsworth was a prominent opponent of the Child Labor Amendment, to Catt's disgust. And he was also an opponent of Prohibition, completing his consistent opposition to Catt's Progressive platform. In the 1926 race Catt worked for the Prohibitionist candidate, who eventually got more than 190,000 votes, a margin exceeding Robert Wagner's plurality over Wadsworth. Seeing Wadsworth lose was undoubtedly the political highlight of the 1920s for her and she took satisfaction that she had played a role in what was for her frankly the politics of revenge.[19]

Even in the presidential realm Catt found it hard to avoid expressing her opinions in public, though usually she kept her views among friends. In 1928 when Herbert Hoover ran for president, Catt endorsed him. Even in 1932 she (like Jane Addams) supported him over F.D.R. Hoover mattered to her because he was such a strong Prohibitionist and, perhaps too, because he was so opposed by the "others."[20]

Catt first got to know Franklin Roosevelt in 1911 when he was a prosuffrage state senator in New York. Once he was elected president, she welcomed his leadership in the New Deal and then in World War II, and she probably voted for F.D.R. in both 1936 and 1944. On the other hand, Catt was very much like many other Progressives who objected to Roosevelt's extreme (as they saw it) affinity for a larger, intrusive, and "political" state. In 1940, when she backed Wilkie, she expected Roosevelt to win since the "tremendous influence of Mr. Roosevelt's bureaucracy will pull him through, I am afraid."[21]

There is no question that, given Catt's distaste for the state-oriented New Deal, her reluctance to oppose Roosevelt publicly derived from her friendship with and devotion to Eleanor Roosevelt. She and Catt were hardly contemporaries, Catt being a generation older. Nor were they intimates. But they became friends working together on assorted causes in the 1920s. Eleanor Roosevelt admired Catt for her leadership in the fight for votes for women, as well as for Catt's concern for world peace. She dedicated one of her books, *This Troubled World*, to Catt. For her part Catt frequently and extravagantly praised Eleanor Roosevelt as First Lady and she basked in the support and recognition that Mrs. Roosevelt frequently accorded Catt in her old age. To Catt she was "the First Lady of all the First Ladies of the land for 150 years." Catt once publicly told Mrs. Roosevelt, "when people ask me 'Do you like Mrs. Roosevelt?' my answer is 'Yes, and I think she's the queen bee of the universe.' "[22]

For Catt, of course, as for so many other women, what made Eleanor Roosevelt so special was not her husband. It was her own life as a woman. Catt admired her "for having been a loyal member of our army,"[23] a reference to Eleanor Roosevelt's cooperation with Catt on a number of 1920s causes (not the earlier suffrage movement, since the young Eleanor was not a suffragist). She also meant much more. She felt so much of Mrs. Roosevelt's life was a demonstration of what Catt dreamed modern women (and men) could do. She was her kind of independent person. She stood her ground as she acted in (and out) of politics to advance the causes of peace, justice, and women, among many others. She was the liberated woman, as Catt visualized that ideal, helping others and seeking to improve the world, a Progressive woman in politics. It was in this light that Eleanor Roosevelt won Catt's emphatic approval, regardless of her husband's political faults.

On balance, and despite her own advice, Catt mostly stayed on the sidelines of conventional party and electoral politics. She heard the call, but she just could not ordinarily square it with her Progressive idealism. She could not join a party not only because she did not like either one, but because she was her own ideal — an independent-minded citizen whose adherence to specific principles and policy goals found no consistent echo in either party. Catt was as political a woman as the United States has seen, but always in the Progressive mode: skeptical of parties and devoted to principle and yet, within these constraints, able to operate in public life to promote her objectives.

The League of Women Voters

Catt perceived the necessity for an institutional forum for her dream of a reformed democracy (as well as for her hopes for organized women in political life). To that end she founded the League of Women Voters (L.W.V.). It was never just another political organization for Carrie Catt. It was a very special one, dear to her heart and mind, central to her dreams for a transformed American polity. Though Catt typically disavowed such a view — "You asked what hope led to the foundation of the League of Women Voters. None at all. . . . It was not a hope, but a job, a hard disagreeable job" — the truth was quite different.[24]

Catt saw it (at least at first) as her own, fond creation, and one with great potential. For Catt, the L.W.V. would bring independent women who cared about the commonwealth together for education and issue politics, always avoiding partisan politics. It was to be an alternative to the reality of the old democracy, a model of Catt's vision of democracy and independent citizenship in action. Indeed, in proposing the L.W.V., Catt was proposing her ideal for America, her deepest dreams, her utopia.

Catt first presented the idea of a League of Women Voters (the name was her invention) to the N.A.W.S.A. before Congress had passed woman suffrage and even before three-quarters of the states had ratified the Anthony amendment. This was typical of Catt's tendency to plan for the future while actively working on current causes and campaigns. Exactly when Catt first thought of such an organization to embody her ideal we do not know. Possibly she had long dreamed of its existence, since she had always believed woman suffrage was merely a matter of time.

There was no self-evident logic to her idea of the League. In no other western nation was there any significant effort or success in continuing (or refashioning) women's organizations after the achievement of women's enfranchisement. Only in the United States did Catt's dream for American democracy lead to the creation of the League of Women Voters and only here did Alice Paul's vision for women lead to the birth of the National Woman's Party.[25]

In 1919, with the success of woman suffrage manifestly on the horizon, Catt actively began promoting the idea of the League.[26] The *Woman Citizen* was filled with articles by Catt and her acolytes boosting the idea. She touted it as a logical continuation of the work of the N.A.W.S.A., but also as a "memorial" to the great crusade, a memorial to impending victory and the struggles that had gone into it. Others went further and viewed it as a memorial to Catt herself, the sort of thing that Catt had no interest in, she said, but that she knew how to use to speed what she wanted.

In her glory days of 1920, when suffrage was achieved, Catt moved directly to take advantage of the attendant euphoria and found the League of Women Voters.[27] It was apparently never Catt's intention to run the organization herself, at least not directly. Her interest in the international woman suffrage and peace campaigns came first, but it was a mark of her serious intentions for the organization and that of others' around her that she took an aggressive role in getting it afloat. One important example was her search for qualified leadership for the League. At first she wanted to have the League operate with an elected board and a hired manager, a typically Progressive conception in its combination of democracy and professional expertise. But she soon decided that an elected president would be a better idea.[28]

While Maud Wood Park was not her first choice for the job, Catt eventually convinced her old comrade-in-arms to be the first leader. Catt wanted as many new faces as possible to be active, but she concluded that the League would need the talents and shrewd practical experience that Park possessed.[29] Catt agreed to be honorary chair of the League, a post that she held without dispute till her death in 1947, but this was merely a symbolic arrangement. It honored not only her, but the suffragist origins of the League.

Maud Wood Park was in important ways a good choice for the first years of the League (she served as leader from 1920 to 1924). Somewhat younger than Catt, she shared Carrie Catt's aspirations for women to count in politics. Because of her prominence in the suffrage crusade she was able to attract and hold many of her fellow campaigners in the League, giving it a base on which to build. She was also used to leadership and able to play politics effectively, both the politics within an organization and on the national scene. She had, after all, risen to head the congressional lobbying effort in the last years of the struggle, and there was all but unanimous agreement that Park did remarkably effective work in that role.[30]

As Catt conceived of the League of Women Voters, it was to be something of an experiment — as indeed it was. To be sure, the Woman's Christian Temperance Union, the General Federation of Women's Clubs, and, indeed, the National American Woman Suffrage Association demonstrated that the drive towards organization in the late nineteenth and early twentieth centuries had a great many expressions among women. In this sense the League was hardly anything new. As Catt knew, though, the League did represent a new stage in the new age of national woman suffrage, and it remained to be seen if the League could last and could serve.

Her proposal was that the L.W.V. try its wings for five years and then face an evaluation of its continuing worth. She wanted to ensure that it lived up to her aspirations, that it became a living, active force ready to strike boldly toward her ideal democracy. She also had a specific policy agenda that she expected the League to pursue, but the first challenge it would have to face would be whether it was necessary at all for any purpose. Some questioned whether women, now armed with the vote, required such a group. Others wondered how the League fit with Catt's other recommendation, entering political parties. Still others questioned whether many women had, or could have, enough in common to become a political force. Finally, and importantly, antisuffragists attacked the League, trying to kill it before it could get started. In their publications it was nothing less than an attempt to overthrow America by unstable feminists, led by the worst of them, Carrie Chapman Catt.[31]

To say the least, this was a misunderstanding of Catt's vision, though it was testimony to Catt's once widespread reputation as something of a radical. Instead, Catt's more specific policy objectives for the L.W.V. went in other directions. It was to press for women's full participation as political equals. It should educate women to become voters and to become voters of the independent, rational type Catt so admired. It should educate women as to political inequities, especially at local and state levels, and get them moving to end them. Moroever, Catt wanted the League to create a "department of efficiency" to address political corruption and manipulable election laws. Her League was also to work for civil service reform, a direct primary by voters to nominate political candidates, and reform of city governments. In short, it was to continue the Progressive political reform package that meant so much to Catt. After all, for Catt, woman suffrage was partly

about improving American democracy and thus the L.W.V. should
assist in bringing its potential to life.[32]

The last objective Catt wanted the League to pursue was economic
and social reform. Despite her attacks on assorted economic interests,
Catt never appears to have objected to capitalism. Nor did she suggest
any radical changes in it. She was never a socialist. But Catt had an
agenda which she worked for in the 1920s that included the Child
Labor Amendment to the Constitution, the Sheppard-Towner Act to
aid pregnant women and reduce infant mortality, minimum wage legislation for women, and other protective laws for employed women.
She urged the League to join the battle for these reforms, assuming
not that they threatened capitalism, as their critics said, but that they
would help women be independent and free, just the sort of thing the
League of Women Voters should care about.

The League followed Catt's expectations on all fronts, though the
fact is that Catt's hand was not closely held to the heart of its operations.[33] While she crusaded for world peace, it moved along. In one
instance this caused a good deal of trouble. In 1921 Catt zealously
rushed in to give her League the bulk of the credit for the passage of
the Sheppard-Towner Act, provoking a storm of criticism of Catt and
the L.W.V. from other sponsors. In fact, the League had participated
with a host of other organizations in a coalition that achieved the victory, and some of the others had done much more than the League.
Recognizing the potential damage Catt's uninformed claims might
cause to the fledgling League, Maud Wood Park smoothed ruffled
feathers by giving generous credit to the League's partners, and calm
was restored.[34]

From the beginning, however, Catt had definite opinions that she
continued to advance in League circles on two internal issues which
eventually affected what the L.W.V. would be like. She was vitally concerned with how political the League should be and whether it should
be strictly nonpartisan. She cared far more about these matters than
the many other internal issues that bothered Maud Park,[35] because
they affected how closely the League would realize her dream as a
model of a new democracy.

Catt wanted the League of Women Voters to be a quasi-political
organization. "Is it political? Certainly but not partisan," she said.[36]
She meant that the League would certainly educate and lobby for programs it favored, but that it would do so by focusing on *issues*. It must
be "united for principles" and never degenerate into yet another political party routinely in the business of endorsing and supporting candidates. In theory she did not object to League women also being
Republicans or Democrats. But Catt believed that the L.W.V. could

not be an attractive vehicle for those benighted souls for whom "party loyalty is a superstition and a fetish." She was partly motivated by the practical fear that partisan involvement would ensnare the L.W.V. in petty local quarrels sapping the organization's overall strength. But mostly it was a matter of her principles, her conviction that the L.W.V. must represent a different model of politics, one that left old parties and old ways behind.[37]

In its beginning years some of the League's local branches did stray away from Catt's vision of nonpartisanship. The national League stayed out of the endorsement business, however, and soon all local Leagues did as well. Catt was glad, though she never meant for a minute that the League should not have an impact at the ballot box. On the contrary. She never respected any group that could be dismissed as "a parlor uplift movement." She was much too tough and much too political for that. She expected members of the L.W.V. "to use their ballots fearlessly." They were to offer another ideal of organization than the parties she hated. But she wanted members to be sufficiently educated to recognize the reality that elections mattered, and she wanted opponents of the L.W.V.'s objectives to understand that League members knew that elections mattered. In short, what Catt had in mind was education and lobbying backed by determination of League members to aid those who agreed with them and to punish those who didn't — without the necessity of endorsing candidates. The League was to be "above" parties and their corrupt practices, but no so far above that its educated and informed members could not force parties to do their bidding.[38]

One might wonder, what politician would seriously worry about this kind of an organization, the chary, half-political League? But in its very early years a great many were concerned. The main reason was the possibility that large numbers or even most women might rally to the L.W.V., making its support a prize to catch and its opposition a force to fear. Some party politicians tried to kill the L.W.V. from the start, sometimes charging its nonpartisanship was phony, sometimes asserting its devotion to nonpartisanship was hurting the party system. A few women activists, usually connected with the Woman's Party, were equally critical. They saw the League Catt envisioned as nothing more than a toothless training organization for women before entering the old system of politics and political parties. They saw no evidence that the League of Women Voters was to be a serious woman's party, focused on *women's* concerns and determined to exercise its full political muscle on behalf of candidates who cared about feminism. Another view was that of Jane Addams and those like her for whom Catt seemed too political. For them, women needed to enter politics much less than they needed to turn to the social needs crying for action all around them in their local communities. What was needed was not a League of Women Voters but more Hull Houses.[39]

Despite the disagreement, Catt pushed for the League to take the path she had always traveled herself. Women would have to go the route of politics, though not the route of partisan or party politics. Their advance towards control of their destiny as well as towards general social and political reform in a Progressive mold could happen, but only if women were armed to participate in the world of practical politics. This was her ideal. This had been her practice. She made the League of Women Voters in this image and it lives on, still much as she would have wished.[40]

C H A P T E R 7

The Gospel of Organization

Robert Wiebe in his now classic study, *The Search for Order: 1877–1920*, argues that America at the turn of the century made a fateful shift towards a world of organization, a shift that was to transform every aspect of life in the United States in the twentieth century. His thesis by now has been tested and frequently confirmed by others who have explored such realms of our collective life as the advance of the modern corporation and the growth of local government administration.[1]

But we can also find its confirmation in the development of the National American Woman Suffrage Association under the direction of Carrie Chapman Catt. Without doubt Catt personified what Wiebe argues was the spirit of the age: faith in organization. She believed completely that organization was the pathway to victory for women's enfranchisement. And she had the remarkable practical talent to translate her faith into reality. Universally acknowledged by friend and foe alike, Catt was the most important organizer of woman suffrage.

The fact that Catt's leadership of the organizational growth of the N.A.W.S.A. was part of a broad movement toward organization throughout American life does not dim Catt's personal contribution. It does place it in perspective, so that we can acknowledge the reality that, as Catt perceptively realized, the time was ripe for suffrage forces if they but chose to take advantage of this tendency and become a group of women united in a serious, effective political organization.

This opportunity was, of course, not only a collective possibility, but also a personal one. As Anne Firor Scott recently noted, "What business and public life were to aspiring nineteenth-century men, the voluntary association was to aspiring women" — especially by 1900.[2] This was obviously true for Carrie Catt and those associated with her, whose prominence in American life was achieved with the rise of their voluntary organization, the N.A.W.S.A.

In fact, within the realm of the volunteer associations, many women grasped the opportunity. Jane Cunningham Croly had somewhat earlier founded Sorosis and deserves acknowledgment as the most significant pioneer of the women's club movement. Frances Willard's remarkable leadership of the Women's Christian Temperance Union in the latter part of the nineteenth century also provided an important model. Both of these efforts, however, preceded the major era of organization in American life as it flowered in the late nineteenth and early twentieth centuries, when Catt made her decisive impact on the National American Woman Suffrage Association. A contemporary example of the general movement to organization among women, complementing the N.A.W.S.A., was the General Federation of Women's Clubs. Born in 1890, by 1912 it had over a million members.[3]

Yet it was the far more controversial National American Woman Suffrage Association that became the women's group of that day, surpassing all others in numbers and in organization. Its internal engineer was Catt, who stoked it in theory and practice until the N.A.W.S.A. became the most powerful women's organization in American history. Kraditor describes Catt's role directly and accurately: "She transformed the huge, disorganized, and aimless group of women into a purposeful organization, each part of which carried out its assigned task in its leader's grand strategy for victory."[4]

Catt's celebration and practice of organization in the suffrage struggle evolved gradually. The first phase was the decade of the 1890s, when Catt emerged as a powerful force in the N.A.W.S.A., as a tireless advocate of the value of organization. As she said in 1895, "The great need of the hour is organization . . . the size of our membership is not at all commensurate with the sentiment for woman suffrage. The reason for this condition is plain; the chief work of suffragists for the past forty years has been education and agitation, and not organization."[5]

Her goal was to encourage the movement to become practical. The N.A.W.S.A. had to turn away from its past when suffragists preferred to get "hold of some interesting phrase about woman suffrage and talked about that," and had to concentrate instead on "the way to get the vote."[6] After all, how much had the earlier approach gained in terms of women's enfranchisement? A few, very lightly populated western states had adopted woman suffrage. That was about it. To start winning, there had to be a more structured organization. Being reformers was not enough; indeed, it could be counterproductive, because reformers usually both disdained politics and did badly when they tepidly tried to play its game. Catt insisted that people like herself were needed, individuals who could combine commitment to reform with an ability to work hard in a disciplined, focused, organized fashion. They alone would build the organization that could bring victory.[7]

To be sure, Catt always argued that the relationship between organization and victory would not be neat. She appreciated that in the forty-year period after 1870 the record could be read to indicate that, the more organized its campaigns were, the more certain it was that suffrage would be defeated in one state or another. She noted that the first victories in the West came where there was usually little organization, whereas massive efforts in the East resulted in repeated failures. Yet she was convinced that it was all merely a matter of time. As organization developed, as it grew stronger and stronger, it would win more and more often. Its presence might not guarantee victory at first, but in the end it would simply overpower its opponents even in the resistant East, where success by any other effort had proven hopeless.[8]

To build an organized movement Catt knew it was essential to effect "a change of sentiment concerning the possibilities of organization."[9] Changing suffragist opinion was Catt's real mission within the N.A.W.S.A. in the 1890s, though she simultaneously tried to craft a serious organization. Both steps, Catt argued strenuously, simply had to be taken. No matter how uncomfortable she made her elders, Catt returned to this theme again and again, insisting that organization was the absolute, irreplaceable necessity for arousing apathetic women and defeating active enemies.[10]

Catt's work as an organizer in the 1890s took her to many states and into many campaigns, some victorious (for example, Colorado in 1893) and many more defeats (beginning with South Dakota in 1890). But it can best be followed through her annual reports to the N.A.W.S.A. conventions, mostly from the Organizational Committee, which she headed. They detail the specific steps taken and contain both harsh words for the past and gradually increasing optimism as organization slowly spread.[11] Also available are some of Catt's detailed reports on work in individual states, which illuminate the ebb and flow of concrete organizational work.[12] All of them illustrate Catt's first efforts to organize groups, cultivate the press, encourage "education," distribute literature, start petition drives, lobby legislators, raise money, and the rest of her efforts, which we will consider shortly in discussing her principles of organization. By 1900 Catt felt she had accomplished a great deal even though victories were not numerous. A major start towards a serious national organization was in place and, above all, "suffragists are beginning to see the truth . . . that organization is the watchword of the hour."[13]

During her first presidency (1900–1904) Catt made only modest progress toward her organizational goals, and her unexpected departure from leadership of the N.A.W.S.A. temporarily ended her pursuit of organization in the N.A.W.S.A. The second important phase of her organizational work began about a decade later when she gradually turned her energies towards obtaining women's enfranchisement in her adopted New York State. While organization of women for this purpose was hardly new in the state, Catt and her associates began a distinctly more hopeful era when they established the Woman Suffrage Party in New York City in 1909. Its first president was Carrie Catt and her right-hand woman was her intimate, Mary Hay.[14] Over the next few years a number of suffrage groups sprung up in both the city and the state, and in 1913 Catt led the way to their effective coalition under the rubric of the Empire State Campaign Committee, which she chaired. Two years later, as the suffrage forces moved towards their initial statewide New York referendum on women's enfranchisement, Catt won agreement from all the cooperating groups to merge into a single organization rather than a cooperating coalition. This became the New York State Woman Suffrage Party. Catt again was selected as leader. Under its banners Catt fought (and lost) the 1915 referendum and started planning for the 1917 referendum until she was persuaded to assume the N.A.W.S.A. presidency.[15]

It was during this phase that Catt refined ideas she had tried in the 1890s and developed new ones towards building an organization for the tremendous challenge of winning resistant New York to woman suffrage. Here she consciously began to model her organization "exactly after the dominant political parties in order to measure swords with them."[16] In particular, she stressed the importance of forming her organization precinct-by-precinct throughout the state so that all areas, indeed all houses, would be canvassed and as much as possible be "educated." We possess a great deal of material demonstrating how Catt promoted this kind of organization and how she handled the bewildering array of problems and details that her overall direction required her to treat.[17]

Catt's focus on the election-district model of the then well-organized political parties necessarily included a willingness to reach out to all sorts of people, all sorts of precincts, including those where

few middle-class WASPS were to be found. Indeed, Catt vigorously encouraged recruitment in the vast areas of New York City where
immigrants dominated, arranging for literature, speakers, and
organizers in appropriate tongues. She also urged serious efforts to
organize precincts where people were poor, no matter what their
nationality, as part of her recognition that to win, the woman suffrage movement had to shed its parochial, elitist reputation. Like a
successful political party, the Woman Suffrage Party would have
to be a coalition of all sectors of the population, and Catt set out to
make it so.[18]

Another important stage in Catt's organizational endeavors came
during her second presidency (1916–1920) when she struggled to win
congressional approval of the Anthony amendment. It required her
to convince state leaders to implement the organizational techniques
she (and others) had fashioned, in order to increase pressure from the
states for federal action.[19] It also required her to oversee the work with
Congress in Washington. Maud Wood Park headed the day-to-day
lobbying of Congress, but she and Catt worked extremely closely, as
their extensive correspondence indicates.[20] Finally, Catt had to deal
with overall national strategy (see chapter 9) and try to persuade the
rest of the N.A.W.S.A. to be as aggressively committed to organization
as she was — a continual concern.[21]

It was an altogether exhausting and complicated regimen. What
was new about it was both her attention to national strategy and her
supervision of the often exasperating congressional lobbying. Both
stood her in good stead in the final phase, which was the national
campaign to win ratification of the Anthony amendment in three-
quarters of the states once Congress gave its approval (1919–1920).
Indeed, everything she had learned about strategy, detailed local organizing, and lobbying was brought to bear by what was then a smooth-
running national machine that any politician might envy — and more
than a few did. As state after state fell in line, Catt had no doubt why.
As she wrote Alice Stone Blackwell, while the "ratifications seem to
come in such a spontaneous way, I beg to assure you there is nothing
spontaneous about them."[22] Organization was the answer — as Catt
had always known it would be.[23]

Principles of Organization

Carrie Catt operated with a definite understanding that there were
basic elements or principles that necessitated attention if organization
was to become more than a watchword without substance. The first

was leadership. Catt assumed that leadership would be tightly held in the hands of one person cooperating with other elite associates and operating in a clearly hierarchical structure. Such a leader would, of course, be democratically elected, but otherwise have a largely free hand, a goal she finally achieved for herself within the N.A.W.S.A. in 1915.[24]

Of course, leaders in some sense were a necessity at every level in the N.A.W.S.A., right down to the smallest precinct committee. Whatever their level, however, Catt insisted that leaders could operate effectively only within an organizational framework. Catt never was enthusiastic about leadership in any romantic or heroic sense. What might be called "media stars" today were not the answer. Such short-term celebrities operated ineffectively because they operated alone. They might flash through a town or a state, stimulating their audiences. But then they were gone, leaving little lasting effect. Leaders were needed to arouse and to teach, but they were equally needed to *organize* and to get others to organize. In Weberian terms, what Catt sought was a new type of leader for the woman's movement, one who could play the charismatic roles of Anthony and Stanton, while also performing the bureaucratic functions that (in her private opinion) they had neglected.

When Catt thought about organization she immediately thought about planning. Planning was a central principle of any impressive organization, she argued, and she followed her own advice. In every one of her campaigns and during both her presidencies, she conceived broad designs — often planning, as she did for the ratification struggle, years in advance. On the other hand, Catt also planned specifically what had to be done state by state, month by month, week by week, day by day.[25] As one admirer put it, she united "what are usually thought to be opposing qualities. She sees large and she sees small. Her plans are of extraordinary scope, but they are worked out to the tiniest detail."[26]

But leadership and planning meant nothing, she discovered, unless there were effective organizers to carry out leaders' plans. For Catt that meant unstinting efforts to find talented organizers for her national campaigns, and she pressured state and local organizations to do the same.[27] Moreover, Catt insisted that organizers be trained systematically. She had no confidence in what mere good intentions could do. Organization was a skilled job and people had to learn the job to do it well. Here as elsewhere, Catt as a Progressive believed in what education could do. In New York and during her second presidency she developed and staffed her "Suffrage Schools"; as early examples of disciplined efforts to train people in political effectiveness, they were serious business for her and for those who studied in them. Although this sort of thing is routine now, then it was an innovation, one of which Catt was quite proud. Participants learned both the history of suffrage and current suffrage (and antisuffrage) arguments, and they were taught how to organize, often down to the last practical detail. Such matters as the different approaches to take when dealing with voters or members of legislatures, how to develop a good relationship with the press, how to use the press for influencing the electorate, and the techniques of public speaking received extensive attention.[28]

In and out of the Suffrage Schools, Catt's accent was undeniably on fostering *professional* organizers. She had no elaborate definition of a professional in mind, but her goal was individuals who were "scientifically" trained as specialists working full-time on their jobs with pride in their services. It was her conviction that such professionals would be a good deal more effective than amateurs.

As Wiebe leads us to predict, Catt's conversion to this approach was gradual and unself-conscious. She displayed no awareness that she was merely one more participant in a much broader movement across the United States towards the growth of a modern professional and bureaucratic ethos.[29]

Catt proudly claimed that her model of professionals was special in a crucial way. Her professionals were to be altruists, a possibility that she assumed would be easy to achieve. And such altruists would prove their commitment, and did, because they would work for free. Catt always bragged that at every level the suffrage movement was a volunteer movement, one where people gave of themselves without any financial compensation (and taint of corrupt self-interest).

Catt never appears to have reflected on the class implications of her standard in terms of who might become an officer or one of her organizers. She preferred to trumpet proudly the fact that during her presidency no national or state officer (with one exception) was ever paid by the N.A.W.S.A. She did, however, have to come to terms with the fact that staff workers and organizers often had to be paid, and were, because they could not serve otherwise.[30]

Nonetheless, the professional she sought was acceptable only if she saw her work as a calling that she answered out of idealism. Catt had no intimation of the future of professionalism, of worlds of professionals without a cause except their profession, or themselves. Nor did she see paid professionals as a fruitful avenue by which some women might achieve the dignity Catt yearned for. Women's dignity could not come from employment, much less professionalization; they might be necessities, but they were not the answers.

Whatever the implications of Catt's model of organizers, she worked for decades to make it a reality. There is no doubt that she succeeded to a remarkable extent with the help and hard work of many of her peers. The eventual result was a national network of women engaged in organizing for the enfranchisement of women. By 1920 this network was an impressive demonstration of what could be accomplished by disciplined organizers. It ranks Catt with Frances Willard, and those who aided her in organizing for temperance, as among the pioneers in crafting organized networks of women for change.[31]

Gerda Lerner challenges us to acknowledge networks among women and recommends we look at them in terms of how women experienced them. She suggests that they had a culture of their own that could tell us a great deal not just about their operation but also about the women in them. Each network could be an important window to a chapter in the history of women.[32]

Catt was the first to agree that her network was more than the individuals who composed it and had a culture or spirit of its own. She thought the organizers and activists of the suffrage movement bonded together in a special way. This subculture was a weapon, she thought, a means to greater effectiveness. Above all, though, for Catt its greatest beneficiaries were the women in the network. As she put it, "while we all toiled long hours, the comraderie [sic] of those days made the work easy."[33] "How do I pity the women who have had no share in the exaltation and the discipline of our workers. How do I pity those who have felt none of the grip of the oneness of women struggling, serving, suffering, sacrificing for the righteousness of women's emancipation."[34]

But what Catt did not explain, nor can a study of her, is whether this "exaltation," "discipline," and "oneness" were, in fact, characteristic of — or essential to — the network as a whole. Catt thought so and, despite occasional conflicts, many of those around her saw the network in like fashion; so did some others in the movement who have shared their thoughts with posterity. "To understand the little world of suffrage, one . . . should bear the scars . . . one should have worked and laughed and sorrowed with its inhabitants. . . . Once of its circle, life was forever deeper and different. . . . It developed a new loyalty — that of woman to woman."[35]

While these bonds were intense at the leadership level, we know very much less about the network's effects among the women in the movement at large. This ignorance about life below the leadership level of the N.A.W.S.A. (which was, despite Catt's effort, always somewhat of "a loose federation of clubs") remains the great gap in the study of the struggle for women's enfranchisement in the United States.[36] What was the texture of relations, thoughts, feelings, culture among the "ordinary" participants and organizers? What was the reality of their corporate life? Lerner's summons to explore the culture of women's networks is timely, but answering it will not be easy. The problem is not simply that little has yet been done, and much is needed, in the unglamorous study of the state and local levels of the suffrage movement; it is the difficulty of defining and recovering the elusive and yet potentially revealing culture of the suffrage struggle.

All that Catt knew, in any case, was that she had to have a network of committed, well-schooled organizers directed by able leaders. If and when she did, it would be possible to have an impact on every state and, through them, on Washington. We know she thought this could work only if directions emanated from the top, but just as crucial, she judged, was the role of the organizers, who had to penetrate every county, every city, every village, every precinct. For organizers, success meant local organization. For Catt it was literally true that victory would be won on the local level and thus it was there that her dreams could come true.

In election districts politicians won or lost and in election districts referenda were won or lost. It was that simple. Organizing them, however, was much less simple. Beginning in Idaho in 1896, Catt spent a lot of time not only doing just that, but later, advising others on how to do it. The task required putting her organizers to work surveying each district, interviewing and lobbying every voter, keeping records of all voter contacts, setting up district meetings, forming committees for publicity and for recruitment of more organizers, educating poll watchers in both election laws and the techniques of corruption, and much more. Moreover, all of this had to be done with the enthusiasm that allowed one to transcend setbacks, insults, or the mundaneness of the job, and to push on.[37]

The objective, of course, was to build a machine that could match and then defeat the machines that so often thwarted her. This she did by concentrating on organizers and local election district organization, laying aside the illusions that impressive statements from national headquarters or even impressive plans on paper were a substitute.

Catt asked few questions about supporters as long as they did not cause personal or ideological tension with other allies and as long as they expected no favors in return. She avoided Prohibitionist groups on this ground. But she favored going after every other women's club on the local level, while she personally undertook to win over national women's organizations, such as the newly founded National Federation of Business and Professional Women's Clubs.[38]

Catt was also eager to get every kind of male support she could. She knew well enough that her success in referenda or in legislatures would depend on men. This obviously was not her preference, but it was a fact of life and Catt saw no choice but to embrace such a political reality. Therefore, recruiting male support was important; she realized this fact early, perhaps because she knew from her personal life what a difference it made when men opposed or favored suffrage for women (her father opposing it, her two husbands favoring it). As early as 1890 in the South Dakota contest she had said: "We must get Dakota *men* in the work: They are not talking woman suffrage on the street."[39] As a result she urged rallying any possible citizen groups to support the cause. She also proposed that every state and locality set up a men's group that would push for suffrage, under the assumption that some men could be convinced only by other men.

While Catt insisted that it was sheer numbers that finally mattered in organizational success, she also strove to get a good many "names" organized behind votes for women. She wanted both the names of influential organizations and the names of influential people behind her.

She told organizers to find out who really counted in their locality and seek their support, just as, when her die-hard opponents took to the courts to block the ratification process, she fought back by enlisting the prominent and esteemed Charles Evans Hughes as her lawyer. Catt prided herself on organizational realism and she appreciated that elites always matter more than average citizens, though she intended to have both, to have everybody she could, marching under her suffrage banner.[40]

To generate support Catt depended on publicity as well as organizers. Each had to complement the other. Under her direction, a massive educational apparatus spread the suffrage word out over the country, spewing what Catt frankly termed "propaganda" into any willing hands. Part of it involved campaigning and part publicity by other means. Catt herself loved to campaign for suffrage and she encouraged others to do so too, as long as it did not serve as a substitute for organizing. Catt was the furthest thing from a mere headquarters figure. She had her headquarters, and she was sometimes there, either in New York City or Washington. But she had an incurable desire to be out on the hustings carrying the word and a well-developed sense that organizational success depended on her role as leader being in the field. She visited almost every state in her tours in an age in which touring took far greater time, money, and energy than it does today.

Sometimes these trips were rough, especially before 1900, when she ventured into parts of the West where neither travel nor accommodations were comfortable. She loved to recount her adventures in frontier South Dakota when she had subsisted mostly on watermelon and bread. But nothing deterred her. By 1900 Catt had already traveled 13,000 miles and visited twenty states. By 1920 Catt had covered over 100,000 miles and spoken about 7,000 times.[41]

For Catt this campaigning was essential to generate publicity (which she always did so well), to educate voters, and to inspire and get feedback from organizers. Catt believed there was no substitute for actually meeting and talking with the faithful, no substitute for her or for them.[42]

Of course there was something painfully prosaic in all this — half a lifetime spent on the road exhorting, conferring, organizing in places remote and not so remote. Surely it was often not just hard, but boring and, at least in the earlier years, a considerable strain for a person as shy as Carrie Catt. Yet there is never a suggestion from Catt of frustration at the problems she experienced. Perhaps a more candid and less private person would have vented these feelings, as presidential candidates often do in their years after victory or defeat. It is unlikely though, because Catt liked the hustings, she admired the discipline it took to endure it all, and she took it as an article of faith that campaigning at the local level was crucial for victory. So she did it.

Campaigning by Catt and others generated some publicity, but it did only part of the job. Much more was required in order to win the battle for the mind of the public at large, so that it could "be made to understand, to arise and to exert its power."[43] How to generate effective publicity was the practical issue Catt faced. If the proper vehicles could be found, Catt took it for granted that the N.A.W.S.A. would triumph in the contest for the public's approval.

A portion of the answer, especially in the last years of the struggle, was Catt's own involvement. But from the first Catt felt that publicity seeking was not something she could accomplish or manage herself. During her second presidency she used, first, Ida Husted Harper, the biographer of the suffrage movement, and, later and more extensively, Rose Young, the editor of the *Woman Citizen*, to direct this aspect of her organization. Under their direction, the already existing publicity department and the Leslie Bureau of Suffrage Education got to work.

One approach was to work with the press: issuing press releases, currying favor, planting favorable stories, challenging "false" ones, and stimulating positive letters to the editor. This was a specialty of Rose Young, who labored hard to win the battle in the press, which both Catt and Young felt had to be waged and won against not only antisuffragists but also Alice Paul and her dissidents.[44]

Meanwhile, the Leslie Bureau of Suffrage Education cranked out hundreds of items promoting the cause to the public and the activists alike. Indeed, virtually any form of propaganda was available and was used during Catt's second presidency. Balloons, buttons, fans, playing cards, even thimbles proclaimed the glory of woman suffrage. So did posters ("It Does Not Unsex Her," reassured one). There were also songs and plays for sale, for those who preferred a more artistic approach. Short flyers ("the best arguments in brief, readable form") were produced in vast numbers. Two-page leaflets were especially popular, as were scores of pamphlets such as Nettie R. Shuler's "A.B.C. of Organization," Alice Stone Blackwell's "Objections Answered," or Ida Husted Harper's "National Amendment for Woman Suffrage." There was even an "Equal Rights Drawing Book" for "little suffragists."[45] Catt, in fact, wrote a number of these publications. But her main contribution lay in understanding their importance and in successfully fashioning a vast publicity machine that reached out to sustain believers and win converts.[46]

Of great importance in communicating with suffragists was the *Woman's Journal.* This magazine was for a long time the province of Alice Stone Blackwell in every sense. As her diaries show, she expended an enormous part of her life on its publication.[47] Much of the time Blackwell did all the work except the actual printing, a demanding and — since it was a weekly — relentless challenge. It is not clear when questions first arose as to its role in the N.A.W.S.A., but they were bound to. The *Woman's Journal* was an independent publication, not under the N.A.W.S.A.'s control, and yet it was the central vehicle for the organization's elite to communicate to its membership. During Catt's first term relations between the N.A.W.S.A. and the *Woman's Journal* went smoothly, perhaps because Blackwell was always so supportive of Catt. By 1910, however, discussions between Blackwell and the National Board were underway regarding ownership and editorial control of the *Woman's Journal.* By then Blackwell was willing to let the National Board determine editorial policy, to make the journal more nationally oriented (some felt Blackwell focused too much on New England and the East in general), and to give the N.A.W.S.A. a share of ownership and complete ownership at her death. In return the N.A.W.S.A. was to finance the *Woman's Journal* and maintain Blackwell as its overall editor. However, by 1912 Blackwell was angry at the National Board because she did not feel it had lived up to its financial promises. Tensions were particularly sharp with Anna Howard Shaw, who Blackwell suspected was trying to seize control of the magazine. On the other hand, Shaw was distressed that Blackwell could not seem to create a truly national journal.[48]

No doubt Blackwell's belief that Catt was highly supportive of her and of the *Woman's Journal* assisted Catt in 1916 as she undertook to achieve the control of the magazine that had eluded Anna Howard Shaw. In that year the N.A.W.S.A. purchased the publication from Blackwell, though Blackwell continued her close association with it. The next step was the *Woman's Journal*'s transformation into the *Woman Citizen* in 1917. The name change reflected, of course, Catt's concerns and symbolically marked Catt's success in bringing this once independent journal under her organizational control. At its masthead was the unmistakable statement: "Official Organ of the N.A.W.S.A." Thus one more part of Catt's publicity machine was cemented in place.[49]

Nowhere was Catt more hardheaded than in her recognition that organization faced failure without the reinforcement of money. Catt and the National American Woman Suffrage Association flourished before the advent of compulsory, elaborate, and enormously expensive television and radio advertising campaigns. And they had the undeniable advantage provided by thousands of women who were willing and able to work for the cause without pay. Nonetheless, as Catt knew, the N.A.W.S.A. always badly needed money for publicity, "education," training, office supplies, travel, and pay for those women it needed who had to make a living at the same time. As a result, throughout her career as a suffragist Catt felt impelled to be a fund-raiser.

Like so many others since, Catt does not appear to have enjoyed this part of her role as a politician. Her first efforts in the middle 1890s were rather pathetic and apparently did not generate much cash for the N.A.W.S.A. She told readers of the *Woman's Journal* in 1895 that if they bought their Christmas presents from particular businesses the firms would contribute to the N.A.W.S.A. In 1896 she advertised in the *Woman's Journal* to encourage women to purchase suffrage calendars as another modest money-making scheme.[50]

These and other efforts raised little money in the 1890s and Catt became increasingly concerned. She recognized that it could not be a serious organization without more financial support than the small dues and an occasional fund-raising idea provided. She struggled with how to pay organizers in the field and with the substantial debt that Anthony allowed to flourish.[51] Early in her first presidency Catt discovered that the traditional suffrage elite was just not very concerned about such mundane matters. She insisted that they had to change.

Grand policies would mean nothing if the money was not there to implement them. At first she had to depend to a large extent on state suffrage organizations for support and she eventually made a rule that she would not enter state campaigns unless they could provide sufficient money to mount a substantial effort. In her leadership of the New York struggles of 1915 and 1917, fund-raising became a priority and she helped raise the million dollars that she calculated would be needed for the 1917 contest. By her second presidency Catt also had within the N.A.W.S.A. a regular fund-raising operation, which garnered millions of dollars in small sums from numerous women (and men), helping to ensure that woman suffrage would have the resources to be taken seriously as a political movement.[52] But this was never an easy business for Catt. The needs always were greater than the money available. It remained a source of continual frustration. As she said, "The National American never found any other way to support its work except by eternal begging."[53]

In addition to paying her own expenses, Catt helped by a good deal of personal giving to the cause. No one knows how much she gave over the decades of her involvement. She kept no records. Yet Carrie Catt never became — and never intended to become — the angel of the suffrage movement. Nor was she temperamentally inclined to part casually with a dollar. As her friend Mary Peck tactfully observed, "C.C.C. herself had a very careful respect for money. She knew how hard it is to raise, and how easy to squander."[54]

After the complicated affairs of her second husband's estate were resolved, by 1910 at the latest, Catt was a wealthy woman, able to live well in New York City and then New Rochelle, New York, travel all over the world, and support herself without working for remuneration for the rest of her long life. But Catt could not carry the financial load of the N.A.W.S.A. herself, and temperamentally she did not want to try.[55]

What made a tremendous difference to the movement was the death of Mrs. Frank Leslie, wife of a prominent publisher, in 1914. She left her estate, which eventually totaled well over $900,000, to Carrie Catt to use as she saw fit to assist the enfranchisement of women. In this single event Catt not only gained substantial potential power within the N.A.W.S.A., but the organization gained major financing, just when it was most needed.

It was not until 1917, however, that Catt got the money. Leslie's relations, understandably eager for all that money in an age in which it was a truly enormous sum, fought her all the way. Catt fought as hard for it. She wanted it for her cause, but it also became another Armageddon for her, another battle in the constant warfare required to defeat the greedy and the selfish by those who served duty and principle. And it was typical of Catt that she waged this war with the conviction that right would win if it had the best practical help available (in this case, the best lawyers).[56]

The contest for the Leslie fund was nasty. Its progress (and later Catt's use of the money) attracted a fair amount of notice from anti-suffragists. They charged she was at best trying to violate the Leslie will and at worst simply stealing the Leslie bequest. They were envious, of course, but that was not the whole story. Antisuffragist leadership clearly perceived how important money was in the contest with Catt and her allies, and they sensed that the Leslie bequest could tip the scales. They also drew sinister conclusions from her final legal victory, emphasizing as always the skill she had in manipulating the world to her evil purposes.[57]

Once she had clear title to the Leslie monies, Catt established the Leslie Woman Suffrage Commission, Inc., which began doling out funds. Fortunately, we have its records and so have a reasonably precise idea of how Catt's organization spent the money. Over $100,000 went to Catt's International Woman Suffrage Alliance, but the two biggest items were connected with the central N.A.W.S.A. office and the *Woman Citizen*. The office took over $200,000, most of which went to salaries of staff and organizers, underlining again that the N.A.W.S.A. crusade was not quite the all-volunteer effort Catt liked to portray it as. Over $400,000 went to the *Woman Citizen*, illustrating just how important Catt judged its role in her publicity machine. Very little went to other aspects of publicity. Literature especially paid its own way and, indeed, was often used as another means to raise money.[58]

The Leslie gift measurably strengthened the N.A.W.S.A.'s crusade in its last years. That it also strengthened Catt's personal hand as leader of N.A.W.S.A. is never mentioned, indeed never noticed, in accounts from those days, but this too must have been part of the story of the Leslie bequest. We know she believed in strong, even tough, centralized leadership. With the Leslie bequest behind her, Catt from 1917 to 1920 obtained an important lever which helped her achieve her organizational ideal in practice. It was one more step toward her goal of building an organizational machine that could not be stopped.[59]

Carrie Catt was a prophet of the new organizational era of the turn of the last century. She reflected and expressed the Progressive Era's drive towards modernization — organization, bureaucracy, control, discipline, and the rest. She knew what she was doing. Sharing none of Mark Twain's doubts, she quoted him approvingly: "In our days we have learned the value of combination. We apply it everywhere — in railway systems, in trusts, in trade unions . . . we organize . . . we have found that that is the only way."[60]

For Catt, as for some other Progressives, commitment to organization — to "modernization" — was not necessarily evidence of broader reform goals, even if these were subjective, definitional matters. But any distinction between modernization and reform would probably not have interested Catt. She agreed organization was not a remarkable good in itself, despite its valuable lessons of discipline and comradeship. It was, in her mind, simply a necessity. The creation of efficient and bureaucratic organizational structures was essential for addressing the world as she knew it, not just to protect women but to forge a world in which they had dignity equal with men's.

In later life she laughingly explained the story of woman suffrage as how "we stumbled on for three generations,"[61] but she did not believe for a moment that that was the entire story. It left out organization, which produced victory.

CHAPTER 8

The Mysteries of
Leadership

Carrie Catt's perceptions about good leadership were multifaceted and complex. They were fully developed through a long career in which she articulated her ideas and practiced them to the applause of an often admiring audience. For Catt the essence of a leader was what the word implied, someone prepared to take charge and lead. She never felt any sympathy with undisciplined, drifting, or easy-going leadership. She only admired forceful doers, activists infused with energy, eagerness, and determination. After all, she was herself yet another Progressive doer, a woman of action, as she felt all real leaders were. She assumed every organization needed and wanted just such leaders.

Implicit in her conception of a determined, activist leader, of course, was the judgment that the woman suffrage movement too rarely had such leaders. There is every reason to believe she meant it when she wrote to Millicent Fawcett in 1912: "What is really needed is a truly great leader, and I, for one, feel that our movement *never* had one."[1] Anthony in fact rebuked Catt after one of her controversial demands for action in the middle 1890s by telling a N.A.W.S.A. Convention, "There never yet was a young woman who did not feel that if she had had the management of the work from the beginning the cause would have been carried long ago. I felt just so when I was young."[2] The audience laughed, but one may doubt if Catt was entirely amused by this remark.

121

Yet Anthony picked Catt as her successor because she knew Catt
had the skills and the determination for the job. Both knew determination was as important as skill. Catt over and over said leadership was
in good part a matter of drive. When asked for advice, she told women
to have a vision — but a vision backed by serious commitment. Her
commitment was never in doubt after 1890: "I have enlisted for life."[3]
Her favorite saying was Anthony's "Failure is Impossible," and she
often proclaimed what she believed heart and soul: "no chance, no
destiny, no fate can circumvent or hinder or control the firm resolve
of a determined soul. Gifts count for nothing; will alone is great. All
things give away before it soon."[4] Will was the word, the magic for a
leader.

She carried the message to the woman suffrage movement as a
whole. It had to will its fate, will to act, will to win. This was Catt's
constant litany. She never altered it from the time of her controversial
1898 Organization Committee Report, which blasted some women
suffragists as the major problem the N.A.W.S.A. faced: "We find
them everywhere, doing practically nothing themselves but throwing cold water." "It cannot be done" was their motto until the day the
struggle was over.[5] Catt's motto was that it could be done. Indeed, it
would be done just as soon as people were prepared to put forth
the effort. It was a matter of will and it was her job to lead others to
make it happen.[6]

Of course, there were problems and obstacles. But action rather
than naysaying was the remedy — for leaders and for followers. Her
own example was steady, unending work. "Never hurried or flurried,
she went on her carefully thought-out way, turning out a colossal
amount of work, much of it in harassing detail."[7] It was also work with
unashamed confidence. As she told her fellow suffragists before the
1915 vote in New York State, if defeat comes, "we shall keep right on.
We shall not pause for a moment."[8]

She was the aggressive actor she exhorted others to be, energetic
and driving throughout her career. Even in her earliest work, in Iowa,
she acted this way, insisting on aggressive, public action for women's
enfranchisement when others counseled that sedate, unobtrusive
work in the churches was the proper approach. And she continued
this approach right up through 1920, in her direct lobbying of Tennessee state legislators to obtain their approval of the Anthony amendment and thus complete the last step in the ratification of the
Nineteenth Amendment.[9]

Given Catt's affection for an aggressive activist leader, it followed
for her that a good leader should lead and others should follow the
leader. She tried and failed to clarify her authority at the start of her

first presidency.[10] The result was both considerable frustration during her first term *and* her stipulation before her second election as president that in both structure and practice heirarchy would be the norm and she as leader would be firmly in place at the top. She exacted this as her condition for accepting her second period as president from those who begged her to be the leader. As she put it, "they promised to do anything and everything possible to support my administration," and Catt called on them to fulfill their promise without hesitation.[11] Catt was quite candid in private: "all matters which concern organization or the carrying out of policies . . . I want to keep in my own hands," which is just what she did — and she adopted the same stance regarding most substantive policies as well.[12] Meanwhile, others, such as the state branches, were expected to do what they were told.

Under her tutelage, the N.A.W.S.A. was to be a tightly administered, almost military-like organization with Catt as the supreme commander.[13] This military analogy is a fitting one. Catt may have had pacifist leanings, but she unconsciously thought in military terms regarding leadership and organization. Moreover, that a great deal of elitism was implicit, indeed explicit, is no surprise given the ambivalence about democracy that she shared with many Progressive reformers.

Catt, however, did not believe that a centralized leadership was antidemocratic. For Catt, as for many of her fellow Progressives, approval of centralization of authority was partly defended in terms of democracy. Only a centralized authority could really speak for the people and only it could be accountable to them. The behavior of local politicians with limited power and corrupt practices was the alternative model. They, Catt argued, had nothing whatever to do with democracy, no matter how it was defined.

For Catt centralization was also an advantage in terms of efficiency. It encouraged getting things done in an expeditious fashion. And in no sense was efficiency antidemocratic. Efficient action, in a government or the N.A.W.S.A., promoted democracy by serving its constituency.

In terms we associate with the Progressive Herbert Croly, Catt's idea of leadership was distinctly Hamiltonian rather than Jeffersonian, though even in her second presidency Catt did not rule the N.A.W.S.A. without some internal democracy.[14] She and other officers were subject to yearly election and all major policies had to pass muster at the annual convention composed of delegates elected by local and state branches of the N.A.W.S.A. But there is no doubt that, while president, Carrie Catt judged that she was there to rule the organization and direct the movement to enfranchise women. She did not feel she was president merely to mediate disputes. She was not to be the Progressive arbitrator, but rather the Progressive leader.

What was also implicit in her notions of leadership was Catt's considerable attraction to power. Her idea of a good leader was a power force, within and without (her) organization. Certainly she admired the will to power, if wrapped in a just cause, even as she protested that she feared power and wanted to check it (when it was exercised by her enemies). She never put the case for power quite so bluntly, but it is clear that she took for granted that a leader must seek and use power to succeed personally and politically. And she had no hesitation or apologies about this reality of politics.

Equally important, of course, was the role of communication. Catt was very sensitive to communication's significance and worked hard to be as effective a communicator as she could be. Communication with both the movement and the public at large was obviously vital and this became a cardinal principle as Catt sought to build organizational effectiveness. Communication to her closest aides and workers could not be ignored either. This was at least as important, and it was no easy matter in an era before routine use of the telephone. Catt was well aware of this challenge. She tackled it by the use of personal letters and headquarter newsletters to keep signals clear and spirits high.[15]

While newsletters reached the elites and publications such as the *Woman Citizen* reached the broader suffrage movement, Catt wrote thousands of letters to specific persons about suffrage business. Letters were, in fact, her principal vehicle of communication with individuals. In them Catt explained strategy, laid plans, resolved disputes, and, indeed, addressed every imaginable matter that could arise in a large and complex organization. This very much included one of Catt's most noticeable communication techniques, her generous apportioning of praise. Catt knew full well that communication from a leader had to include much more than facts and orders; there were psychological as well as informational requirements to be met. Catt frequently expressed her gratitude for others' help, however, because she genuinely believed that she ought to, quite apart from practical benefits. She may have had a taste for power and authority, but she agreed a leader was nothing without followers.[16]

At another level Catt communicated constantly through her speeches. Over the decades she gave hundreds of speeches and made 185 speaking tours.[17] Ironically, Catt was more than a little ambivalent about speeches because she felt that words had been all there was to the suffrage crusade for too much of its long history, and words frequently became a comfortable substitute for practical political action. This was not what Catt wanted. But speeches had their value, perhaps

The second generation of leaders, Carrie Catt (left) and Anna Howard
Shaw, ca. 1918. Courtesy of the Library of Congress.

especially as a means to move people from words to action. And as a
leader Catt spoke often to accomplish just this goal.

It was, however, the part of her leadership about which she was
least happy. She did not think she was particularly effective in this role
and often lacked self-confidence in speaking. Susan B. Anthony once
told Catt that she (Anthony) always gave bad addresses, but felt that a
poor speech was better than none at all. Catt liked that consoling view.
She always felt she was not a good speaker; she routinely felt disappointed when she finished any major address, and she laughed at the
idea that anyone might want to imitate her speaking style. But she gave
herself credit for at least doing the speaking.[18] While over time Catt
became more self-confident on public platforms, it was never easy for
her. She wished she could write better, which she thought would make

her a better speaker, and she had other hopes for improving her performances. Yet she did not expect to succeed. She knew she could never match Anna Howard Shaw and become the orator of woman suffrage.[19]

Catt's lack of esteem for herself as a speaker explains why she offered little concrete advice on how to make a good address. Speaking had a part to play, one of great importance, in the leadership of the suffrage movement, but teaching its rhythms was never her department. Her practice was the best model she could offer, though it was a practice now mostly lost to us. Most of her addresses were delivered before audio, not to mention video, recording. Thus we can approach Catt as a speaker only through her written speeches and the reactions of others to them.

When we examine Catt's addresses we can see how they fit into her overall leadership objective. Above all, they are designed to educate, always a central feature of Catt's approach to leadership and organizational success. This much she realized herself. They are also highly rational in tone. They are packed with lucid arguments for her views, arguments which we know she normally delivered in a calm manner with little verbal drama and few gestures. There are few attacks on individuals. Instead, she met opposing arguments, attempting to overwhelm them by logic, facts, and ethical claims. She especially loved to overwhelm her listeners with a barrage of statistics, calling on the world of social science (like the good Progressive she was) to sustain her.

All this sounds like a formula for dullness. Yet Carrie Catt's addresses were not dull, or at least her listeners did not perceive them that way.[20] Perhaps one reason was that her audiences often were eager for her approach. It was a refreshing change from the usual political harangues that many, like Catt, found repugnant. As Rose Young reported:

> [Catt,] never ornate in rhetoric or delivery, seemed to withdraw her personality utterly. . . . To hear her was like listening to abstract thought, warmed by the fire of abstract conviction. To see her was like looking at sheer marble, flame-lit. . . . Hers was the crowning achievement to sway an audience to emotion by the symmetry and force of her appeal to its mind. Again and again salvos of applause stopped her for a moment but again and again the steady rhythm of her strong voice regained control.[21]

As this paean to a 1917 Catt speech also suggests, another reason that Catt had no reputation as a dull speaker was her delivery; she spoke with an air of authority, which was widely admired. Apparently it frequently riveted audiences to her as her words did not. As observers noted over and over, she possessed the mysterious "presence" every effective speaker has. Then too Catt made emotive appeals more often than she claimed. She repeatedly indulged in appeals to the pride of women as women and employed flattery on a regular basis. She was also, when she chose to be, a relentless flag-waver who called on the Constitution, the Declaration of Independence, and any other source from American history to stir her listeners' hearts.[22]

Most of the time, though, in her speeches and elsewhere Catt firmly adhered to her belief that a proper leader had to be "rational" — balanced, thoughtful, impersonal, and open. Close friends and distant newspaper writers saw her in just this way and agreed she practiced a cool rationality in her leadership. She displayed a thoughtful balance in her judgments, as Susan B. Anthony noted, and she consistently shied away from "nervous types" whose rationality was suspect. Normally she was the "rational" pragmatist in action, and proud of it.[23]

Catt's conception of rationality was never developed into a formal philosophy. This was hardly her approach. It did involve "reason, logic, and patience" which she felt "were the weapons which won the final victory."[24] Rationality also centered on the pragmatic and the concrete. It was an empirical breed of rationality. Rationality as abstraction, as theory, as formal mathematics, or as the higher reaches of philosophy was entirely foreign to her definition. While less threatening than emotionalism, these types of rationality were nonetheless equally counterproductive because they were irrelevant. Pragmatic logic was what mattered.

Rationality also meant impersonality, a characteristic Catt emphasized as much, or more, than any other. She was proud of her ability to be impersonal, an orientation she thought was integral to the rational person. "Managers of all sorts should play their helpers like men on a chess board; studying their characters and putting each where she will be of most value. She must be absolutely *impersonal*, disconnected, aloof from the pettiness of the fray."[25] Again and again she advised: "let us be impersonal."[26]

Catt sometimes acknowledged that she thought it was easier for her than for some others to be impersonal since she claimed to be so by nature. Yet how impersonal Catt was is open to question. Certainly she had to work hard to achieve her public impersonality.[27] That she did so is clear. Tributes to her "unusual calm and poise" and her skill in "impersonal consideration of events" are numerous.[28]

One of the chief benefits for a leader with an impersonal approach, she contended, was that such an approach inevitably tempered and often eliminated personal clashes. This, at least, was her own experience. She had relatively few personal fights with others in the N.A.W.S.A. She hated such conflicts and found them acutely painful and always draining. As she conceived it, her job as leader partly involved serving as a kind of transcendent pacifier of personal disputes. One of her constant admonitions to others was to follow her example and eliminate human frictions whenever possible.[29]

Catt thought effective leaders could also reduce conflicts in general by openness of mind. Having a will to power was not enough. Openness was equally essential. Openness for her meant serious study of important questions, welcoming different ideas, and confidently rejecting dogma and "superstitions," whether political or religious.[30]

Her openness and her impersonality, however, did not always preclude conflict. Indeed, she welcomed it, when necessary, if it focused on *issues*. As a young woman in the suffrage movement and even at the beginning of her first presidency, Catt had a reputation for criticizing others — even the powers-that-were in the N.A.W.S.A. — when she thought they were in error about issues.[31]

As she became more the leader and less the impatient, young activist, this reputation faded, but Catt was never afraid of conflict when it was essential. She had goals and she had strategies she believed in and she was a strong, sometimes authoritarian leader determined to see them accomplished. Thus conflicts were bound to arise and they did. As she recognized, every leader "might as well learn now . . . that somebody's gun will be aimed at you all your life if you really stand for causes and attempt to do things."[32]

Almost all of Catt's major conflicts outside the N.A.W.S.A. were impersonal and those within it were usually over organization and tactics rather than personalities. Granted it is sometimes hard to separate one from another, but it is worth noting that even those who clashed with Catt rarely explained the conflict as anything but a dispute over substantive issues. Her reputation as impersonal in this sense is not in doubt.

The more one reads Catt's correspondence and digs deeply into the day-to-day affairs of Catt as an organization leader, the more disputes turn up. Hers was never a serene stewardship either before or during her presidencies. Catt may have been a mother figure to her followers but disagreements were common, even if she did not emerge as a center of endless conflict within the movement as did Shaw.

Catt had, for instance, an awkward dispute in 1897 over the management of the suffrage campaign with the Nevada officers of the N.A.W.S.A. She and Abigail Duniway disagreed over what kind of women to recruit for suffrage in Idaho in the 1890s. She and Annie

Diggs of the Committee on Political Parties of the N.A.W.S.A. quarreled over that committee's work in the same period. In 1916 Catt and a Miss Flora Dunlap, head of Iowa's woman suffrage effort, clashed over the lack of organization in that state. And there were many more such disputes over issues. Some were well-known conflicts, such as the quarrel over *The Woman's Bible* with Elizabeth Cady Stanton, the dispute over a national approach to enfranchisement of women with states' rights suffragist Laura Clay, and, of course, the differences with Alice Paul and the devotees of the Woman's Party.[33]

Perhaps the most trying conflict in personal terms for Catt was the hostility that others in the leadership elite sometimes felt towards Mary Hay. Conflict over Hay and her appropriate role never seemed to end. Catt was forced to keep her out of a number of official positions at the national level to avoid factionalism. Alice Stone Blackwell records in her diaries some of the endless turmoil over Hay, which she found disgusting, as well as Catt's persistent efforts to preserve the peace and defend her. Predictably, the biggest problem lay between Shaw and Hay, who "hated each other devotedly all their lives."[34]

Each of the conflicts obviously marred Catt's dream of unity. She accepted them, though, as the price of goal-oriented leadership. And she was pleased that few of the divisions degenerated into personality clashes. Issues could be, and sometimes had to be, fought out. Yet if they did not become personal feuds much could be saved, she thought, including overall unity.

The great advantage, as Catt saw it, of her style of rational and impersonal leadership was that her mind and energies were left free so that she could be a practical and realistic leader. To be practical one had to take life in a matter-of-fact way, as Catt so often did. One had to avoid the exciting adventure of the mind or the delicious tidbit of gossip — especially the latter. Indeed, Catt was intensely unhappy about gossip in general. People who had complaints about her work, she urged, or about her in any way, should have the courage to "bring it to me instead of passing it along as gossip."[35] She had no sense that someone might enjoy gossip and little appreciation of what it might take to be as straightforward as she proposed everyone should be. The same spirit governed her approach to meetings. She was uncomfortable about them if they were not all business. She hated it when they degenerated into "parlor meetings" with irrelevant social chitchat and gossip.[36] She wanted goal-directed practical behavior and as a leader she tried to impose this standard.[37]

A good example was her impatience with Maud Wood Park, her close ally, when Park began to write plays. This was the sort of thing that struck Catt as slightly absurd, of little importance, and of no interest — "I am not much interested in that line."[38] Catt was never the romantic and never open to the artistic. What she admired and expected others to admire was the practical.

It followed that Catt loved to style herself a realist and believed that realism was an essential companion for the practical leader. Realism involved the ability to see a political situation for what it was and Catt had that ability. This included calling situations hopeless when they were and pushing on, as Catt did, for example, in her first major fight in 1890. She could see as she worked South Dakota that the enfranchisement of women was simply not going to take place there that year. She could tell the truth — "We have not a ghost of a show for success" — and proceed with no false hopes or expectations.[39]

That too was part of being an effective, realistic leader. One had to be able to accept defeats and unpleasant odds and go on. As she observed in 1916, "We are having to learn by hard knocks a good many things . . . but perhaps in the long run the knocks won't hurt us."[40] To be effective as a leader also required realism about oneself. Catt quoted F. B. Silverword's aphorism, "Leaders are ordinary persons with extraordinary determination."[41] There is no doubt she believed this was true of herself as leader. She always argued that she was nothing special. Her closest associates did not agree, but they testified that she was unusually modest and unpretentious as a leader. As a result, she accepted awards in the years after 1920 in a spirit that emphasized what other women and the campaign "army" had achieved together. She was utterly sincere, modest, practical, and businesslike, all of which helped her as a leader. But she never faced one "realistic" fact about herself (and about leaders in general): the role of personal ambition.[42]

As far as one can tell, Catt had no sense of the possibility of mixed motives in herself. She saw herself as a realistic person who required a little self-analysis and a great deal of tough-mindedness. Catt dwelt in a real world where, in fact, struggle against long odds was her life. Thus, emphasis on the leader as a tough fighter made sense. Her decision to face outward also flowed out of her conception of the good person. Good people did not waste time in contemplation, mooning over their souls, or whining over defeats. They acted. Always for Catt Progressive action was the answer, action in a realistic mood. Prepared for rough waters, she was eager to declare: "I am ready for the fray."[43]

She knew that the battle for votes for women was not going to be easy. And she felt there was no room in the struggle for the faint-hearted or those inclined to surrender when things looked grim. She wanted individuals who knew what toughness meant. The struggle required treading on sensitive and sometimes powerful toes. It meant making enemies, no matter how much one tried to avoid personal feuds. It also meant realizing that "the burden and responsibility of administration takes spontaneity and emotion and joy out of one."[44] But a tough leader had no choice.

The qualities she wanted in a leader drew unmistakably on military language. She was always speaking of "warfare" and "battles" and enjoining her disciples to "buckle on your armor anew," to be "brave soldiers," to face "cruel battle" with unflagging courage.[45] At issue was more than what would make an effective leader; it was what made a free, independent person. In life, she thought, Longfellow (though Nietzsche might have been a more appropriate source) had the right idea: "In this world a man must be either an anvil or a hammer." She intended to be a hammer, a tough activist, the kind of person and leader that was necessary. It was in this spirit that she identified herself with the only feminist of the past whom Catt sometimes mentioned, Mary Wollstonecraft. It was not Wollstonecraft's writings that appealed to her. Catt did not care much about the writings, as opposed to the actions, of anyone. Rather it was her understanding of Wollstonecraft's life that attracted Catt. Wollstonecraft, according to Catt, deserved admiration as a person and, in her way, as a leader because she was tough and learned "to stand up before the world and give her testimony."[46]

All this dramaturgy of toughness, however, was best when it need not be practiced. She wanted and practiced a smooth toughness and an authoritative style which encouraged assent rather than stimulated opposition or exacerbated division. Her eventual evolution into a leader with a regal bearing, an authoritative voice, and a poised, controlled demeanor radiated just such an impressive style.[47]

Catt got on well with people, in fact, and her peers judged her to be approachable. This was just the way she was. But she was convinced it was much to her advantage as a leader. The truth was that however lonely a leader might be, she needed others and thus had to get along with them in a spirit of give and take. This meant being easy to work for, as even Catt's opponents within the suffrage crusade agreed she was; it meant being able to delegate authority, sharing opportunities and successes with others; and it meant being respectful of others and their ideas, without necessarily sharing them.[48]

That Catt won devotion from those who worked for her is well known. This devotion merits our attention since obviously not all leaders are so regarded by those with whom they labor most closely. Yet the devotion to Catt, to "the Chief" or "Mother Catt" as they called her, comes through the memories of her associates again and again. For them she was "the incomparable leader" whom they loved.[49] In-

deed, it is not too much to say that her closest campaign workers idol-
ized Catt, which sometimes caused problems. Some of her followers
could not resist criticizing competing leaders within the N.A.W.S.A.,
the sort of thing Catt considered dangerously counterproductive.[50]

That Carrie Catt was "Mother Catt" to most of her close admirers
also symbolizes that Catt did not relate to many of her coworkers, especially by the time of her second presidency, as an equal. She was the
"Mother" and they her "girls." As Mary Peck implies, Catt used their
feeling — "sublimated the affection of her lieutenants into work for
the cause."[51]

For several of her devotees it worked even to the extent that victory for woman suffrage became something they dreamt of for the
happiness of "the Chief" as much as for the cause itself. Maud Wood
Park expressed it so well later when she described their feelings after
ratification had been gained and Catt was in New York City for the
victory parade.

> There is a beautiful picture of her taken just before the proces-
> sion started, when she stood in the car, the flowers in her arms
> and her face alight with the joy of triumphant home-coming.
> No one of us who saw her then will ever cease to be thankful for
> the perfect moment when she must have felt to the full the hap-
> piness of a great task completed.[52]

The devotion that obviously came to surround Carrie Catt was
not, however, entirely a result of her personality or her role as the
Mother-leader. It was also a product of her practical skill in working
with people. She earned many testimonials to her shrewd judgments
about people, about whom to push and whom to conciliate, about
whom to recruit and whom to avoid. She described herself as a "pulse-
feeler" and her written comments on fellow workers, while not numerous, display her sharp eye for who was effective and who was
not — and why. Catt was extremely careful about whom she selected
to be her closest aides, always coolly evaluating their willingness (and
ability) to work hard and their success at what they did. Some people
she appraised very favorably, but appraisals of some others were much
less positive, and Catt winnowed out those who she judged did not
produce. The process succeeded. She became known in the movement
for her ability to get excellent people and, perhaps more significant,
to retain them.[53]

Beyond these requirements for good leadership lay a final and
decisive one. The rock on which Catt believed every effective leader
and every successful journey in leadership must rest was service to
high ideals. Her critics faulted her as a mere technician, but for Catt a

Carrie Catt's arrival in New York City, August 28, 1920, after Tennessee ratified the nineteenth amendment and the struggle for woman suffrage was over. On the far left are Mrs. John Blair, presenting the bouquet, and Governor Al Smith. The women with Catt are, left to right, Mary G. Hay, Mrs. Arthur Livermore, Harriet Taylor Upton, and Marjorie Shuler. Courtesy of the Library of Congress.

worthy leader cared about ethical service far above anything else. Thus action was legitimate only when based on moral principle. This raised no practical problems for her because such an ethical approach had practical advantages. Being idealistic was "Not so hard a task. . . . For the man of vision finds in that vision a buoyant, exhilarating support — an insatiable source of courage — that comes from no other source in life."[54] With conviction and the courage it engendered the model leader would push on to realize her idea.

Yet we still must ask: how seriously did Catt take idealism as the indispensable stimulus for a leader? William O'Neill has attacked Catt and her allies as operators more concerned with political and strategic expediency than one might expect from proclaimed idealists. Catt was no idealist in her strategies, and O'Neill explains this as a casualty that Catt accepted because she thought suffrage, her great goal, would accomplish so much good. Her end justified her means.[55]

O'Neill's explanation does not work. The idea that votes for women would transform everything may have described the view of some of Catt's associates, but it certainly was not her expectation. A more plausible explanation is that Catt did not see her highly political strategies and tactics as wrong. For example, Catt did appeal to nativist and antiforeigner sentiments to help achieve women's enfranchisement. But to her this was no compromise of *her* values. She was convinced that restricting foreigners and their influence was highly idealistic.

Moreover, Catt in general had a rather different understanding of idealism than some do. For her idealism did not imply a superior moral position above vulgar politics and its practical, compromising demands. Purity was not idealism; it was irrelevant nonsense. Idealism by her definition was necessarily something *in* the world, working with the themes of the world, though not in bondage to the world. She saw no abandonment of principle in her immersion in sometimes dark realms of compromise and other political activity, because it was an integral part of what she understood real idealism required.

If "real" idealism was absolutely essential to her and her conception of leadership, so was its companion, sacrifice. Indeed, Catt apparently thought one could identify truly idealistic leaders more by their willingness to sacrifice than by their program or principles. Sacrifice was clearly a crucial test for Catt. Always she urged others to "give yourself" in "*consecration* to an ideal," "*devotion* to the social good," and "*unselfish*" willingness to work.[56] She held that suffrage workers could not operate on a 9-to-5 business schedule, or be interested in limited hours of work or in pay. It was not merely a matter of the need for more effort; it was a matter of what idealism truly required: concrete, selfless sacrifice.

Catt claimed sometimes that idealism required too much sacrifice from her. Yet she appreciated that she could not stop. Her idealism controlled her too tightly for that. Her consolation was not just the practical advantages in furthering "the cause," important as they might be. Perhaps the greater gain, at least for her as a leader and as a person, was the personal results that shared sacrifice and idealism engendered. They fostered a disciplined community of life and meaning. "Dear friends," she wrote, "one and all, I love you dearly because we worked together for a great cause to which we gave our common loyalty."[57] Sacrifice and idealism had personal costs, but to Catt they gave back more than they took.

Such a recognition of the personal dimensions of sacrifice and idealism is the correct note on which to conclude consideration of Catt's conception of leadership. For her leadership was no abstraction nor was it a role that she played out in politics but kept rigorously separate from her private world. Her vision of leadership was her vision of what she demanded for herself as a person. Her ideal leader was her model for herself and for others, and it is only against its demands on herself and others that the depth of her moralism can be appreciated.

C   H   A   P   T   E   R   9

Strategy

Anyone who knows the story of the struggle for the enfranchisement of women in the 1915–1920 period knows that Carrie Catt's strategic decisions were of fateful importance. Their pragmatic wisdom is clear, though their ethical wisdom is now, as it was then, a good deal more controversial.

Catt's Progressive agenda was wide-ranging, and suffrage for her was in large part a *means* to realize other reform objectives. Nevertheless, during the suffrage fight Catt focused all her energies on that issue. Her conscious strategy was to allow no other cause to enter the N.A.W.S.A.'s agenda: "As a matter of fact, we do not care a 'ginger snap' about anything but that Federal Amendment."[1] She did not object when the N.A.W.S.A. Convention adopted all sorts of resolutions favoring a number of this or that measures to assist women in economic, professional, and legal realms. But she insisted that the N.A.W.S.A. would be doing nothing about them. She did not think it could and at the same time promote women's enfranchisement: "we cannot . . . until the Federal Amendment is through, spare any force for the support of any bill. . . . we haven't the power to do anything but merely pass a resolution. It is of no avail."[2]

Catt made sure her wishes were followed as she fashioned her version of that very contemporary phenomenon, the single-issue pressure group. Her rationale was simple. One goal would mobilize women and the N.A.W.S.A.'s resources in a focused direction. It was efficient and—equally valuable—it freed the N.A.W.S.A. of the conflicts and attacks that involvement with other causes inevitably generated.

This was not a self-evident strategic choice, however, and it drew opponents. On the one hand, some earlier feminist leaders, such as Elizabeth Cady Stanton, objected to this approach as too narrow. On the other, some groups, especially the W.C.T.U., the Anti-Saloon League, and, later, peace groups sought alliance with Catt and the N.A.W.S.A. and were not happy when they did not get it. But Catt pushed all such complaints aside, arguing that even hints of such links were a formula for disaster.[3]

A remarkable illustration of Carrie Catt's willingness to pursue this strategy — even at the cost of compromise with other of her values — came in her much disputed strategic moves before and during World War I. All her life, Catt proudly identified with efforts to end war. In the decades after 1920 this became her principal field of public activity. However, when the First World War began in Europe, Catt was caught between her antiwar inclinations and her suspicion that suffragist peace activity could adversely affect the struggle for women's enfranchisement. Catt calculated even before the United States became a direct belligerent in the Great War that the situation was out of control and suffragists' efforts would be a costly venture for nothing. Concerned women, led by Jane Addams, might try, but the unleashed forces of war could not be stopped by their necessarily "puny effort." She doubted that anything could stop "these men in whom the furious beast" had been unchained.[4] Trying to stop them was "like throwing a violet at a stone wall." "There is no power on earth that is going to stop that war until there has been . . . perhaps the most terrible battle that the world has ever seen."[5]

At first Catt tried to have it both ways. While accounts differ as to whom credit belongs for initiating organized opposition to the war among women, in 1914 Catt and Addams worked together in this cause. In general, Catt worked behind the scenes lest she create the kind of backlash toward suffrage that so worried her. She specifically refused to accept a public leadership post. On the other hand, Catt did not avoid public appearances altogether, and her participation with Addams and others undoubtedly lent peace forces prestige without which its modest endeavor might have collapsed even sooner than it did. Catt did, for example, go to the White House on several occasions in 1914 to urge American neutrality to Woodrow Wilson and to Secretary of State William Jennings Bryan. She felt that she took a great risk in such public actions. That risk certainly did not diminish when Catt continued, albeit as quietly as possible, to support Addams when she founded the Woman's Peace Party.[6]

Nonetheless, Catt's heart was not in the Woman's Peace Party or any other part of the active but tiny women's peace movement in the United States from 1914 to 1917. She insisted she had to be concerned about votes for women above all else. She observed with dismay the barrage of attacks on her and woman suffrage by antisuffragist publications once war broke out in Europe. She feared that if she were more active in the peace cause she might confirm their propaganda that the woman's movement was a harbor for pacifists at best and for disloyal American women at worst. Most of the main organs of the antisuffragists were early on the bandwagon of United States preparedness and outspoken hostility to Germany and they ridiculed every effort of peace groups and every peace plan. Such ideas, they charged, were dangerous and had had a large part in encouraging the weakness that led to war in the first place. Moreover, as time went on, antisuffragists lost the distinction between pacifist "disloyalty" and outright support for Germany and the kaiser. It all became rather ugly and the charges specifically toward Catt were as ugly as the rest.[7]

As war approached for the United States, Catt moved with the tide. She had no intention of allowing enemies of her crusade to get away with their antiwar, pro-German charges and thus damage it. In February 1917, Catt convened the N.A.W.S.A., recognizing that war for the United States was imminent. It was necessary for the N.A.W.S.A. to get its house in order because "The future of our movement depends upon the right action being taken now."[8] What Catt wanted was a willingness on the part of the N.A.W.S.A. to support national war readiness. She got it, successfully steering past both extremist doves and hawks. In her terms the convention was a great success also because it attracted favorable publicity from the growing prowar segments in American society and brought the N.A.W.S.A. into contact with such influential government notables as Secretary of War Newton Baker and Secretary of the Navy Josephus Daniels.

When the United States did declare war on Germany and the contest she had long expected (and dreaded) began in earnest, Catt quickly offered her personal endorsement; she made sure that the N.A.W.S.A. was in line with national war policy in every way; and she repudiated suffragists who disagreed, notably Montana Congresswoman Jeannette Rankin, who voted against the war.[9]

These actions led to Catt's ejection from the Woman's Peace Party and a good many hard feelings between her and its small cohort of pacifists. Her decision could not have come as a surprise to them, but it still led to some bitter denunciations. They did not really bother her because she had absolutely no hesitation about paying this price. For her, opposition to the war, once the United States had entered it, was courting martyrdom and taking the suffrage movement down in the process. And so Carrie Catt began her war work, publicly working to get women involved in the Red Cross, canteen service, food production, and the like. She campaigned in Liberty Loan drives, and she accepted appointment to the Woman's Committee of the Council of National Defense (under Anna Howard Shaw's leadership).[10]

These activities, especially service on the Woman's Committee of the Council of National Defense, were not easy. Catt hated war and now she found herself busy supporting one, albeit one she eventually convinced herself was legitimate. Equally difficult was the treatment Catt, along with the other members of the committee (especially Shaw), received from the male leaders of the Council of National Defense and assorted government agencies. They found themselves, once again, treated as second-class citizens, bossed, patronized, or ignored. The situation was often acutely frustrating, but Catt remained convinced that working for the war was vital to the suffrage cause.[11]

There clearly were a great many enemies waiting to pounce. Once the United States entered the war, they crossed the already thin line between criticism of suffragists and wild, even frenzied accusations. Without any shame, critics called suffragists disloyal and pro-German. "Woman suffrage . . . is proving of more potent assistance to the Kaiser than his wonderful army." In addition, antisuffragists repeatedly tried to tar them with the brush of socialism, bolshevism, and just about anything that might make suffragists seem anti-American in what became a time of unpleasant xenophobia.[12]

Once again, the antisuffragists singled out Catt for special charges and smears. How intensely the antisuffragists, now garbed in the most patriotic of uniforms, hated Catt is difficult to comprehend unless one actually reads the flood of denunciatory articles on her in their press during World War I. In their portrait Catt was a knowing opponent of the war, a virtual traitor who continued to criticize her government in disgusting fashion during wartime. Her work for the war was a sham, hiding her conspiratorial actions for woman suffrage, and often for the Germans. In at least one article deportation was suggested as the way to deal with Catt.[13]

It is only in this context that Catt's own strategy can be understood. And it is only in this context, despite the loud cries of the antisuffragists, that its success can be understood. For, despite the cries of the antisuffragists Catt's strategy regarding World War I worked. All over the country she gained praise as a patriot actively behind the war effort. Though publicly abused, Catt and the N.A.W.S.A. escaped the almost unbelievable hostility that befell some others, Jane Addams in particular, which undercut their political influence for a time. When

Carrie Catt, left, and Jeanette Rankin in 1917. Courtesy of the Library of Congress.

charges of disloyalty and other ugly words flew, Catt could and did reply with her war record and that of the N.A.W.S.A.

It would be wrong, however, to portray Catt's strategic purposes in World War I as only defensive. She looked in this direction, but she also realized that there was another, much more positive side to her strategy. Patriotic service could create "opportunity" for the cause of women's enfranchisement. It could greatly increase the respectability of suffragists and their cause, and thus advance the cause, which is exactly what happened, both with the public at large and with many Washington decision-makers, including Woodrow Wilson. It happened in part because Catt made sure every contribution by the N.A.W.S.A. and prominent members of N.A.W.S.A. received as much publicity as possible. The not very subtle point was that the vote for women was American, was patriotic. Meanwhile, Catt sought to foster the impression that women, while they gave their service freely, nonetheless deserved something in return, and that something, of course, was the vote.[14]

Catt did not hesitate to make sure that people got the point that suffragist war service deserved repayment with enfranchisement. In fact, Catt relentlessly kept up the pressure for woman suffrage throughout the war. A frequent argument was that women's enfranchisement was needed "as a war measure."[15] Her argument that, if it was to fight a war for democracy, the United States should advance democracy at home by making women full citizens was effective — just how effective is indicated by the outrage it provoked from antisuffragists. They stormed at Catt, accusing her of being a monomaniac, pursuing her cause at all costs, and thus threatening American democracy when such divisive matters ought to be laid aside in the name of wartime unity.[16]

Catt paid no attention. Just as she spurned those who expected her peace concern would lead her to oppose the war, so she rejected those who urged she drop the cause of the vote during the war. For her the central issue never changed.

Overall, Catt was proud of her strategy during the Great War, though she hoped it would never be required again and dreamed that once women got the vote they might well end all wars. But questions were raised then — and have been since. Shouldn't she of all people have known the shortsightedness of her strategy? After all, from her own perspective, war corrupted progressive impulses in history. Some historians agree, regarding World War I.[17] But this analysis does not apply to votes for women. World War I hardly killed the chance for enfranchisement.

The uneasiness over Catt's strategy mostly derives from a sense that it was cynical. Cynical it was, but Catt did not see it this way. She never had any interest in a politics of purity in the impure world. To her the fact was that she could not stop the war, but the N.A.W.S.A.'s opposition to war could seriously delay women's enfranchisement. And her belief was that she was called to help women. Her devotion in subsequent decades of her public life to the cause of world peace was not an act of expiation. It was rather a resumption of the peace mission, which she had never lost sight of. But it was a long-range goal and she had no intention of losing momentum for women's enfranchisement because of it.

Much less controversial in retrospect, but much more so at the time, was the adoption of "The Plan," in 1916, to push for congressional passage of the Anthony amendment to the United States Constitution, giving women the right to vote. Catt had long looked toward the Anthony amendment as a way of overcoming the slow and cumbersome process of achieving women's enfranchisement state-by-state.[18] But by 1915–1916 she was sure it was absolutely necessary to concentrate N.A.W.S.A. resources on this strategy, a major shift in N.A.W.S.A. focus.

"The Plan" was adopted in 1916 at an emergency meeting of the N.A.W.S.A., which Catt had called at Atlantic City, New Jersey.[19] Catt was by then president of the N.A.W.S.A., and she reflected dissatisfaction with the N.A.W.S.A.'s drift during Shaw's long reign towards (unsuccessful) campaigning for the extension of suffrage at the state level, including support for the Shafroth-Palmer constitutional amendment intended to encourage opportunities for state electorates to vote on woman suffrage. The Shafroth-Palmer proposal would have required any state to hold a vote on woman suffrage where eight percent of the voters in the previous presidential election petitioned for such a referendum.

The drift during the Shaw years towards action on the state level was the result of several factors. One was fealty to those in the N.A.W.S.A., including Catt, who had been struggling for success state-by-state. Another was the necessity of placating southern members of the N.A.W.S.A. who were states' rights oriented and strongly against the Anthony amendment. A third was anger at Alice Paul and her supporters, who were committed exclusively to the federal strategy— a knee-jerk resistance on N.A.W.S.A.'s part to whatever Paul and her faction favored.[20]

But by 1916 Catt was convinced that reversal of strategy was essential. She based her strategic judgment on what she thought was the practical situation. The old approach now seemed what Catt frankly called "negative — not positive."[21] It simply was not working, certainly not fast enough. No doubt, the memory of the loss of the suffrage referendum in New York State in 1915 was a painful factor in this assessment. As she looked ahead, moreover, Catt increasingly doubted the state approach alone could ever work. Its chances in many states were nearly hopeless. State election laws and constitutional provisions often made state constitutional revision almost impossible. Even worse, Catt doubted whether there was a majority of men in many states who would soon vote for women's enfranchisement if they got the chance. She continued to be haunted by "the others," the "groups of recently naturalized and even unnationalized foreigners, Indians,

Negroes, large numbers of illiterates, ne'er-do-wells, and drunken loafers," who she felt resisted women's enfranchisement.[22] Catt also worried that even if she was wrong, and some states did begin to approve enfranchisement, this might represent a victory of distinctly mixed blessings. Concern with national enfranchisement might decline in every state that granted women the vote. Valuable energy and talent might be lost to the N.A.W.S.A. and "disintegration" would increase.[23] Thus, from every angle it seemed imperative to Catt to redirect attention to the national effort to obtain congressional passage of the Anthony amendment.

Catt's expectation was that Congress would prove more cooperative than many of the resistant states. She understood that this was a gamble and intended to keep some pressure on the states while hoping that suffrage states and those with strong prosuffrage forces would help by pressuring Congress. Pressure from the states was needed, after all, to impress Congress that there was popular support for woman suffrage. Moreover, the states could not be ignored because, when Congress finally capitulated, the Anthony amendment would need approval by three-fourths of the state legislatures. Yet Catt was convinced emphasis had to shift to the federal level. Victory there would lead to victory everywhere.[24]

Catt also argued that the national approach best fit her long-run ideal for women. It acknowledged women's dignity, she insisted, because it took them seriously. It made the issue of woman suffrage a national matter, as it should be, and it left behind the image of women pleading state-by-state for something that was basic to democracy and human rights.[25]

At the Atlantic City convention Catt pushed her strategy through largely on the force of her personal and political leadership. In a mood for strong leadership and attracted by her effective plea for her strategic gamble, the convention swung behind "The Plan" with an enthusiasm that overcame earlier positions and earlier doubts.[26]

Undoubtedly, Catt was aided in her coup by the decision of Anna Howard Shaw to back her plan fully (except for moving the national headquarters to Washington). While Shaw had lost much respect within the N.A.W.S.A. during her presidency, she was still, second only to Catt, the most formidable force to be reckoned with. Her enthusiasm for "The Plan" was strong. She helped arrange the special Atlantic City meeting, in fact, and thereafter repeatedly backed its decisions, probably in part because she thought it would undermine the appeal of the Woman's Party.[27]

On the other hand, there were costs. There were personal costs: Catt drove herself night and day as she built support within the

N.A.W.S.A. for her shift in strategy There were organizational costs: there was serious opposition to "The Plan" from significant southern voices in the N.A.W.S.A. Kate Gordon, of Louisiana, and Laura Clay, of Kentucky, both prominent during the Shaw presidency, argued that suffrage could (and should) have appeal in the South only if it did not remind southerners of earlier national attempts to change the South at the behest of federal edicts. And they feared that if a national effort were successful in this instance a similar attempt to dictate to the South on the subject of race might follow.

Moreover, opponents of several stripes felt that Catt bulldozed her plan through in Atlantic City with precious little concern for them or for a diverse N.A.W.S.A. From their perspective, they were quite right. But Catt wanted action in response to the strategic imperative at hand. They had had their way for a long time; now their day was over. Indeed, Catt believed it should have ended long before, since an honest evaluation would have revealed that the "littleness of the view[,] which our states' rights' [sic] plan has stimulated for a hundred years, is the greatest enemy of woman suffrage."[28]

Privately, Catt had arranged to resign if "The Plan" was not adopted by the N.A.W.S.A. She insisted there just was no point in continuing the struggle in the old, humiliating, and ineffective fashion. This issue went beyond compromise or temporizing. But Catt won in Atlantic City and she used "The Plan" as her vehicle towards victory, defending it as she went.[29]

Dealing with Divisiveness

Catt's strategic analysis is further illuminated by her attitude towards and dealings with "the militants" in the later suffrage movement. The first major sign of division in the suffrage crusade occurred in 1907 when Harriot Stanton Blatch, daughter of Elizabeth Cady Stanton, turned against the N.A.W.S.A. Influenced by the more active and more militant movement in Great Britain, Blatch founded a more radical organization in 1907, which became the Women's Political Union in 1910. While Blatch's tiny splinter movement played a minor role, it was a harbinger of the future.

A far more serious split in the suffrage forces became apparent in 1913 with the emergence of the remarkable Alice Paul. Paul's first serious work for votes for women began in England, where she associated with the British militants and went to prison for her militancy.[30] With this background, the young Alice Paul arrived in Washington in 1913 and went to work for the N.A.W.S.A.'s Congressional Commit-

tee. Through the force of her charismatic personality, Paul soon transformed the committee. She changed it from the inactive, sleepy arena
it had been under Anna Howard Shaw's regime into a permanent
committee that was a busy lobbying center determined to push the
Susan B. Anthony amendment through Congress. In spite of the
changes, Paul became dissatisfied with the unwieldy committee, linked
as it was to the "conservative" N.A.W.S.A. and its multileveled strategies. As an alternative, Paul set up the Congressional Union to concentrate exclusively on the Anthony amendment, ignoring state efforts
for suffrage and efforts to get Congress to encourage enfranchisement of women by the states. At first Paul acted within the N.A.W.S.A.
and with the approval of President Shaw, but Paul's focus and her
sometimes brash style soon aroused opposition within N.A.W.S.A.
circles. Moreover, as the Congressional Union took on the unmistakable appearance of a separate and independent organization, still
others within the N.A.W.S.A. became uncomfortable. Aware of the
criticisms by the end of 1913, Paul defended herself by claiming that
the Congressional Union existed only to assist the Congressional
Committee.

In reality, however, the Congressional Union was an almost
separate organization — empire, critics charged — which used
N.A.W.S.A. stationery to raise money and recruit membership while
not accepting direction from the N.A.W.S.A. board. Indeed, as Anna
Howard Shaw eventually argued, it pursued policies never approved
by the N.A.W.S.A. Not surprisingly, the N.A.W.S.A. board sought to
force Paul to do its bidding. The result was that in 1914 Paul was asked
to resign as head of the Congressional Committee. She did so and she
soon took the Congressional Union with her, feeling very much that
she had been rejected and forced to secede. While in later years Paul
conceded that she had erred in not communicating along the way with
the N.A.W.S.A. leadership, she doubted at the time that compromise
was possible — and it was not, in fact.[31]

Paul did not act alone. She had support from others who had tired
of the N.A.W.S.A.'s largely fruitless pursuit of votes for women via
state referenda. They wanted to get the Anthony constitutional
amendment passed, and they wanted to move fast. Among them were
Blatch, whose Women's Political Union fused with the Congressional
Union in 1916, and Alva Belmont, who contributed a great deal of her
considerable wealth to the cause. By 1916 the Woman's Party had
emerged, with Anne Martin as first chair. Martin was a former
N.A.W.S.A. board member from Nevada who, like a number of others
from western states where woman suffrage was a reality, was impatient
with the slow progress of the N.A.W.S.A. towards national enfran-

chisement of women. Finally, in 1917 the National Woman's Party was founded with Alice Paul as its acknowledged leader.[32]

It was Anna Howard Shaw who took the role of chief and consistent opponent and who rallied those within the N.A.W.S.A. seeking to control Paul. Shaw detested Paul. "I wish something would happen to Miss Paul," she wrote, and one senses she did not mean something pleasant.[33] But her larger complaint went to Paul's followers, who were "blank fools"[34] and who, Shaw insisted, hurt the suffrage cause by their divisiveness, disloyalty, and tactical militance.

Shaw blamed herself for not attacking Paul's tendency to go her own way from the first, stopping her before she was in a position to make a cause célèbre out of the affair. Paul suspected that would have ended the entire affair, since in her judgment it was not at bottom a fight over tactics or policy but a matter of willful ambition on the part of Paul and her coworker Lucy Burns.[35]

Shaw's opinion was widely shared among other suffragists. One of the most important, and most hostile, was Alice Stone Blackwell, who was still denouncing the Woman's Party in the late 1920s. She would not forgive them for the divisions she felt they had brought to the suffrage cause, and she thought it incredible that they blithely took credit for the passage of the Anthony amendment. And yet even Blackwell acknowledged their appeal. They might be "pestiferous," but they had "cleverness and enthusiasm" — which made them continually "dangerous."[36]

In 1913 and 1914, while Catt shared Shaw's doubts about the organizational loyalty of the Paul group, Catt did not join President Shaw in her assault on them.[37] Nor did she share the antagonism that some in the N.A.W.S.A. felt toward Paul and her allies because they wished to push Congress to adopt the Anthony amendment. Indeed, Catt favored the same approach. This fact explains why informed critics of the N.A.W.S.A. did not single out Catt nearly as much as they did Shaw as a major cause of the split.[38]

Nineteen-fifteen was a decisive year in Catt's relations with the Alice Paul group, by then gone from the N.A.W.S.A. On the one hand, Catt made efforts to heal the wounds between the N.A.W.S.A. and Paul. She met with Paul, despite Shaw's intense disapproval and fear,[39] though to no good result.[40] And she moved rapidly, upon her election to the presidency of the N.A.W.S.A. in 1915, towards adoption of a national strategy for women's enfranchisement (which Paul had supported with no success within the N.A.W.S.A.), a goal she accomplished when "The Plan" was approved in 1916.

By then, however, the split was too deep, too personal, and too institutionalized for the two groups to get back together. Moreover, new conflicts arose that sealed a split between Catt and her N.A.W.S.A. and Paul and her associates. As a consequence, while all of Catt's contacts with Woman's Party supporters did not dissolve,[41] Catt made her decision: Alice Paul and her group — soon to be the National Woman's Party — were a destructive influence on the cause, and the N.A.W.S.A. must keep free from them. While never denying that they sometimes were "doing some good work," Catt concluded that there was a fundamental split and all suffragists had to choose: "No one can carry water on both shoulders."[42] At the same time Catt unrealistically hoped to avoid open warfare. A choice had to be made but that did not mean each group should continually waste energy "battling each other when they should be more concerned to help the big cause on."[43]

The source of conflict between Catt and Paul concerned tactics, and whether Paul and her allies had a realistic understanding of practical politics. The question Catt asked of any strategy or tactic was: will it help the cause, will it maximize votes in referenda and in Congress? In Catt's judgment this pragmatic sense was missing among people such as Alice Paul. A "sharp tongue," radical pronouncements, radical actions did not produce votes. They were the products of those who chose self-indulgence over practicality.[44]

In the suffrage fight two tactics of the Paul group drew Catt's opposition, partisanship and picketing. The militants' eagerness to abandon nonpartisanship, enter the world of party and electoral politics, and campaign against political enemies appealed to some women activists more than nonpartisanship did.[45] Catt claimed to appreciate appeal of activism by recognizing that nonpartisanship "lacks the avenger's satisfaction."[46] She could also agree with those such as Rose Young who thought more in terms of positive action and wondered if using a "big stick" such as electoral politics might not speed progress by striking fear into politicians.[47]

But Catt thought this was a dangerous idea, a judgment undoubtedly encouraged by her natural suspicion of partisan politics in every situation. Catt insisted, first, that alliances for or against a political party invariably proved costly in terms of independence. In this case, she feared that suffrage would be swallowed up by other party concerns and the compromising, self-promoting ethic of all parties. Second, even if one were to enter party politics to the extent of endorsing candidates — which was too much involvement to begin with — the endorsements had to cross party lines or else one would find oneself saddled with a partisan label and the bitter opposition of at least one political party.

Catt's position was faithful to the long-time gospel of the women's movement, especially the ideas of Susan B. Anthony. Had there been a party prepared to endorse "Freedom to Women" on its banner, Anthony and, later, Catt would have rallied to it. In the meantime, Catt was prepared to follow Anthony's classic advice to appeal to both parties and to serve as "a balance of power" when possible, never accepting a marriage to one party or a crusade against another.[48] It was incredible to her that Paul and her allies sought to go after *all* Democrats in the 1914 and 1916 elections, blaming Democratic President Wilson and all congressional Democrats for the failure of Congress to pass the Anthony amendment. The policy of nonpartisanship failed to distinguish between Democrats who favored suffrage and those who did not. Moreover, it was bound to alienate desperately needed Democrats in Congress where the Anthony amendment had to gain a two-thirds majority if it were to start its way to final enactment.

It was also bound to alienate President Wilson, whose support was needed, especially to persuade reluctant southern Democrats in Congress to give their support. Nor was it the way to promote success in state referenda. As she wrote Jane Addams, any crusade against the Democrats was "exceedingly distasteful to most of us . . . because it committed the stupendous stupidity of making an anti-democratic campaign when the suffrage question was pending in eleven states and depending for success upon Democratic votes."[49]

Instead, Catt preferred to work closely with friends in both parties while exerting pressure in all legal (but nonelectoral) ways on senators, members of the House, and the president. She gave full support to Maud Wood Park's direct lobbying work on Capitol Hill and kept in close lobbying touch with Park's "Front Door" effort, the joint strategy sessions, and "machinations," which were (and are) part of the game there. She worked the White House personally, convinced that dignified lobbying was the way to get results.[50]

Yet Catt did not object only because she considered entering partisan, electoral politics a strategic mistake. The Woman's Party's strategy also offended her ideals. It was natural for her to skate away from playing partisan electoral politics. Such a strategy clashed with her nonpartisan ideal for a democracy and activated her substantial ambivalence about politics in general and party politics in particular. The Woman's Party was guilty of a tactical blunder, in her mind, but it also seriously offended Catt's dream for a politics without politics. Catt fought for her perspective with all her energy, challenging Charles A. Beard when he defended the Woman's Party's partisanship in that bosom of Progressivism, the *New Republic*. And she fought back against other critics. A lot was at stake for her that went beyond strategy, though her replies invariably stressed her claim that only her approach would work — and was working. And Catt had the considerable satisfaction (if that is the word) of watching the radicals' adventures into partisan electoral politics fail in both 1914 and 1916.[51]

Nonpartisanship remained a fixed star in her belief, but by 1918 Catt became open to the idea of bringing women's muscle to bear on congressional opponents of women's enfranchisement through the electoral process. Her impatience with the manifest dilatoriness of Congress from 1915 to 1917 had grown. She began to issue unmistakable warnings that votes for women was an idea that would "not perish," but "the party which opposed it may," and she told the 1917 convention to expect to take action against individual senators who were up for re-election in 1918 if they opposed woman suffrage.[52] When the 1918 campaign came, Catt led the N.A.W.S.A. into a carefully circumscribed, nonpartisan battle to defeat four recalcitrant senators (three Republicans and one Democrat), and was delighted by the defeat of one of them in November. Of course — though not for the first time — this move reflected the adoption of a part of Paul's strategy, yet it did so only within Catt's nonpartisan strategic constraints, which, she asserted once again, preserved the N.A.W.S.A.'s freedom while advancing its effectiveness.[53]

A far more rigid position was adopted by the head of the N.A.W.S.A. towards the other major "radical" tactic of the Woman's Party, the aggressive picketing of the president which began in 1917. Women picketers caused a sensation and, in many circles including within the N.A.W.S.A., they created a scandal. Nor were the Woman's Party picketers necessarily modest and sedate. As time went on they became more aggressive in pursuit of their mission, refusing to cooperate when police arrested them.[54]

Once again the issue here was not solely a matter of strategic effectiveness. Catt put it this way. So did her opponents. Interminable arguments followed over whether militant picketing and what became civil disobedience were, or ever could be, effective. Catt was convinced that suffrage was past its strictly agitational phase. What it needed now was male support, and especially the support of the male who was president of the United States. Picketing could not accomplish this goal. It was better to work mostly on education, particularly during the war, as that would produce more male acquiescence or support.[55]

Though Catt and everybody else treated the matter in these terms, the enormous national controversy over a few picketers suggested much more was at stake. The fight over the picketers actually involved an intense and significant dispute over the definition of a good woman. Were women pushing for suffrage always to be proper ladies and law-abiding citizens? Or was it appropriate for free women in control of their lives to break convention and law in pursuit of the

vote? Most of the leadership and members of the N.A.W.S.A. were
outraged at the tactics of the picketers, in part because they seemed
brash and unfeminine — and thus were detrimental to their cause.

Carrie Chapman Catt, however, was not among those who joined
the assault on the picketers as unladylike women. Given Catt's resent-
ment over undignified treatment of women, indeed their daily humiliation, it is no surprise that she had more than a sneaking sympathy
with the picketers' tactical militance — especially when they were
safely located in Great Britain. At home the problem for Catt, as always, concerned their political effectiveness.[56] She knew the public
reaction would be negative — as it was. She also observed the picketers' negative effects on Congress.

As a result, Catt publicly appealed in 1917 for the Woman's Party
to stop damaging the chances for passage of the Anthony constitutional amendment by its picketing. She privately wrote Alice Paul
deploring the "futile annoyance to the members of Congress."[57] She
worried too about picketing as "an insult to President Wilson," which
could alienate his needed support. (She tried to compensate by quietly
notifying the White House of planned embarrassments to Wilson,
which her friends in the Woman's Party leaked to her.) Finally, Catt
saw only unfortunate effects on the state level also, since she was certain that "the picket party" had hurt the 1917 New York campaign for
the enfranchisement of women.[58]

Everywhere she heard opponents denouncing the picketing.
They charged it showed the danger of women in politics and the fool-
ishness of granting women the vote. They insisted that to give women
the ballot while they were picketing would reward tactics that should
have no place in American politics. At another, lower level, antisuffragists consciously used the uproar over the picketers as an opportunity to denounce the suffragists as exemplars of "fanaticism," and as
"freaks" and "spoiled" children undeserving of suffrage. Moreover,
intent on destroying all suffragists through public disapproval of the
picketers, they worked as hard as they could to collapse any distinction
between them and Catt and the N.A.W.S.A. Over and over they asserted that Catt and the N.A.W.S.A. were in league with the militants,
equally deserving of popular condemnation.[59]

Throughout much of 1917 and thereafter Catt tried to repair the
continuing damage she believed the picketers caused the movement.
Her private assistance to the White House was an illustration of this,
but mostly Catt did her work in public. She succeeded in getting the
N.A.W.S.A. to disavow the picketing tactic and she led the N.A.W.S.A.
to publish its objections in some 350 newspapers across the country.
She spoke out personally, arguing that all suffragists should not be

judged by what she correctly insisted was a tiny minority. She was especially anxious to establish that suffragists were not against Wilson (and thus not unpatriotic) in what was wartime.

Catt's course offended (and still does) those who contended that Catt should have embraced the picketers as fellow participants in the struggle who were determined to get action quickly. Such judgments did not impress Catt. Her constant refrain was that one had to be practical, to make trade-offs, and to ask about the consequences of tactics. Catt thought she, and not the Woman's Party, recognized how to play politics. And those who did not know its rules had to be neutralized because, though naive, they could hurt the work of those who did. The danger was always that the Woman's Party might become the tail that wagged the suffrage dog, that the work of two million women might be lost in the actions of a group that never was larger than 50,000.[60]

Pragmatism was not the only root of Catt's objections to the picketers, however. She may not have found their "unladylike" activities offensive to her ideal of womanhood, but their actions did clash with her ideal of the kind of politics she wanted suffragists to model for society at large. When Carrie Catt looked at the Woman's Party, she saw individuals who had already proven themselves "untrustworthy and extremely disloyal."[61] They operated by churning up dark forces of emotion and conflict, not at all the kind of politics she wanted anything to do with. After all, Catt was to devote almost as many years of her life to world peace as to woman suffrage. She could not see how promoting "warfare" in any realm for any reason was acceptable. In this Catt's thought was identical to that of Jane Addams and many other Progressives. Conflict was their enemy. It could not and did not facilitate a harmonious democracy or a peaceful world. In effect, Catt's complaint was that the militants were merely reflecting the world in their tactical moves. They did not represent change and were not reformers at all. They had surrendered to the world and were trying to beat men at their own game.

Of course, Catt respected toughness and employed military language often enough that she had no business being too self-righteous in condemning the Woman's Party. Moreover, all along she suspected that emotional appeals could at times be more effective than rational ones. Yet none of these things were quite to the point in Catt's calculations. To her, the Woman's Party gloried in confrontation and seemed to operate under the illusion that conflictual emotionalism was somehow laudatory. It would not work, nor, she thought, should it work if the woman suffrage movement was to herald the new politics of Catt's Progressive dreams.[62]

Another factor that alienated Catt from the radicals was clashing temperaments. It cannot be neatly separated from more straight-forward issues. We know Catt loved order and organization; that inclination automatically recoiled from the milieu of Alice Paul and the Woman's Party, which Catt believed housed a good many unconventional souls, organizational arrangements, and, of course, tactics. Even the N.A.W.S.A. sometimes attracted what Catt saw as strange people, but Catt was pleased that they rarely stayed long. She felt they were welcome in the Woman's Party, where disorder was a way of life.

Catt misunderstood how the Woman's Party actually functioned. It may have been unconventional in many ways, but it was not disorganized. In practice Alice Paul commanded it in a remote but far tighter fashion than Catt ever dreamed of doing with the N.A.W.S.A. Moreover, the picketers were extremely disciplined generally. But to Catt the Woman's Party was another part of America out of control in a country already blighted by too many other instances of the same thing.[63]

Eventually Peck and Catt concluded that both the N.A.W.S.A. and the Woman's Party had contributed to the success of the suffrage crusade. While it was true that "an icy gulf existed" betweeen the two groups, "the two organizations worked side by side" in effect.[64] Each had done so by compensating for the limitations of the other. The limitations of the N.A.W.S.A. spurred the creation of the Woman's Party as a home for militants who could not work for suffrage elsewhere and provided a base for the development of more radical and experimental tactics and strategies. For instance, the Woman's Party and its predecessors created the idea of the suffrage parade and it argued for the federal amendment strategy, both of which Catt's N.A.W.S.A. adopted. Above all, the Woman's Party's tactical radicalism helped enormously to legitimate the N.A.W.S.A.: it turned the N.A.W.S.A. into a respectable vehicle for reform and increased its effectiveness both in attracting women and the public at large. Catt went a bit far in later years when she pretended that "there was no serious quarrel between the two." She was more convincing in her perception that each organization had nothing to apologize for in its respective endeavors.[65] By her lights neither organization was flawless, neither was totally "right," and neither deserved full credit for the adoption of the suffrage amendment.[66]

In reflecting on Carrie Catt as a strategist, we can see how much strategy mattered to her and how much she was involved in its formulation and defense. Thinking strategically was natural to her, integral to Catt's very being. No one can have a sense of her as a politician, or recognize her as one, without understanding that strategy was foremost on her mind. This is what it means to say she had an intensely political mind. She had goals, of course, and they meant a lot to her, but she never visualized them apart from strategy. It was not just that she did not approve of "unrealistic" or "unstrategic" idealists. She was totally different from such people just as, in turn, her Progressive form of idealism prevented her from being merely another politician.

Her single-minded pursuit of woman suffrage led her to be flexible in strategy and tactics, so flexible indeed that she sometimes seemed to compromise far too much, as in her response to World War I or her tolerance of racism. But she insisted that being practical in this fashion was being moral. It was not the whole of morality, but without it moral idealism was more a self-righteous pose than a relevant program to change the world.

Conclusion

From a contemporary perspective, important questions remain about Carrie Catt as a feminist politician, one of which must concern Catt's judgment in tying her feminist goal so closely to woman suffrage. After all, the enfranchisement of women did not produce much change in women's economic, political, or familial status in the United States in her long lifetime.

Did Catt overpromise regarding woman suffrage? And did she give it too much weight in her program for women?[1] The benefits of women's enfranchisement was a topic she addressed often, for skeptics were always numerous. This was true before 1920 when antisuffragists insisted that it would accomplish little while simultaneously suggesting that its enactment would seriously disrupt American society. It was true after 1920 when even some of her allies were deeply disappointed. Alice Stone Blackwell, for instance, wrote Catt that not much had come from the ballot, "women being fools because God made them to match the men."[2]

In later years Catt reflected extensively on what suffrage had brought. She argued that suffrage had made a difference for women, though she never thought its results on their own were, or could be, revolutionary. She was always enthusiastic about the suffrage struggle itself: "Once upon a time there was a great movement for the liberty of a subjected class and it was won," but when she got down to specific results she put it differently.[3]

155

She saw women's enfranchisement as an opportunity. Alone it guaranteed nothing. "Winning the vote is only an opening wedge," she wrote, "to learn to use it is a bigger task."[4] The challenge lay in taking advantage of the opportunity, and Catt assessed suffrage's value after 1920 in terms of the possibilities it had opened for activists to change women's lot and to improve society as a whole.

When she looked to what *political* good woman suffrage had effected, Catt had few illusions. But then she never believed that votes for women would ensure her kind of reformed politics. Indeed, she had seen disturbing signs even before the final enactment of the Anthony amendment that in western states voting women allowed themselves to become absorbed into the status quo as women's auxiliaries to existing parties.[5]

During the 1920s and thereafter Catt perceived that no great transformation in American politics had happened as the result of woman suffrage. There had been some progress, but the battle for American democracy was far from over. She had appreciated all along that somehow some observers had expected women voters to usher in clean, issue-oriented, nonparty politics. She had her own hopes, but Catt was not among those who believed, as she put it, that suffrage (or anything else) was a "short cut to the millenium."[6] Evolutionary change didn't work that way. Moreover, such a view was absurdly idealistic about women, an attitude that Catt never shared. She knew long before 1920 that women did not behave perfectly as voters, though she expected them to do much better than men had. They voted "not like oracles of infallible wisdom, but like human beings moved by very human motives."[7]

Nor was she astonished when woman suffrage did not lead to many elected women officials, especially members of Congress. This further advance would not be easy. Those who thought otherwise just had not fully appreciated what she always knew, that "the battle for equality has only just begun."[8] Nor was she shocked to learn that some suffragists found political life or even voting far less enthralling than they had earlier dreamed it would be. She had often predicted that this would be a common reaction at first. Yet her faith in the long-term possibilities of woman suffrage remained unshaken throughout her life, as did her sense of women's responsibility to act to better their world.[9]

The larger question, however, is the extent to which Catt equated the enactment of the Anthony amendment and the opportunity it represented with a broad-ranging program to alter women's condition — and whether, indeed, she favored such a program at all. After 1920 Catt had no need to stress a single-issue campaign for strategic reason.

But she did not join many further movements aimed at addressing the conditions of women. Instead, she regularly denounced Alice Paul's Woman's Party, which did try.[10]

Catt frequently claimed that achieving woman suffrage was the heart of what had to be done — at least through the law. Her joy at getting the vote also led her to make extravagant declarations about the dawn of women's freedom that were simply wrong. The world of American women changed so much less than she had predicted.

On the other hand, Catt was inconsistent. As often as she was sanguine, she denied that women had achieved self-mastery after 1920. As early as 1921, she defended continuing publication of the *Woman Citizen* because winning the vote could not end the woman's campaign for equality and justice: "Many a hard fought battle lies ahead."[11] As she put it in 1927, woman suffrage was really "no more than an episode in an age-old battle."[12]

In this vein, she insisted there was much more to be done before women obtained more than "the usual 'fetch and carry' work."[13] They needed to advance everywhere towards "more share in government, more share in party control, more share in church administrations, the peace societies, the welfare movements."[14] In her eighties, during the 1940s, Catt was still insisting that the road ahead was long. Women remained too dependent on men and could not easily do such ordinary things as eat alone in a respectable restaurant.[15] Women's groups needed to push ahead and forget their disappointing taste for what Catt saw as "ultra-conservative" programs for women. She was "still looking for a militant gathering of women to assert their claims and work for the equality of the sexes."[16] When the draft of the report of the Woman's Centennial Conference of 1940 seemed to her too cautious in the face of all that had to be done, Catt signed it only reluctantly. Women had to be challenged to go on: "where there are barriers, break them; where there is opposition, beseige it. . . . Keep the banner of women's rights flying."[17]

Exactly what Catt wanted women to do is less clear than her exhortations to further struggle. She did, as we have seen, want a fuller participation by women in governing and, always, she hoped they would come to exercise influence toward her ideal political system. In addition, Catt's program focused to some extent on women in economic life. This included defending and enhancing the opportunity for women to enter employment on an equal footing with men. However, Catt was less concerned with women who wanted to work than with women who had to work.

Before and after 1920 Catt insisted that women who entered the workplace deserved support from other women.[18] Moreover, the law must ensure that working women got what they so obviously lacked: equal treatment with men in most areas of employment, including wages and promotions. At the same time, Catt felt, albeit somewhat vaguely, that concern with working women meant that the state must protect them from excessive hours and too demanding conditions of labor (without ever considering how this fit with her general objectives of equality).

A great deal of Catt's effort in this area came before 1920, especially during World War I, when she tried hard to open a number of occupations to women, promote equal pay, and in general advance employed women when so many men were in the army.[19] But Catt spoke out frequently on this theme after 1920 as well.[20]

Predictably, Catt was convinced that women's enfranchisement provided working women and those sympathetic to their cause the opportunity to do something through the political system to improve their condition. She did not agree for a minute that in her age women's rights (including the right to vote) were largely irrelevant for employed women.[21]

But her economic program was very modest, on balance, and it had a way of inexorably returning to an affirmation of women's voting as the answer. One part of her program was not, however, support for the Equal Rights Amendment. From the first Catt strongly objected to the E.R.A. when the idea began to be discussed in the 1920s and she never wavered in her objections. The most important reason was her understanding of how to help working women. Believing they needed all the assistance they could get, she thought it essential to defeat the E.R.A. It would, she insisted, rob working women of the special, protective legislation that progressive states had passed to aid them and to prevent their all-too-common abuse in the workplace.[22] Catt also opposed the E.R.A. because it became the principal plank of the Woman's Party, which she detested.[23]

There was, of course, nothing unusual in her judgment among leading activist women. Many agreed with Catt that opposition to the E.R.A. was a practical expression of concern for women. Florence Kelley, Frances Perkins, Eleanor Roosevelt, Helen Gahagan Douglas, as well as the leaders of the League of Women Voters, the Consumers League, the Women's Trade Union League, among many, fought the E.R.A. as a scheme that would hurt working women. "All the largest women's reform groups enthusiastically advocated protective labor legislation" in the 1920s and opposed the E.R.A.[24] They were joined by the forces of organized labor. "By the 1920s, most union officials viewed protective labor legislation for women as a complement to unionization for men and actively promoted it."[25]

Carrie Catt in 1929. Courtesy of the Library of Congress.

Catt's position was not absolute or eternal. As she saw it, employed women needed protective legislation. She had felt that way since being exploited as a young woman in San Francisco. Women were inferior in the economic culture of the United States and they had to have protection against exploitation. When, and if, they worked in an environment in which they were not vulnerable, protective laws would be unnecessary and the E.R.A. would be fine. It was a practical matter of power. Of course, a consequence of her view was reinforcement of the reality that women had a secondary status in the American economy, one that limited them as much as or more than it protected them. Some male union leaders favored protective legislation and opposed the E.R.A. for this very reason.[26] But this was not Catt's perspective. She thought in immediate terms, of what she felt were the real conditions women faced now without power and she believed the E.R.A. would have been a disaster.[27]

The one area where women's enfranchisement was not likely to be decisive, according to Catt, was altering men's — and women's — basic attitudes. Catt's analysis, we should remember, was that woman's position in society originated neither in natural nor in legal inequality. It was cultural. While legal changes in politics and economics could help reverse matters, they would only complement, indeed often follow, changes in the basic culture. Thus it was essential to change both men's and women's attitudes to effect a truly significant alteration in woman's place.[28]

The fact is, though, that Catt had little advice about how to change men's attitudes. And she made no systematic efforts to do so. This is surprising of one who thought changing men's attitudes so important and who was so enamored of the possibilities of education for political citizenship. Certainly it was not because Catt thought men's change was hopeless nor because she forgot her resentments of males: "we . . . women waded through the torrential current [the suffrage struggle] with precious little help from men when the tide was wildest."[29]

Yet Catt's analysis, or her vision, failed her at this point. She had nothing to offer to address her image of male selfishness, warlike aggressiveness, and pride, which she resented all her life. She lapsed into characteristic, vague optimism based on her confidence that male supremacy was not natural and evolution guaranteed a better future.[30]

Clearly she was uncomfortable with confronting the issue of males. She liked men on the whole. She married twice. She had experiences even in the suffrage movement in which there "was no hostility between men and women."[31] Moreover, she did not see how faulting men as a group could possibly help women in practical terms. It might have its psychological advantages, but it was likely to become an unproductive substitute for the practical analysis and hard work that were the only means to actual change.

She also believed that harping on male inadequacies could lead women to ignore how much change women needed to undergo. Indeed, Catt could be critical of women who were not prepared to break with their cultural dependency. She had no patience with a cult of sisterhood and she unsympathetically deplored women who had "slave souls" and were mere "clinging vines." She particularly detested women's cultural enslavement to the fashion industry. Paris ruled women (of her class) too often, rather than the simplicity that she naively thought all rational people would admire. The "true woman" was very different from "one of the delicate little dolls or the silly fools . . . slave to society and fashion."[32]

Another issue that should not be ignored is Catt's disinterest in restructuring basic family life, challenging its traditional patriarchal and segregated structure, not to mention her silence on sexual and reproductive freedom. While the suffrage movement in Catt's era was a women's movement that, by and large, argued sincerely for women's enfranchisement as a means to sustain the family and woman's traditional role within the family,[33] Catt's arrangement with her second husband showed that she was no traditionalist. In fact, there is little in Catt's vast public and private writing that celebrates the family, in any form.

Moreover, despite her two successful marriages, Catt had little praise to offer for marriage as an institution. Eventually Catt came to regard marriage as a confining human relationship and its alternative as a "release" to "freedom."[34] When she first traveled in New England she encountered older unmarried women who had no economic reason to be married. To her they "had their freedom and were very happy. I thought I had at last found the most perfectly located human being in the world. I have never lost this opinion."[35] She tried to create such a world for herself in her "retirement" decades in New Rochelle. She fashioned a world of independent (financially and otherwise) women in which men played no role.

Nevertheless, for Catt women's condition had its roots in general cultural attitudes, economic conditions, and political oppression. Family structures and roles were not central to her analysis. Critical of the patriarchal family and eager to end women's submission within it, she was at the same time unwilling or unable to confront the importance of the family for women's estate, much less address the question of whether its radical alteration was integral to the achievement of women's self-mastery. It is a curious, and important, limitation in Catt's analysis.

Catt was simply uninterested in questions of sexual liberation and preference. Sexual liberation, defined narrowly as a woman's freedom to have sexual relations according to her choice, was not an idea new to Catt. She was a woman of the world and she had some contact with Emma Goldman and with the so-called Greenwich Village feminists, who openly proclaimed sexual liberation as an ideal.[36] To be sure, advocates of sexual liberation were a small and suspect part of the larger women's movement in the early twentieth century and had no place among those close to Catt. Nonetheless, it was not ignorance that separated Catt from the sexual liberationalists.

The truth is that Catt did not like considering, much less discussing, the entire sexual dimension of life. What references there are establish that Catt was unmistakably a sexual conservative who adhered to conventional sexual proprieties. Part of her avoidance of the subject and part of her conservatism here were simply reflections of the Victorian norms of her class and background. Part, though, seems to have had to do with her conclusions about who won and who lost in a sexually liberated environment. She had no doubts that women usually turned out to be the losers, given social attitudes and economic realities. "I had never known a woman who stepped out of the path of regularity who did not, herself, have to pay the cost."[37] The implication was that sexual liberation was yet another abstract ideal that when concretely applied was no ideal at all for women.

She drew on her extensive experience in South America to argue that cultures where sexual relations were not circumscribed (or so she perceived) led to exploitation of women. The large number of women who opted to become nuns in the Roman Catholic Church in South America reinforced her conclusion. They were seeking an escape from a free and easy sexual world where women were invariably victims. Women's independence was possible through their minds; chasing after pleasure with their bodies would lead to a new form of enslavement.[38]

Catt's argument is far from lacking interest today. But it establishes again that, for Catt, women's self-mastery was to take place within distinct boundaries. Virtually the only times Catt discussed the explicitly sexual aspects of the women's movement came when anti-suffragists suggested the movement would encourage "free love" or was led by proponents of free love. Catt always denounced such charges as absurd fabrications. Her strategic sense, sensitive to the potential damage the charge of "free love" could have to women's enfranchisement, dictated her indignant response. Yet it probably was a sincere position for Catt. She had no interest in sexual liberation or preference questions and no belief that they mattered on woman's road to self-mastery.[39]

While Catt was an advocate of birth control, perhaps as much to control the numbers of "the others" as to give women more choice in life, she spent no effort rallying women to practice birth control until she was an old woman. When sharp disagreement broke out over the subject at the Woman's Centennial Conference in 1940, Catt vigorously backed its legitimacy in the Commission on Ethical and Religious Values against a disapproving Roman Catholic minority.[40]

On the other hand, Catt had nothing whatsoever to say about abortion. Margaret Sanger and her tiny band of supporters were active in New York City in her time, and she must have known about them, given the notoriety that attended Sanger's endeavors. Yet, while her silence can be explained in terms of strategy, it went far beyond that. Once again, Catt was conventional. Reproductive rights were not, to say the least, a part of her overall Progressive agenda (nor that of most other feminists of her day).[41]

Catt turned away from these tough issues about women, issues that had to be faced in order to progress towards her own ideal for women. What is crucial to appreciate in understanding her is that her feminism was very much influenced by her Progressivism. Her Progressivism directed her to approach the transformation of women's existence in the public realms such as politics and economics while shying away from the more "private" areas such as sexuality and reproduction. As a committed Progressive, Catt was concerned not only about women in themselves but about the overall social good. Freedom for women was important, but not if it impeded her aim of fashioning a woman and a society serving the public interest. Personal freedoms that she assessed to be unrelated to such a focus had no attraction for her and may have frightened her. Self-determination for men as for women was a right, but a right to be used for society, not for oneself. Feminism was not about "doing one's thing" but doing the social thing. She thought more in terms of community rather than the individual woman (or man) and rather naively thought that self-mastery and community could serenely travel together down the same road.[42]

From our perspective, Catt's approach to feminism has much to contribute. Catt was a classic proponent and practitioner of politics and political organization and one who has relevance today for feminists who hold that there can be no escape from conventional politics. In this sense her claim that "there is much to be learned from the Woman's Campaign . . . for future battles" has turned out to be prescient.[43] We know that, for Carrie Catt, being serious about change inevitably meant becoming political and practical. This is not always obvious to reformers, of course, though her approach is increasingly popular within contemporary feminism. The last years of the battle for the E.R.A. have involved a significant shift in the present-day women's movement towards acceptance of the necessity of "practical" politics — as did feminist support for the Geraldine Ferraro campaign for vice-president in 1984. More and more feminists at all levels are running for political office and in numerous localities women's groups have entered conventional politics to create or support rape crisis centers, homes for battered women, day-care facilities, marital property change, comparable worth legislation, and much more.

Even so, Catt's uncritical enthusiasm for "practical" politics, her caution in style and strategy, her limited program for woman's self-mastery, and her resolute avoidance of all sexual and reproductive dimensions of freedom for women distance her from many present-day feminists. Her own view, however, was that she was very much a feminist, involved in the ongoing feminist struggle: "A world-wide revolt against all artificial barriers which laws and customs interpose between women and human freedom." And she felt her instincts were intensely radical, as she confessed to Mary Peck on several occasions. She knew there was and would be a tremendous gap between her public image, influenced by her pragmatic strategy, and her inner passions. "I am only restrained and walking the chalkline to get the vote," she said, but inside she felt differently. She was aware that "I shall die respectable and my descendants think of me as a conservative. . . . To you privately I will say that I can keep up with you in radicalism and if I should decide to unleash myself I might outstep you."[44]

She never did unleash herself. Her ideal was a down-to-earth, "rational individuality," as she had said on many occasions and demonstrated as often.[45] She opted to stand on her record as a practical activist. This was her great strength — and her great weakness — as she struggled to help women achieve the self-mastery she sought for herself all her life.

Notes

(Please refer to the Bibliography for a key to the abbreviations used in the Notes.)

NOTES TO THE PREFACE

1. C.C.C. to Mary G. Peck (August 30, 1926), LC 8.

2. C.C.C. to Mary G. Peck (September 23, 1916), LC 7.

3. C.C.C. to Mary G. Peck (October 12, 1922), LC 8.

4. C.C.C. to Edna Stantial (May 21, 1945), LC 9.

5. Alice Stone Blackwell to C.C.C. (November 21, 1937), LCB 12.

6. Alice Stone Blackwell to Maud Wood Park (November 7, 1937), LCB 20.

7. C.C.C., "Woman Suffrage Only an Episode in Age-Old Movement," *Current History Magazine* 27 (October 1927): 1–6.

8. C.C.C. to K.B. (June 8, 1943), Catt Collection, Box 4, folder 29, SSL.

9. C.C.C.to Edna Stantial (May 1945), Edna Stantial to C.C.C. (October 6, 1941), and Mary G. Peck to Edna Stantial (January 14, 1948), all cited in *The Blackwell Family, Carrie Chapman Catt, and the National American Woman Suffrage Association: A Register of Their Papers in the Library of Congress* (Washington: Library of Congress, 1975), p. iv.

10. For example, C.C.C. to Ima Fuchs Clevenger (August 20, 1946), LC 4.

11. Lola Carolyn Walker, "The Speeches and Speaking of Carrie Chapman Catt" (Ph.D. dissertation, Northwestern University, 1950) and Ima Fuchs Clevenger, "Invention and Arrangement in the Public Address of Carrie Chapman Catt" (Ph.D. dissertation, University of Oklahoma, 1955).

12. Mary G. Peck to Franciska Schwimmer (July 17, 1949), LCN 27.

13. Gerda Lerner, *The Majority Finds Its Past: Placing Women in History* (New York: Oxford University Press, 1979), chapter 10.

14. See Mari Jo Buhle, *Women and American Socialism: 1870–1920* (Urbana: University of Illinois Press, 1981); Susan Estabrook Kennedy, *If All We Did Was To Weep At Home: A History of White Working-Class Women in America* (Bloomington: Indiana University Press, 1979); Meredith Tax, *The Rising of the Women: Feminist Solidarity and Class Conflict: 1880–1917* (New York: Monthly Review Press, 1980), chapter 5 and p. 184.

15. June Sochen, *The New Woman in Greenwich Village: 1910–1920* (New York: Quadrangle, 1972).

16. Ruth Bordin, *Woman and Temperance* (Philadelphia: Temple University Press, 1981); Barbara Leslie Epstein, *The Politics of Domesticity: Women, Evangelism, and Temperance in Nineteenth-Century America* (Middletown, Conn.: Wesleyan University Press, 1981).

17. Besides the antisuffragist periodicals and books I read which are cited throughout this manuscript, see "Suffrage: U.S." Collection, Boxes 17, 18, and 18a in SSL for many useful pamphlets and other antisuffragist materials.

18. Jane Jerome Camhi, "Women Against Women: American Anti-Suffragism 1880–1920" (Ph.D. dissertation, Tufts University, 1973); Aileen Kraditor, *The Ideas of the Woman Suffrage Movement: 1890–1920* (1965; New York: Norton, 1981), chapter 2.

19. Robert Crunden, *Ministers of Reform: The Progressives' Achievement in American Civilization: 1889–1920* (New York: Basic Books, 1982), p. ix; David R. Colburn and George Pozzetta, ed., *Reform and Reformers in the Progressive Era* (Westport, Conn.: Greenwood, 1983), p. 7.

20. Vernon L. Parrington, *Main Currents in American Thought* (New York: Harcourt, Brace & Co., 1930); Eric Goldman, *Rendezvous with Destiny* (1952; New York: Vintage, 1956); Richard Hofstadter, *The Age of Reform: From Bryan to F.D.R.* (1955; New York: Vintage, 1960).

21. Crunden, *Ministers of Reform*, p. ix.

22. James Weinstein, *The Corporate Ideal in the Liberal State: 1900–1918* (Boston: Beacon, 1968).

23. Otis L. Graham, Jr., *The Great Campaigns: Reform and War in America: 1900–1928* (Englewood Cliffs: Prentice-Hall, 1971), pp. 152–154.

24. A nice sensitivity to presence of both strains among Progressives is in David P. Thelen, *The New Citizenship: Origins of Progressivism in Wisconsin: 1885–1900* (Columbia: University of Missouri Press, 1972), p. 312.

25. Hofstadter, *Age of Reform*, pp. 257 and 203.

26. Samuel P. Hays, *The Response to Industrialism: 1885–1914* (Chicago: University of Chicago Press, 1957); Hofstadter, *Age of Reform*, p. 216.

27. Robert H. Wiebe, *The Search for Order: 1877–1920* (New York: Hill and Wang, 1967), p. 156.

28. Graham, *Great Campaigns*, p. 2.

29. Evelyn Fox Keller, address, conference on "Writing Women's Lives," October 12, 1984, Wingspread, Wisconsin.

NOTES TO CHAPTER 1

1. Mary G. Peck, *Carrie Chapman Catt* (New York: Wilson, 1944), pp. 17–35; Louise R. Noun, *Strong-Minded Women: The Emergence of the Woman-Suffrage Movement in Iowa* (Ames, Ia.: Iowa State University Press, 1969), pp. 227–228 and 231–232; Walker, "Speeches," pp. 15–53; Constance Buel Burnett, "Carrie Chapman Catt," *American Girl* 29 (April 1945); Robert McHenry, ed., *Liberty's Women* (Springfield, Mass.: Merriam, 1980), pp. 67–68. There is no dispute among authorities about the basic facts of C.C.C.'s early life.

2. See Lillian Faderman, *Surpassing the Love of Men: Romantic Friendship and Love Between Women from the Renaissance to the Present* (New York: Morrow, 1981), pp. 186–189, for her discussion of the family patterns of nineteenth-century feminists; see Ruth Barnes Moynihan, *Rebel for Rights: Abigail Scott Duniway* (New Haven: Yale University Press, 1983), p. 6, for an example of a Catt contemporary who reflected the common pattern (which Catt apparently did not follow) of identification with the father.

3. Walker, "Speeches," pp. 36–37 and 59; C.C.C., "Why I Have Found Life Worth Living," *Christian Century* 45 (March 29, 1928): 6; Constance Buel Burnett, *Five For Freedom* (New York: Abelard, 1953), pp. 263–270.

4. Constance Buel Burnett, "The Great Feminist: Carrie Chapman Catt," in *Topflight: Famous American Women,* ed. Anne Stoddard (New York: Thomas Nelson, 1946), p. 184; Walker, "Speeches," p. 23.

5. C.C.C., "A Biographical Sketch," LC P80-5458; Walker, "Speeches," p. 32.

6. Much of the little we know about Catt's family relations when she was young was learned from her in very old age by Constance B. Burnett. C. B. Burnett to C.C.C. (February 28, 1945), C.C.C. to C. B. Burnett (December 18, 1944, and March 13, 1945), all in Dillon Collection, Box 1, folder 7, RL; C.C.C., speech, Luncheon on her Eighty-fifth Birthday (January 10, 1944), Box 1, SSL.

7. For the earlier period see Ellen DuBois, *Feminism and Suffrage: The Emergence of an Independent Women's Movement in America: 1849–1969* (Ithaca, N.Y.: Cornell University Press, 1978), chapters 1–5, and the discussion in Eleanor Flexner, *Century of Struggle: The Woman's Rights Movement in the United States* (1959; New York: Atheneum, 1973), chapters 5–8 and 10–11; Mari Jo Buhle and Paul Buhle, ed. *The Concise History of Woman Suffrage* (Urbana, Ill.: University of Illinois Press, 1978), pp. 151–212; Andrew Sinclair, *The Better Half: The Emancipation of the American Woman* (New York: Harper & Row, 1965), chapters 17 and 20; also see Loretta E. Zimmerman, "Alice Paul and the National Woman's Party: 1912–1920" (Ph.D. dissertation, Tulane University, 1964), pp. 14–59; also see notes 9 and 10.

8. DuBois, *Feminism and Suffrage,* pp. 200–201.

9. On the usually neglected A.W.S.A., see materials in LCN 38; Alice Stone Blackwell, *Lucy Stone: Pioneer of Woman's Rights* (Boston: Little, Brown, 1930), chapter 15; Elinor Rice Hays, *Morning Star: A Biography of Lucy Stone: 1818–1893* (New York: Harcourt, Brace & World, 1961), chapters 17–26; DuBois, *Feminism and Suffrage,* chapter 6; also see note 7.

10. Mary Ann B. Oakley, *Elizabeth Cady Stanton* (Old Westbury, N.Y.: Feminist Press, 1972), chapter 8; Elisabeth Griffith, *In Her Own Right: The Life of Elizabeth Cady Stanton* (New York: Oxford University Press, 1984), chapters

8–9; Alma Lutz, *Created Equal: A Biography of Elizabeth Cady Stanton* (New York: John Day, 1940), chapters 15–17; Alma Lutz, *Susan B. Anthony* (Boston: Beacon, 1959), pp. 138–148; Lois Banner, *Elizabeth Cady Stanton, A Radical for Woman's Rights* (Boston: Little, Brown, 1980), chapters 6 and 7.

11. C.C.C. to Edna Stantial (October 1941), LCN 39; Alice Stone Blackwell to Mary Hunter (August 13, 1938), LCN 38; Robert E. Riegal, *American Women: A Story of Social Change* (Rutherford, N.J.: Fairleigh Dickinson University, 1970), pp. 232–233: Hays, *Morning Star*, p. 297; Blackwell, *Lucy Stone*, pp. 228–230; also see "National American Annual Meeting," *Woman's Journal* 21 (March 1, 1890): 68.

12. Theodore Stanton and Harriot Stanton Blatch, *Elizabeth Cady Stanton As Revealed in Her Letters, Diary and Reminiscences*, 2 vol. (New York: Harper, 1922), 2: 261–262 and 254; Oakley, *Elizabeth Cady Stanton*, chapters 11 and 12; C.C.C. to Eileen T. Morrissey (March 4, 1933), LC P80-5458; Banner, *Elizabeth Cady Stanton*, chapters 7 and 8; also see Elizabeth Cady Stanton papers, LC P80-5300–P80-5304.

13. C.C.C. to Eileen T. Morrissey (March 4, 1933), LC 5458; Lutz, *Created Equal*, p. 316; Lutz, *Susan B. Anthony*, p. 278; Miriam Gurko, *The Ladies of Seneca Falls: The Birth of the Woman's Rights Movement* (New York: Macmillan, 1974), p. 282.

14. For example, see "Proceedings" of the 1893 Convention, pp. 41–53, "Suffrage: U.S." Collection, Box 6, folder 104, SSL.

15. Elizabeth Cady Stanton, *The Woman's Bible, Parts I and II* (1895; New York: Arno, 1972), 2: 115 and passim.

16. Ibid., pp. 10–11.

17. Lutz, *Created Equal*, chapter 25; Oakley, *Elizabeth Cady Stanton*, chapters 11 and 12; Paul E. Fuller, *Laura Clay and the Woman's Rights Movement* (Lexington: University of Kentucky Press, 1975), pp. 76–77; Lutz, *Susan B. Anthony*, pp. 278–280; Katharine Anthony, *Susan B. Anthony* (Garden City, N.Y.: Doubleday, 1954), p. 438; Susan B. Anthony to Elizabeth Cady Stanton (July 24, 1895) and Susan B. Anthony to Clara B. Colby (February 10, 1896), both letters quoted in Kraditor, *Ideas*, pp. 78–95; also see "Proceedings" of the 1896 Convention, pp. 91–96, "Suffrage: U.S." Collection, Box 6, folder 111, SSL. The vote against the Anthony–Stanton position was 53 to 41, which shows not only a fairly even division, but also the small size of N.A.W.S.A. conventions in those days.

18. Lutz, *Susan B. Anthony*, p. 274; Susan B. Anthony diary entry (November 7, 1895), quoted in Lutz, *Susan B. Anthony*, p. 274.

19. Kraditor, *Ideas*, p. 11.

20. Burnett, "Great Feminist," pp. 192–194; Walker, "Speeches," pp. 40–41; Minnie J. Reynolds, "Carrie Chapman Catt," *New Idea Woman's Magazine* 31 (November 1909).

21. C.C.C., speech, dedicating Bronze Tablet for Iowa Suffrage Pioneers in Capitol Building, Des Moines, Iowa (May 10, 1936), Catt Collection, Box 1, folder 14, SSL.

22. Peck, *Carrie Chapman Catt*, pp. 58–59; Burnett, *Five for Freedom*, pp. 278, 282, 285, 290, 291; Noun, *Strong-Minded Women*, p. 235.

23. Mary G. Peck, "Changing the Mind of a Nation: The Story of Carrie Chapman Catt," *World Tomorrow* 13 (September 1930): 358–361; Mary G. Peck, "Carrie Chapman Catt" (1943), for Woman's Rights Collection, RL; C.C.C. to Mary G. Peck (March 26, 1920), LC 8; Noun, *Strong-Minded Women*, pp. 41–54, 225, and 230–231; also see Catt, "Biographical Sketch," LC P80-5458.

24. C.C.C., speech, dedicating Bronze Tablet.

25. C.C.C. to Mrs. Quincy Shaw (January 1916), LCN 27.

26. Wiebe, *Search for Order;* Anne Firor Scott, "On Seeing and Not Seeing: A Case of Historical Invisibility," *Journal of American History* 71 (June 1984): 7–21.

27. Dorinda Riessen Reed, *The Woman Suffrage Movement in South Dakota* (Pierre, S.D.: State University of South Dakota, 1958), chapter 2; N.A.W.S.A. Convention, 1890, "Suffrage: U.S." Collection, Box 6, folder 104, SSL: Catt first appears; Peck, *Carrie Chapman Catt,* pp. 53–69; Noun, *Strong-Minded Women,* pp. 233–237.

28. Susan B. Anthony and Ida Husted Harper, *The History of Woman Suffrage: 1883–1900,* vol. 4 (New York: Arno, 1969), throughout; Peck, *Carrie Chapman Catt,* pp. 85–102; Alice Stone Blackwell, "Washington Notes," *Woman's Journal* 25 (February 24, 1894): 60; Helen Reynolds, "How Colorado Was Carried," *Woman's Journal* 24 (November 18, 1893): 361, 364–365; Helen Reynolds, "The Colorado Campaign," *Woman's Journal* 24 (October 7, 1893): 316; "The Washington Convention," *Woman's Journal* 27 (February 1, 1896): 33–34; Anthony, *Susan B. Anthony,* pp. 397, 418, and 425; "Conference with Mrs. Catt," *Woman's Journal* 30 (May 27, 1899): 164.

29. Many references to Catt appear in Blackwell's diaries by the late 1890s; see, for instance, July 24, 1897, and January 1, 1899, LCB 1.

NOTES TO CHAPTER 2

1. C.C.C. to Catharine W. McCulloch (July 24, 1899), Dillon Collection, Box 9, folder 235, RL.

2. Anthony and Harper, *History,* vol. 4, pp. 387–388; Walker, "Speeches," pp. 174–176; "The Washington Convention," *Woman's Journal* 31 (March 3, 1900): 67.

3. For example, Susan B. Anthony, "Proceedings" (1896), p. 66, "Suffrage: U.S." Collection, Box 6, folder 111, SSL.

4. Lutz, *Susan B. Anthony,* pp. 276–277 and 294; Clevenger, "Invention and Arrangement," p. 5; Flexner, *Century of Struggle,* p. 237.

5. Anthony, *Susan B. Anthony,* p. 502; C.C.C. to Alice Stone Blackwell (August 4, 1900), LCB 12.

6. Blackwell, "Washington Notes," *Woman's Journal* 31 (February 24, 1900): 60.

7. Lutz, *Susan B. Anthony,* p. 275; "The Washington Convention," *Woman's Journal* 31 (March 3, 1900): 66; Anthony, *Susan B. Anthony,* pp. 423 and 453; Susan B. Anthony to Catharine W. McCulloch (July 24, 1900), Dillon Collection, Box 8, folder 226, RL.

8. Anna Howard Shaw to Lucy Anthony (1900), Dillon Collection, Box 18, RL.

9. C.C.C. to Alice Stone Blackwell (August 4, 1900), LCB 12. Blackwell later explained that this was a factor in 1900 only and that Shaw and Catt generally got on much better both before and after this period, LCB 12.

10. Anna Howard Shaw, *The Story of a Pioneer* (New York: Harper, 1915), pp. 284–285.

11. Lutz, *Susan B. Anthony,* pp. 291–292; McHenry, *Liberty's Women,* p. 37; Sinclair, *Better Half,* p. 296; Walker, "Speeches," p. 5.

12. Sharon Hartman Strom, "Leadership and Tactics in the American Woman Suffrage Movement: A New Perspective From Massachusetts," in Jean E. Friedman and William G. Shade, ed., *Our American Sisters* (Boston: Allyn & Bacon, 1976), p. 267.

13. Mary G. Peck to Edna Stantial (February 28, 1951), LCN 24; Lutz, *Susan B. Anthony,* pp. 291–294; Fuller, *Laura Clay,* p. 81; "Proceedings" (1900), pp. 50–51, "Suffrage: U.S." Collection, Box 6, folder 115, SSL.

14. Susan B. Anthony to Catharine W. McCulloch (March 14, 1900), Dillon Collection, Box 8, folder 226, RL; Alice Stone Blackwell diaries (May 30, 1905), LCB 2. Catharine W. McCulloch's letters and notes from Business Committee meetings give a good sense of the early period of Catt's first presidency; see Dillon Collection, Box 9, RL; Elizabeth Cady Stanton to Susan B. Anthony (September 15, 1902), and other relevant materials, Stanton Papers, LC 5300–5304.

15. Susan B. Anthony, quoted in "The Washington Convention," *Woman's Journal* 33 (March 22, 1902): 91; Ida Husted Harper, ed., *The History of Woman Suffrage: 1900–1920,* vol. 6 (New York: N.A.W.S.A., 1922), pp. 459 and 800; Peck, *Carrie Chapman Catt,* pp. 122–123; Noun, *Strong-Minded Women,* p. 246.

16. "Mrs. Catt's Resignation," *Woman's Journal* 35 (February 6, 1904): 42; Walker, "Speeches," p. 182; Peck, "Carrie Chapman Catt," Woman's Rights Collection, 1943, RL; C.C.C. to Eileen T. Morrissey (March 4, 1933), LC 15; Anthony, *Susan B. Anthony,* pp. 476–477; Lisa Sergio, "Carrie Chapman Catt," WOV Radio (March 10, 1947), pp. 1–7, LC 15; Shaw, *Story of a Pioneer,* p. 287.

17. See Maud Wood Park, "The Row in The National" (1912), LCN 81; Abigail Duniway to Alice Stone Blackwell (December 12, 1913), LCN 10; James R. McGovern, "Anna Howard Shaw: New Approaches to Feminism," *Journal of Social History* 3–4, no. 2 (Winter 1969): 135–153; Anthony, *Susan B. Anthony,* p. 477; Shaw, *Story of a Pioneer,* pp. 230–231, 285–286, and 335–336; Flexner, *Century of Struggle,* pp. 268, 270–272; McHenry, *Liberty's Women,* p. 379; David Morgan, *Suffragists and Democrats: The Politics of Woman Suffrage in America* (East Lansing: Michigan State University Press, 1972), p. 84.

18. Anna Howard Shaw to Harriet Laidlaw (June 10, 1914), Laidlaw Collection, Box 7, folder 115, RL; Anna Howard Shaw to C.C.C. (March 6, 1914), LCN 27. Shaw had a similar set of problems during her World War I work as chair of the Woman's Committee of the Council of National Defense, though in that instance her service was better rewarded; see Wil A. Linkugel and Kim Griffin, "The Distinguished War Service of Dr. Anna Howard Shaw," *Pennsylvania History* 28 (October 1961): 372–385.

19. "Great Welcome to Mrs. Catt," *Woman's Journal* 43 (November 16, 1912): 361.

20. Shaw, *Story of a Pioneer,* p. 287; Peck, *Carrie Chapman Catt,* pp. 137–167 and 171–211.

21. "Mrs. Catt at the Helm," *Woman Voter* 1 (September 1910): 5; C.C.C., letter (September 26, 1910), LC P80-5453; also see articles relevant here: "Mrs. Catt Getting Better," *Woman's Journal* 41 (May 28, 1910): 85; "Mrs. Catt Doing Well," *Woman's Journal* 41 (June 11, 1910): 95; "Mrs. Catt Much Better," *Woman's Journal* 41 (July 9, 1910): 109; Walker, "Speeches," p. 191.

22. "Welcome Home to Mrs. Catt," *Woman Voter* 3 (December 11, 1912): 6 and 8.

23. Some of Catt's reports are: "The Victory in Denmark," *Woman's Journal* 39 (April 8, 1908): 61; "Mrs. Catt in Bohemia," *Woman's Journal* 40 (May 1, 1909): 72; "Some Suffrage Experiences Abroad," *Woman's Journal* 40 (July 10, 1909): 109; "Mrs Catt in Norway," *Woman's Journal* 42 (June 3, 1911): 169 and 171; "More About Mrs. Catt in South Africa," *Woman's Journal* 43 (January 13, 1912): 13–14; "The New China," *Woman's Journal* 43 (October 5, 1912): 314; "Mrs. Catt in Burmah," *Woman's Journal* 43 (July 13, 1912): 221; "Mrs. Catt Under Equator," *Woman's Journal* 42 (May 18, 1912): 157; "World Progress of Women," *Woman's Journal* 45 (June 20, 1914): 197; "The Latest Suffrage Victory," *Woman's Journal* 40 (January 2, 1909): 1.

24. Harper, *History,* vol. 5, p. 123; "Mrs. Catt Talks of State Tour," *Woman Voter* 6 (February 1915): 57–58; also see reports on Catt in *Woman's Journal* 36 (August 26, 1905): 135, 43 (February 21, 1914): 173, and 46 (December 11, 1915): 393; Noun, *Strong-Minded Women,* p. 248; Brown, "On Account of Sex" (ca. 1956), chapter 11, p. 2, SSL; C.C.C. to Harriet Laidlaw (October 8, 1912), Laidlaw Collection, Box 7, folder 101, RL; also see the extensive materials on the New York State campaigns in the "Suffrage: U.S." Collection, SSL.

25. Flexner, *Century of Struggle,* p. 272; C.C.C., *Woman Suffrage by Federal Constitutional Amendment* (New York: National Woman Suffrage, 1917), chapter 4.

26. Brown, "On Account of Sex," chapter 11, pp. 5–7; also see the assorted letters to Anna Howard Shaw expressing regret at her departure: Dillon Collection, Box 20, folder 472, RL.

27. Alice Stone Blackwell, notes regarding C.C.C. (1915), LCB 36; Harper, *History,* vol. 5, p. 456.

28. C.C.C. to Mary G. Peck (December 30, 1915), LC 7.

29. Zimmerman, "Alice Paul," p. 28.

30. C.C.C., "New York's Victory Convention," *Woman Citizen* 2 (December 1, 1917): 12; Flexner, *Century of Struggle,* p. 273; Inez H. Irwin, *Angels and Amazons: A Hundred Years of American Women* (1933; New York: Arno, 1974), pp. 370–373; Maud Wood Park, *Front Door Lobby* (Boston: Beacon, 1960), pp. 15–17; C.C.C., "Acknowledgements," *Woman Citizen* 1 (November 17, 1917): 469; C.C.C. and Nettie Rogers Shuler, *Woman Suffrage and Politics: The Inner Story of the Suffrage Movement* (New York: Scribner's, 1923), pp. 295 and 299.

31. C.C.C., *War Aims* (New York: N.A.W.S.A., 1918), pp. 1–16; Harper, *History,* vol. 6, p. 617; C.C.C., "Be Joyful Today," *Woman Citizen* 4 (February 21, 1920): 885.

32. Catt's own role is detailed in chapter 10, and the general conflict is discussed in chapter 7, of J. Stanley Lemons, *The Woman Citizen: Social Feminism in the 1920s* (Urbana: University of Illinois, 1973).

33. Peck, *Carrie Chapman Catt,* pp. 402–470, gives the overview.

34. C.C.C. to Gertrude Brown (February 28, 1946), Catt Collection, Box 4, folder 30, SSL. The best secondary source guide to Catt and pacifism is David H. Katz, "Carrie Chapman Catt and the Struggle for Peace" (Ph.D. dissertation, Syracuse University, 1973).

35. C.C.C., "Woman Organized for Peace," *Missionary Review of the World* 49 (August 1926): 631; C.C.C., speech, "The Price of Peace," Cause and Cure of War (February 14, 1935), Catt Collection, Box 1, folder 10, SSL.

36. C.C.C., "What Happened to the Treaties?" *Woman Citizen* (March, 1928): 22; C.C.C., "Dare to Do Right," *Woman Citizen* (June 18, 1921): 12; C.C.C., "While Europe Burns," *Woman Citizen* (July 28, 1928): 16.

37. C.C.C., speech, "Fourteen Points in My Faith for Permanent Peace" (May 25, 1925), Catt Collection, Box 1, folder 10, SSL.

38. C.C.C., "Elements in a Constructive Foreign Policy," *Annals of the American Academy of Political and Social Sciences* 132 (July 1927): 187–189; C.C.C., "Friction in International Opinion," *Annals of the American Academy of Political and Social Sciences* 126 (July 1926): 49–50; C.C.C., speech, Luncheon on Eighty-fifth Birthday (January 10, 1944), Catt Collection, Box 1, SSL; C.C.C. to Edna Gellhorn (August 18, 1927), Gellhorn Collection, folder 7, RL.

39. C.C.C., "Disarmament," *Missionary Review of the World* 54 (December 1931); C.C.C., "The Outgrown Doctrine of Monroe," *World Tomorrow* 9 (November 1926): 193–194; C.C.C., "What Is the Monroe Doctrine?" *Woman Citizen* 14 (March 1929): 12–13 and 46; C.C.C. "Friction in International Opinion."

40. The best original source guides to the Cause and Cure of War effort are in the Schain Collection, Box 5, RL, and LC 19.

41. Susan Becker, "International Feminism between the Wars: The National Woman's Party versus the League of Women Voters," in Lois Scharf and Joan Jensen, ed., *Decades of Discontent: The Women's Movement: 1920–1940* (Westport, Conn.: Greenwood, 1983), pp. 223–242.

42. Joan Jensen, "All Pink Sisters: The War Department and the Feminist Movement in the 1920s," in Scharf and Jensen, *Decades of Discontent,* pp. 199–222.

43. C.C.C. to Mary Anderson (May 7, 1945), Mary Anderson Collection, Box 2, folder 54, RL; see Woman's Centennial Congress documents in LC 20, 21, 23, and 24; Catt charged that Nazism was also repugnant because it was antifeminist in a radio speech, eighty-fifth birthday (January 10, 1944), Catt Collection, Box 1, folder 13, SSL.

44. Regarding the Protest Committee, see LC P80-5461; regarding the Committee of Ten, see Gellhorn Collection, Box 10, RL; C.C.C., speech, American Jewish Congress (March 30, 1938), Catt Collection, Box 1, folder 12, SSL; "Mrs. Catt Gets 1933 American Hebrew Medal," *New York Herald Tribune* 93 (November 24, 1933): 12; other materials relevant to C.C.C.'s award of the American Hebrew Medal are in Catt Collection, Box 1, folder 2, SSL.

45. Regarding the Women's Action Committee, see LC P80-5464; C.C.C., "An Action Program for Peace," *New York Times* (April 11, 1943), Catt Collection, Box 1, folder 9, SSL; C.C.C. to Margaret Corbett Ashby (April 9, 1945, and July 6, 1945), LCN 16; C.C.C. to Mary Anderson (May 1, 1943), Mary Anderson Collection, Box 2, folder 45, RL; C.C.C. to Hon. Champ Clark (March 5, 1943), Dillon Collection, Box 24, folder 586, RL.

46. My discussions of antisuffragist points here and elsewhere are based largely on my own reading in original materials, but I have also been influenced by the able Jane Jerome Camhi study, "Women Against Women," especially chapters 1 and 2.

47. "When You Double the Radical Vote, You Surrender Democracy's Front Line Trenches to Socialism," *Woman Patriot* 1 (May 11, 1918): 8; Margaret Robinson, "Suffrage and Socialism, The Kaiser's Allies," *Woman's Protest* 11 (February 1918): 10; Alice Wadsworth, "For Home and National Defense Against Woman Suffrage, Feminism and Socialism," *Woman Patriot* 1 (April 27, 1918): 7–9.

48. "Mrs. Catt and the Schwimmer Peace Plan," *Woman's Protest* 11 (October 1917): 10–11; "The First Suffrage 'War-Measure': Demanded Referendum on our Army in Austria to Defeat Draft," *Woman Patriot* 1–2 (August 10, 1918): 1–2. These are only two examples of a flood of articles and denunciations.

49. Some examples: "Shall Bolshevist-Feminists Secretly Govern America?" *Woman Patriot* 5 (January 1, 1921): 1–2; "Organizing and Financing Revolution," *Woman Patriot* 6 (August 15, 1922): 1–2; masthead, *Woman Patriot* 5 (January 1, 1921): "Germany Thanks Jane Addams," *Woman Patriot* 5 (August 15, 1921): 8; "The Suffrage-Socialist Alliance in Action: Is Nicolai Lenin Using the Suffragist Card Index?" *Woman Patriot* 4 (December 25, 1920): 5.

50. Lemons, *Woman Citizen*, chapter 8; C.C.C., "An Open letter to the D.A.R.," *Woman Citizen* 7 (July 1927): 10; C.C.C., "Lies At-Large," *Woman Citizen* 7 (June 1927): 10; C.C.C., "The Lie Factory," *Woman Citizen* 9 (September 20, 1924), LC P80-5457; "Mrs. Catt Assails D.A.R. 'Red-Hunt,' " *New York Times* (July 1, 1928), LC P80-5465; "D.A.R. Head Makes Reply to Mrs. Catt's Criticisms," *San Francisco Chronicle* (July 22, 1927), LC P80-5465; for the 1946 point, see Mrs. Raymond Burr to A. L. Miller (August 21, 1946), LC P80-5464.

51. C.C.C., speech, "Then and Now" (1939), LC 10; C.C.C. to Alice Blackwell (November 6, 1908), LC 4; C.C.C. to Edna Stantial (May 14, 1940), LC 9; C.C.C. to authors of *Victory* (August 18, 1940), LC P80-5455.

52. C.C.C. to Mary G. Peck (December 8, 1944), LC 8; C.C.C. to Mary G. Peck (April 20, 1943), LC 8.

53. "Women, Great Affairs," *Time* 7 (June 14, 1926): 8–9; also see, for example, "Too Many Rights," *Ladies Home Journal* 39 (November 1922): 31 and 168; "World Politics and Women Voters," *Woman's Home Companion* 47 (November 1920): 4; "The League of Women Voters," *Woman's Home Companion* 47 (May 1920): 4 and 152; "The Old Order Changeth," *Woman's Home Companion* 48 (July 1921): 24.

54. On the Woman's Centennial Congress, see "Fight Dictators, Mrs. Catt Pleads," *New York Times* 90 (November 26, 1940), and "Woman's Congress

Looks to Future," *New York Times* 90 (November 27, 1940); there are extensive internal documents relating to the Woman's Centennial Congress in LC P80-5462 and LC P80-5463; see C.C.C. to Josephine Schain, letters regarding the Woman's Centennial Congress, Schain Collection, Box 5, SSL.

55. See materials regarding Chi Omega Award (May 16, 1941) in LC 14.

56. Mary G. Peck to Caroline Slade (January 11, 1948), LCN 27; three of the many obituaries: *Newsweek* 29 (March 17, 1947): 59; *Nation* 164 (March 22, 1947): 330–331; *Time* 49 (March 17, 1947): 96; others are in LC P80-5458 and WRC, folder 39, RL.

NOTES TO CHAPTER 3

1. "Mrs. Carrie Chapman Catt — Constructive Decisionist," *Everyone's Magazine* 35 (November 1916): 640.

2. For example, see her 1912 journals on Java or her India and Burma diaries of 1912, LC 2; C.C.C. to Mary G. Peck (April 13, 1919), LC 8; C.C.C. to Mary G. Peck (April 26, 1910), LC 7; Peck, "Carrie Chapman Catt," for Woman's Rights Collection.

3. C.C.C., speech (March 20, 1905), LC 10; C.C.C., Baccalaureate speech, University of Wyoming (1921), LC P80-5466; C.C.C., "Miscellaneous Quotations," LC P80-5466.

4. Mary G. Peck to C.C.C. (February 6, 1929), LC 8.

5. Catt's letters, especially to Mary Peck (LC 7 and 8), are the best source on her assorted illnesses over the years as well as on her reactions to them; for the Hyde view see Clara Hyde to Mary G. Peck (March 17, 1918), LCN 24; for the South Dakota start, see Reed, *Woman Suffrage Movement in South Dakota*, pp. 46–47; also, Mary G. Peck, "Changing the Mind of a Nation: The Story of Carrie Chapman Catt," *World Tomorrow* 13 (September 1930): 360; for the 1920s see the Hyde–Peck Letters, LCN 24.

6. Anthony, *Susan B. Anthony*, pp. 403 and 500; "The Washington Convention," *Woman's Journal* 27 (February 1, 1896): 1; "Organization Committee's Report," *Woman's Journal* 27 (February 1, 1896): 37–40.

7. For instance, Brown, "On Account of Sex," chapter 7, p. 9.

8. Anna Howard Shaw to Lucy Anthony (October 31, 1917), Dillon Collection, Box 18, RL.

9. Mary G. Peck to C.C.C. (February 6, 1929), LC 8.

10. C.C.C. to Anna Howard Shaw (February 2, 1916), Dillon Collection, Box 20, folder 461, RL.

11. C.C.C. to Mary Hay (November 17, 1911), LC 5.

12. C.C.C. to Clara Hyde (November 1920), LC 6; C.C.C. to N.A.W.S.A. officers (Thanksgiving, 1920), Catt Collection, Box 4, folder 32, SSL.

13. Mary G. Peck to C.C.C. (January 19, 1912), LC 7; Mary G. Peck to C.C.C. (February 6, 1929), LC 8.

14. For example, C.C.C. to Mary G. Peck (June 15, 1912), LC 7; C.C.C. to Clara Hyde (April 10, 1910), LC 6.

15. On humor see C.C.C. to Mary G. Peck (October 18, 1915), LC 7; C.C.C. to Mary G. Peck (November 8, 1926), LC 8.

16. *Mrs. Carrie Chapman Catt and Charles City*, LC 16; C.C.C. to Mary G. Peck (October 23, 1917), LC 7; C.C.C. to Alice Stone Blackwell (August 4, 1900), LCB 12; Alice Stone Blackwell, diary (April 10, 1899), LCB 1; also see Schain Collection, Box 5, SSL.

17. C.C.C., "Too Many Rights," p. 168; C.C.C. to Catharine W. McCulloch (April 19, 1901), Dillon Collection, Box 9, folder 235, RL.

18. C.C.C. to Harriet Laidlaw (December 26, 1934), Laidlaw Collection, Box 7, folder 101, RL.

19. C.C.C. to Rose Powell (November 9, 1938, and February 2, 1935), Powell Collection, Box 2, folder 32, RL; C.C.C. to N.A.W.S.A. Board (November 4, 1946), Woman's Rights Collection, folder 41, RL. C.C.C. to N.A.W.S.A. Board (July 16, 1946), Box 4, folder 32, SSL.

20. See, for example, Alice Stone Blackwell diaries (March 19, 1903), LCB 2; (February 9–16, 1900), LCB 1; Blackwell, "Washington Notes," *Woman's Journal* 25 (February 24, 1894): 60; "Conference with Mrs. Catt, *Woman's Journal* 30 (May 27, 1899): 164; Blackwell, "Washington Notes," *Woman's Journal* 31 (February 24, 1900): 60; C.C.C. to Alice Stone Blackwell (August 4, 1900), LCB 12.

21. Anna Howard Shaw to Harriet Laidlaw (June 10, 1914), Laidlaw Collection, Box 7, folder 101, RL.

22. See, for example, Anna Howard Shaw diaries (February 15, 1908, and February 14, 1910), Dillon Collection, Box 20A, RL; Anna Howard Shaw to Lucy Anthony (April 27, 1888), Dillon Collection, Box 18, RL; Anna Howard Shaw to Harriet Laidlaw (June 10, 1914), Laidlaw Collection, Box 7, folder 115, RL; C.C.C. to Mary Anthony (March 25, 1943), Anderson Collection, Box 4, folder 88, RL.

23. C.C.C. to Anna Howard Shaw (February 2, 1916), Dillon Collection, Box 20, folder 461, RL.

24. See, for example, C.C.C. to Anna Howard Shaw (December 12, 1892; February 14, 1897; and February 15, 1905), Dillon Collection, Box 20, folder 461, RL; C.C.C. to Anna Howard Shaw (June 30, 1918, and February 2, 1916), Dillon Collection, Box 20, folder 461, RL. There are also many letters between Catt and Shaw in LCN 27, which yield a similar sense of their normal relationship as warm coworkers.

25. C.C.C. to Caroline Reilly (July 3, 1919), Catt Collection, Box 4, folder 29, SSL; C.C.C. to Mary Anderson (March 25, 1943), Anderson Collection, Box 4, folder 88, RL; C.C.C. to Mary Anderson (September 1, 1943, and September 21, 1943), Anderson Collection, Box 4, folder 90, RL.

26. Examples other than those to be mentioned include: C.C.C. to Edna Gellhorn (September 20, 1930), Collection A-113, folder 7, RL; C.C.C. to Gertrude Brown (July 18, 1945), Catt Collection, Box 4, folder 30, SSL; C.C.C. to Katharine Blake (May 21, 1941, and June 3, 1943), Catt Collection, Box 4, folder 29, SSL; C.C.C. to Mary Anderson (September 21, 1943), Anderson Collection, Box 4, folder 90, RL; C.C.C. to Mary Anderson (May 7, 1945), Anderson Collection, Box 2, folder 54, RL.

27. There are many letters between Hyde and C.C.C. in LC 6; Hyde's letters to Mary G. Peck make clear how close Hyde felt to C.C.C. (for example, February 17, 1929; October 23, 1918; June 26, 1922; and October 2, 1928), LCN 24.

28. Folders of correspondence between Catt and Schain in the 1930s are in the Schain Collection, Box 5, SSL.

29. See the Catt–Stantial letters in LC 9.

30. C.C.C. to Harriet Laidlaw (May 23, 1912, and January 4, 1926), Laidlaw Collection, Box 7, folder 101, RL.

31. Catt–Hooper correspondence is in LC 5.

32. C.C.C. to Maud Wood Park (February 17, 1947), Woman's Rights Collection, folder 41, RL.

33. Some of the best illustrations of Park to Catt are the following letters: July 15, 1918; April 30, 1918; and September 3, 1918, Catt Collection, Box 4, folder 39, SSL; for Catt to Park see the following examples: Easter, 1922; September 1, 1929; October 31, 1930; April 11, 1931; March 16, 1938; and August 10, 1945, Woman's Rights Collection, folder 41, RL; Park's poems to Catt are in Dillon Collection, Box 24, folder 586, RL; this is only the start of a truly voluminous correspondence over decades; many other letters are in the sources already cited here, as well as elsewhere in RL, SSL, and LCN 23.

34. There are a number of letters that reflect the strained relationship in the 1920s: for example, Rosika Schwimmer to C.C.C. (October 12, 1921; December 16, 1924; and December 12, 1925); there are also a number of letters reflecting a much warmer relationship beginning in the 1930s—they began with Rosika Schwimmer to C.C.C. (August 11, 1932); outside confirmation comes in letters such as C.C.C. to Elaine Sanders (August 22, 1936); for post–World War II citizenship developments, see LCN 27, the source for these letters also; a negative view of Schwimmer appears in Mary G. Peck to Edna Stantial (June 4, 1947), LCN 24.

35. On Wilson, see correspondence with and regarding Wilson (including the fact that she was co-executor of Catt's estate) in LC P80-5466 and LC P80-5455; also relevant is *The Blackwell Family, Carrie Chapman Catt, and the National American Woman Suffrage Association,* p. v; John William Leonard, ed., *Women's Who's Who of America* (New York: American Commonwealth Co., 1914), p. 891.

36. On Hay and on Hay and Catt, see "Mary Hay," in Edward T. James, *Notable American Women,* vol. 2 (Cambridge: Harvard University Press, 1972), pp. 163–165; Maud Wood Park, "Biographical Sketch — Mary G. Hay," Dillon Collection, Box 24, folder 592, RL; Maud Wood Park, "Supplementary Notes," LCN 55. Entry on Hay in LCN 55 is also helpful; for some references to Hay and N.A.W.S.A., see "Convention Proceedings," 1899, 1902, and 1917, "Suffrage: U.S." Collection, Box 6, SSL; Brown, "On Account of Sex," chapters 7 and 9, discusses Hay in New York State; letters detailing Hay's work in the Republican Party are in the Margaret Roberts Collection, Box 1, folders 9 and 10, RL.

37. Anna Howard Shaw to Harriet Laidlaw (September 29, 1916), Laidlaw Collection, Box 8, folder 133, RL.

38. Anna Howard Shaw to Mrs. Stewart (January 11, 1909), Dillon Collection, Box 18, RL; Anna Howard Shaw diary (March 26, 1903), Dillon Collection, Box 20A, RL.

39. Anna Howard Shaw to Mrs. Stewart (January 11, 1909), Dillon Collection, Box 18, RL.

40. Peck, *Carrie Chapman Catt*, pp. 110 and 436–437.

41. C.C.C. to Mary Hay (November 21, 1911), LC 5.

42. There are a good many letters between Hay and Catt, especially during 1911–1912 when Catt was abroad, in LC 5.

43. For Peck and the suffrage movement, see entry in LCN 69 and 81; also see Mary G. Peck to Helen Owens in Helen Owens Collection, Box 1, folder 13, RL; to get a sense of Peck, see her correspondence in LCN 24.

44. C.C.C. to Gertrude Brown (November 1, 1928), Catt Collection, Box 4, folder 30, SSL.

45. C.C.C. to Mary G. Peck (May 24, 1922); among many other Catt thank-you letters to Peck are January 9, 1937, and October 18, 1928, LC 8.

46. Mary G. Peck to C.C.C. (January 9, 1936), LC 8.

47. Mary G. Peck to C.C.C. (October 12, 1928), LCN 24.

48. Mary G. Peck to C.C.C. (1928), LCN 24.

49. Mary G. Peck to C.C.C. (October 21, 1928), LCN 24.

50. Mary G. Peck to C.C.C. (February 6, 1929), LC 8.

51. Mary G. Peck to C.C.C. (December 5, 1928), LCN 24.

52. Faderman, *Surpassing the Love of Men*, p. 16.

53. C.C.C. to Mary G. Peck (for example, February 26, 1925; August 30, 1926; and early 1928), LC 8.

54. C.C.C. to Mary G. Peck (September 23, 1929), LC 8.

55. See C.C.C. to Mary G. Peck (October 18, 1928, and late 1928), LC 8.

56. C.C.C. to Mary G. Peck (September 8, 1926), LC 8.

57. C.C.C. to Mary G. Peck (February 26, 1925), LC 8.

58. C.C.C. to Mary G. Peck (April 3, 1922), LC 8.

59. C.C.C. to Mary G. Peck (October 12, 1920), LC 8.

60. Faderman, *Surpassing the Love of Men*, pp. 16–18.

61. C.C.C., "Why I Have Found Life Worth Living," *Christian Century* 45 (March 29, 1928): 406–408; C.C.C., "Evolution — Fifty Years Ago: A Reminiscence," *Woman Citizen* 10 (July 11, 1925): 7–8, 29; C.C.C., *Then and Now* (New York: Leslie Woman Suffrage Continuing Committee, 1939), p. 22.

62. See Richard Hofstadter, *Social Darwinism in American Thought: 1860–1915* (New York: Braziller, 1959).

63. C.C.C., speech, National American Woman Suffrage Association (1902), p. 8, "Suffrage: U.S." Collection, Box 13, SSL.

64. For a thorough discussion of religion and the woman's rights movement in the nineteenth century, see Donna Behnke, *Religious Issues in Nineteenth Century Feminism* (Troy, New York: Whitston, 1982); also see "Menace of Feminism to Women and the Church," *Woman Patriot* 4 (June 12, 1920): 6; Catt's opponents did try to link her with religious radicalism, specifically the *Woman's Bible*, see LC P80-5465.

65. C.C.C., "Woman Suffrage and the Bible" (1890), Catt Collection, New York Public Library, cited in Kraditor, *Ideas*, pp. 88–89.

66. C.C.C., Ceylon and Burma diaries, LC 1 and LC 2; C.C.C. to Mary G. Peck (February 20, 1912), LC 7.

67. For example, C.C.C., "Women Organized for Peace," p. 631 and passim.

68. Arthur Mann, *Yankee Reformers in the Urban Age* (Cambridge: Harvard University Press, 1954), p. 147.

69. C.C.C., "Statement on the Proposed Equal Rights Amendment," *Congressional Digest* 22 (April 1943): 118.

70. Maud Wood Park on C.C.C. in "Remember the Ladies," Dillon Collection, Box 24, folder 586, RL.

71. For example, "Mrs. Catt's International Address," *Woman's Journal* 39 (June 27, 1908): 101–103; C.C.C., "What Every Senator Knows," *Woman Citizen* 2 (March 2, 1918): 263; C.C.C., "Convention Week in Albany," *Woman Voter* 7 (December 1916): 12; C.C.C., "Be Joyful Today," *Woman Citizen* 4 (February 21, 1920): 885; C.C.C., speech, U.S. Senate hearing (1900), LC 10; "Mrs. Catt's Tribute," *Woman's Journal* 40 (October 23, 1909): 171; "National-American Convention," *Woman's Journal* 25 (February 24, 1894): 58.

72. C.C.C., speech (June 12, 1921), LC 10.

73. C.C.C., "Evolution — Fifty Years Ago: A Reminiscence," *Woman Citizen* 10 (July 11, 1925): 7–8 and 29.

NOTES TO CHAPTER 4

1. Kraditor, *Ideas*, p. vii.

2. Kraditor, *Ideas;* Janet Zollinger Giele, "Social Change in the Feminine Role: A Comparison of Woman's Suffrage and Woman's Temperance: 1870–1920" (Ph.D. dissertation, Harvard University, 1961) especially pp. 109–146 and 210–233; also see the controversial view in William O'Neill, *Everyone Was Brave: The Rise and Fall of Feminism in America* (Chicago: University of Chicago, 1969).

3. Kraditor, *Ideas*, chapter 3; Giele "Social Change," pp. 178–179, 185, and 224–233.

4. C.C.C., "The Nation Calls," *Woman Citizen* 3 (March 29, 1919): 917–921; C.C.C., speech, Chicago School of Citizenship (1920), LC 10; C.C.C., speech, Woman's Centennial Congress (November 25, 1940), LC P80-5456; Eliza D. Armstrong, "What Are The Very Latest Suffrage Arguments?" *Woman's Protest* 6 (April 1915): 4; "How Has It Worked Where They Vote?" *Woman's Protest* 7 (May 1915): 9–10.

5. C.C.C., "Why New York Women Want to Vote," *Woman Voter* 6 (January 1915): 5.

6. C.C.C. to Everett P. Wheeler (October 26, 1915), LC 9; Camhi, "Women Against Women," chapter 3.

7. "Mrs. Catt Believes Women Should Continue in Chosen Career, Although Married," *Wichita Eagle* (November 29, 1933), LC 14.

8. Some of the innumerable critical comments here: Brooklyn Auxiliary New York State Association Opposed to the Extension of Suffrage to Women, "Copy of Preamble and Protest," in *Why Women Do Not Want The Ballot* (Massachusetts Association Opposed to Further Extension of Suffrage

to Women, 1903); Grace D. Goodwin, *Anti-Suffrage: Ten Good Reasons* (New York: Duffield and Co., 1912), chapters 5, 7, and 10; "Equal Suffrage and Equal Obligation," *Woman's Protest* 1 (July 1912): 4; Minnie Bronson, "How Suffrage States Compare with Non-Suffrage," *Woman's Protest* 4 (January 1914): 7–9; Lucy J. Price, "Why Wage Earning Women Oppose Suffrage," *Woman's Protest* 2 (January 1913): 7; "Laws of Suffrage and Non-Suffrage States Compared," *Woman's Protest* 1 (June 1912): 3.

9. For some sample critiques: "Petition Against the Child Labor Amendment," *Woman Patriot* 5 (May 15, 1921): 1–5; "Origin of the Children's Bureau," *Woman Patriot* 5 (August 15, 1921, and September 1, 1921); *Woman Patriot* 5 (October 15, 1921), entire issue devoted to denunciation of Sheppard-Towner Act.

10. C.C.C., "The Further Extension," *Woman Voter* 4 (May 1913): 17 and 20; C.C.C. to Everett P. Wheeler (October 24, 1915), LC 9; Mary G. Peck, "The Secretary Has Signed the Proclamation," in *Victory: How Women Won It*, p. 149.

11. See Jane Addams, "Women and Public Housekeeping," "Suffrage: U.S." Collection, Box 6, folder 121, SSL.

12. For an able, recent discussion of Jane Addams, see Anne Firor Scott, *Making the Invisible Woman Visible* (Urbana: University of Illinois Press, 1984), pp. 107–141; C.C.C., speech, Harrisburg, Pa. (March 7, 1916), pp. 16–17, Box 1, folder 2, SSL.

13. C.C.C., "Annual Address," N.A.W.S.A. (1902), Catt Collection, Box 1, folder 13, SSL.

14. For instance, Metta Folger Townsend, "Good Reasons for Opposition," *Woman's Protest* 3 (June 1913): 3; "Statement of the Illinois Association Opposed To The Extension Of Suffrage To Women," Brooklyn Auxiliary, "Copy of Preamble and Protest," Frances M. Scott, "Extension of the Suffrage to Women," and Priscilla Leonard, "A Help or A Hindrance?" all in *Why Women Do Not Want The Ballot;* Mrs. Simeon H. Guilford, "Woman's 'Emancipation' — From What?" *Woman's Protest* 7 (July 1915): 5; Helen Kendrick Johnson, "The End of Suffrage: A Social Revolution," *Woman's Protest* 7 (June 1915): 10–11; "Up-to-Date," *Woman Patriot* 1 (May 25, 1918): 4; "The Suffragist's Ideal of Womanhood," *Woman Patriot* 3 (August 23, 1919): 4–5.

15. Kraditor, *Ideas*, pp. 15, 24, and 41–42.

16. C.C.C. "Feminism and Suffrage" (1917), leaflet, Catt Collection, Box 1, folder 9, SSL.

17. C.C.C., "By Way of a New Beginning," *Woman Citizen* 5 (August 28, 1920): 329; C.C.C., "The Home and the Higher Education," *Woman's Journal* 33 (July 26, 1902): 234–235; C.C.C., "Woman's Place," *New York Herald Tribune* (August 22, 1914), in LC 14; C.C.C. to Everett P. Wheeler (October 24, 1915), LC 9; Anthony and Harper, *History*. vol. 4, p. 371; Lillian E. Taaffe, "Man's Superiority Complex Called Bar to Equal Rights," *Minneapolis Tribune* (November 8, 1923), LC 14.

18. Ellen DuBois, "The Radicalism of the Woman Suffrage Movement: Notes Toward the Reconstruction of Nineteenth-Century Feminism," *Feminist Studies* 3 (Fall 1975): 63–70.

19. For example, "Feminism and Insanity," *Woman Patriot* 3 (October 18, 1919): 8.

20. C.C.C., Oklahoma Report #2 (November 4, 1898), Catt Collection, RL.

21. Mrs. John B. Heron, "Feminism a Return to Barbarism," *Woman's Protest* 6 (April 1915): 5–6; "Men Becoming Effeminate," *Woman Patriot* 3–4 (March 20, 1920): 6; "God Give Us Men," *Woman Patriot* 3–4 (April 10, 1920): 3.

22. "Mrs. Catt's Address," *Woman's Journal* 30 (June 10, 1899): 178; "Mrs. Catt's Address," *Woman's Journal* 35 (February 20, 1904): 57–59, 61, and 64; C.C.C., speech (1903), LC P80-5456; C.C.C., *Woman Suffrage by Federal Constitutional Amendment,* pp. 89–91.

23. Mary A. J. M'Intire, "Of What Benefit To Woman?" in *Why Women Do Not Want The Ballot;* "Woman Suffrage, the Enemy of Good Government," *Woman Patriot* 3 (May 10, 1919): 8.

24. Catt was an environmentalist through and through; see, for example, "Annual Address," N.A.W.S.A. (1902), Catt Collection, Box 1, folder 12, SSL.

25. C.C.C., "God and the People" (1915), p. 2, LC 12.

26. C.C.C., "Our New Responsibilities," *Woman's Journal* 29 (October 1, 1898): 317.

27. "Giving Or Forcing?" *Remonstrance* (January 1914): 1; "Their Fundamental Error," *Woman's Protest* 8 (April 1916): 8–9; Marjorie Dorman, "Suffragists Traitors To Democracy," *Woman's Protest* 8 (December 1915); C.C.C., "Will of the People," *Forum* 43 (1910): 599; Goodwin, *Anti-Suffrage,* chapter 2.

28. For example, see Mrs. John B. Heron, "Why Suffragists Prefer to Face Legislatures Rather Than Voters-At-The-Polls," *Woman's Protest* 6 (January 1915): 8–9; "A Referendum To Women," *Woman's Protest* 10 (January 1917): 4, one of many calls for a vote by women.

29. C.C.C., "Two Systems," *Woman Citizen* 3 (June 29, 1918): 85; "Two Letters and Sunday Senators," *Woman Citizen* 2 (May 4, 1918): 445–446; C.C.C., "Forward March!" *Woman Citizen* 1 (September 22, 1917): 305–306; C.C.C., speech (1918), LC P80-5455; C.C.C., speech, "Woman Suffrage As A War Measure" (1918), LC 10; C.C.C., *War Aims,* pp. 1–16.

30. C.C.C. to Margery Corbett Ashby (April 9, 1945), Catt Collection, Box 4, folder 29, SSL.

31. C.C.C. to Katharine Blake (June 1, 1937), Catt Collection, Box 1, folder 29, SSL.

32. For example, C.C.C. "Surplus Women," *Woman Citizen* 6 (October 22, 1921): 12; "Mrs. Catt Tells View on War," *Woman's Journal* 45 (August 15, 1914): 234.

33. Mrs. J. T. Waterman, "Women and War," *Woman's Protest* 5 (September 1914): 5–6; C.C.C., speech, "Woman Suffrage Now Will Stimulate Patriotism," LC 10; C.C.C., speech, "Woman Suffrage As A War Measure" (1918); C.C.C., *Home Defense,* pp. 1–16.

34. For example, Elizabeth Cady Stanton to E.B.H., Dillon Collection, Box 2, folder 27, RL.

35. On Catt and rights, for example, see C.C.C., speech, "An Appeal for Liberty" (1915), LC 10; Harper, *History,* vol. 5, pp. 144–145; Clevenger, "Invention and Arrangement," p. 86; C.C.C., "Why Women Want to Vote,"

Woman's Journal 46 (January 9, 1915): 11; C.C.C., "Why New York Women Want to Vote," *Woman Voter* 6 (January 1915): 5.

36. Walker, "Speeches," pp. 282–286.

37. Harper, *History*, vol. 5, pp. 745–746; Anthony and Harper, *History*, vol. 4, p. 213; Clevenger, "Invention and Arrangement," p. 95.

38. C.C.C., "Too Many Rights," pp. 31 and 168.

39. C. H. Kent, "Arguments For Suffrage Weighed and Found Wanting in Logic and Justice," *Woman's Protest* 2 (February 1913): 3, 5, and 6; "No 'Natural Right' to Vote," *Woman Patriot* 1–2 (October 26, 1918): 7–8; Mrs. George P. White, "Taxation Without Representation — Misapplied," *Woman's Protest* 6 (February 1915): 8–9; Mrs. H. A. Foster, "Taxation and Representation," in *Why Women Do Not Want The Ballot*.

40. Kraditor, *Ideas*, chapter 2.

41. See Carl Degler, *At Odds: Women and the Family in America* (New York: Oxford University Press, 1980), pp. 352–361, for an interesting, alternative view on this issue; for a discussion in present day terms, see Jean Elshtain, "The New Porn Wars," *New Republic* 190 (June 25, 1984): 15–20.

42. C.C.C., "Feminism and Suffrage," leaflet (1917), Catt Collection, Box 1, folder 9, SSL.

43. For example, C.C.C., "Why New York Women Want to Vote," *Woman Voter* 6 (January 1915): 5, and "Mrs. Catt's Address," *Woman's Journal* 42 (July 15, 1911): 217, 219, and 239; C.C.C., *An Address to the Legislature of the United States* (New York: National American Woman Suffrage Publishing, 1919), pp. 1–23.

44. C.C.C., "Anti-Feminism in South America," *Current History Magazine* 18 (September 1923): 1034.

45. For example, regarding Lucy Stone, see Gurko, *Ladies of Seneca Falls*, p. 128.

46. C.C.C. to Hon. Gilbert Hitchcock (January 24, 1919), Catt Collection, Box 4, folder 37, SSL.

47. C.C.C., "Annual Address," N.A.W.S.A. (1902), Catt Collection, Box 1, folder 13, p. 9, SSL.

48. C.C.C., "The Cave Man Complex vs. Woman Suffrage," *Woman Citizen* 8 (April 5, 1924): 16–17.

49. Jill Conway, "Women Reformers and American Culture: 1870–1930," *Journal of Social History* 5 (Winter 1971–1972): 166–167.

50. Leonard, "A Help or A Hindrance?" in *Why Women Do Not Want The Ballot;* Goodwin, *Anti-Suffrage*, pp. 23 and 91–92; "Another Danger Demonstrated," *Women's Protest* 10 (November 1916): 8–9; Paul Morris, "The Feminine Viewpoint," *Woman Patriot* 3 (April 26, 1919): 8; "Women Competing With Men," *Woman Patriot* 3 (May 31, 1919): 4; Mary A. J. M'Intire, "Of What Benefit to Woman?," Frances M. Scott, "Extension of the Suffrage to Women," and Frances J. Dyer, "A Remonstrance," all in *Why Women Do Not Want The Ballot;* Mrs. George P. White, "Taxation Without Representation — Misapplied," *Woman's Protest* 6 (February 1915): 8; also see Camhi, "Women Against Women," pp. 25–47.

51. C.C.C., speech at National Executive Council, National American Woman Suffrage Association (December 19, 1915), LCB 36.

52. C.C.C., "Annual Address" (1902), p. 11.

53. C.C.C., "Bringing the Victors Home," *Woman Citizen* 5 (September 4, 1920): 362–363; C.C.C., speech, "What the Vote Will Do For the Woman" (1917), LC 13.

54. For example, C.C.C., "What the N.A.W.S.A. Has Done," *Woman Citizen* 3 (November 9, 1918): 487; "Mrs. Catt's Norwegian Maid," *Woman's Journal* 38 (June 22, 1907): 98; Anthony and Harper, *History*, vol. 4, p. 369.

55. "Mrs. Catt vs. Mrs. Meyer," *Woman's Journal* 39 (March 21, 1908): 48; Clevenger, "Invention and Arrangement," p. 224.

56. C.C.C., "A True Story," *Woman's Journal* 44 (January 25, 1913): 26; "Mrs. Catt Tells of Slave Traffic," *Woman's Journal* 44 (January 11, 1913): 16; "Mrs. Catt on Woman Traffic," *Woman's Journal* 44 (January 25, 1913): 32; "Mrs. Catt Tells of White Slaves," *Woman's Journal* 44 (February 1, 1913): 40; C.C.C., speech, "The Traffic in Women" (1899), LC 10; C.C.C., "The Traffic in Women," *Women Voter* 4 (March 1913): 14–15; "Mrs. Catt and Mrs. Barry," *Woman's Journal* 41 (November 12, 1910): 204.

57. C.C.C., "Too Many Rights," p. 31; C.C.C., "Will of the People," p. 601.

58. C.C.C., speech, Harrisburg, Pa. (March 7, 1916), p. 10, Catt Collection, Box 1, folder 2, SSL.

59. C.C.C., *An Address to the Legislature of the United States* (1919), pp. 1–5 and 20; C.C.C., *An Address to the Congress of the United States* (New York: National American Woman Suffrage Publishing, 1917), pp. 1–7 and 19–21.

60. C.C.C., "An Address to the Congress of the United States" (December 13, 1917), in Walker, "Speeches," pp. 331–347; C.C.C., *Home Defense*, p. 14; "Mrs. Catt Scents State Victory," *Woman's Journal* 47 (September 9, 1916): 289; C.C.C., *An Address to the Legislature of the United States*, pp. 1–23; C.C.C., "Will of the People," pp. 595–599; "By No Means 'Sure To Come,' " *Remonstrance* (April 1914): 1; C.C.C. to Margaret Roberts (August 16, 1915), Margaret Roberts Collection, Box 4, folder 4, RL.

61. C.C.C., "The Crisis," *Woman's Journal* 47 (September 16, 1916): 299 and 301–303.

NOTES TO CHAPTER 5

1. C.C.C. to Mary G. Peck (October 15, 1910), LC P80-5453.

2. C.C.C., speech (March 7, 1916), Harrisburg, Pa., Catt Collection, Box 1, SSL.

3. For example, see Alice Stone Blackwell on Catt regarding the danger of referenda, LCB 36.

4. C.C.C. to Margaret Roberts (January 23, 1918), Margaret Roberts Collection, Box 1, RL.

5. C.C.C., "Annual Address" to N.A.W.S.A. (1904), Catt Collection, Box 1, folder 13, SSL.

6. C.C.C. to Helen B. Owens (November 19, 1915), Helen B. Owens Collection, Box 4, folder 37, RL.

7. C.C.C., "Are You A Normal?" (1924), LC 12; C.C.C., speech, Suffrage Committee of the Senate of the United States (1900), LC 10; see Taaffe, "Man's Superiority Complex," *Minneapolis Tribune* (November 8, 1923), LC 14; Katz, "Carrie Chapman Catt and the Struggle for Peace," p. 174.

8. Anthony and Harper, *History,* vol. 4, p. 274; C.C.C., speech, "College Women As Citizens," *Arrow* 38 (June 1922): 613–620.

9. "Mrs. Catt's Address," *Woman's Journal* 35 (February 20, 1904): 61; "Mrs. Catt's Address," *Woman's Journal* 42 (July 15, 1911): 217–219; C.C.C., "We the People," *Woman Citizen* 7 (December 2, 1922): 14; C.C.C., "College Women," pp. 613–620.

10. Mary G. Peck to C.C.C. (February 6, 1929), LC 8.

11. C.C.C. to Mary G. Peck (October 23, 1917), LC 7.

12. "Mrs. Carrie Chapman Catt — Constructive Decisionist," *Everybody's Magazine* 35 (November 1916): 640.

13. C.C.C. to Mary G. Peck (April 23, 1918), LC 7.

14. Park, *Front Door Lobby,* p. 212.

15. "Mrs. Catt Describes New York Opposition," *Woman's Journal* 46 (November 13, 1915): 361.

16. For example, C.C.C. and Shuler, *Woman Suffrage,* pp. 331–333; "Mrs. Catt's Address," *Woman's Journal* 35 (February 20, 1904): 57–59, 61, and 64; Walker, "Speeches," pp. 288–305; C.C.C., speech, "On the Inside" (February 14, 1920), LC 10.

17. C.C.C., speech, Pan-Hellenic Program, New York World's Fair (July 13, 1939), p. 4, Catt Collection, Box 1, SSL.

18. For example, C.C.C. to Catharine W. McCulloch (November 24, 1916), Dillon Collection, Box 9, folder 235, RL.

19. Wiebe, *Search for Order,* p. 164.

20. C.C.C. to Charles Curtis (January 15, 1919), LC 4.

21. "Catt on Suffrage Foes," *Woman's Journal* 44 (May 24, 1913): 166; "Mrs. Catt Makes Stirring Speech," *Woman's Journal* 44 (May 24, 1913): 161 and 163.

22. C.C.C., speech (March 7, 1916), pp. 11–14; Camhi, "Women Against Women," pp. 1–2.

23. C.C.C. to Anna Howard Shaw (March 7, 1916), LC 8; C.C.C. and Shuler, *Woman Suffrage,* chapter 10.

24. C.C.C., "Statement," Committee on Judiciary, United States House of Representatives (1904), p. 19, Catt Collection, Box 1, folder 13, SSL.

25. C.C.C. to Catharine W. McCulloch (July 24, 1899), Dillon Collection, Box 9, folder 235, RL; on the general subject of suffrage and Prohibition, see Paulson, *Women's Suffrage and Prohibition.*

26. C.C.C., "Liquor and Law," *Woman Citizen* 13 (October 1928): 10–11 and 47–48; C.C.C., "If Not Prohibition, What?" (ca. 1931), LC 12; C.C.C., speech, "Observance and Enforcement — Not Repeal," LC 12; C.C.C., "Page Horatio!" LC 12; C.C.C., speech (August 26, 1926), LC 10; "Mrs. Catt Describes New York Opposition," *Woman's Journal* 46 (November 13, 1915): 361.

27. O'Neill, *Everyone Was Brave,* pp. 71–75.

28. "The White Woman's Peril at Washington," *Woman Patriot* 3 (July 12, 1919): 4; "Where Black and White Women Vote," *Woman Patriot* 3 (August 16, 1919): 2–3; "The Vote of 2,000,000 Negro Women," *Woman's Protest* 4 (April 1914): 16; Mrs. Walter D. Lamar, "The Menace of Suffrage In the South," *Woman's Protest* 5 (July 1914): 5–7.

29. "Letter from Mrs. Catt," *Woman's Journal* 32 (March 16, 1901): 82; C.C.C. and Shuler, *Woman Suffrage,* p. 46; C.C.C., speech, "The Nation Calls," *Woman Citizen* 3 (March 29, 1919): 917–921.

30. Elinor Lerner, "Working-class and Immigrant Involvement in the New York Woman's Suffrage Movement," paper, Mid-South Sociological Association (1980).

31. C.C.C., "The Nation Calls."

32. C.C.C. and Shuler, *Woman Suffrage,* pp. 44 and 42; C.C.C., "The Nation Calls"; C.C.C., "The Parting of the Ways" (1903), LC 12; Harper, *History,* vol. 5, pp. 90–91; Alice Stone Blackwell quotes Catt in 1915 in LCB 36.

33. C.C.C., "The Parting of the Ways" (1903), LC 12.

34. C.C.C., speech, Suffrage Committee of the United States Senate (1900), pp. 1–7, LC 10; C.C.C., "The Nation Calls." From the beginning, plans for the League of Women Voters reflected a commitment to education; see *Minutes of the Jubilee Convention* (New York: N.A.W.S.A., 1919), p. 37.

35. Wiebe, *Search for Order,* pp. 212–214.

36. This conclusion regarding socialists is central to the entire argument of Aileen Kraditor, *The Radical Persuasion: 1890–1917* (Baton Rouge: Louisiana State University Press, 1981).

37. For example, C.C.C., "Let's Talk It Over," *Good Housekeeping* 86 (March 1928): 56.

38. Rosalyn Terborg-Penn, "Discontented Black Feminists: Prelude and Postscript to the Passage of the Nineteenth Amendment," in Scharf and Jensen, *Decades of Discontent,* pp. 261–278.

39. "Letter from Mrs. Catt," *Woman's Journal* 32 (March 16, 1901): 82; "Comparisons are Odious," referred to in "National American Convention," *Woman's Journal* 24 (January 28, 1893): 26; Goldman, *Rendezvous With Destiny,* p. 63.

40. C.C.C., speech (June 15, 1908), LC 10; "Mrs. Catt's Address," *Woman's Journal* 35 (February 20, 1904): 57 and 59.

41. Buhle and Buhle, *Concise History,* p. 312.

42. For example, C.C.C. to Adella Hunt Morgan, Dillon Collection, Box 9, folder 235, RL.

43. A. Elizabeth Taylor, *The Woman Suffrage Movement in Tennessee* (New York: Bookman, 1957), p. 117.

44. Alice Stone Blackwell, notes on 1903 Convention, LCB 2.

45. C.C.C. to Elizabeth Blackwell (August 4, 1900), in Sinclair, *Better Half,* p. 294.

46. Mary G. Peck to Maud Wood Park (July 2, 1943), LCN 24; Riegel, *American Women,* p. 300.

47. "Mrs. Catt's Address," *Woman's Journal* 34 (April 25, 1903): 133; Harper, *History,* vol. 5, p. 83.

48. C.C.C. to Mary G. Peck (August 15, 1920), LC 8.

49. C.C.C., "Votes For All: A Symposium," *Crisis* (November 1917): 19–21.

50. A good late expression of her views is in the "Tentative Draft of Purpose of the Woman's Centennial Congress of 1940," LC P80-5462.

51. C.C.C., "Are You A Normal?" (1924), LC 12.

52. See Anthony and Harper, *History*, vol. 4, p. 371.

53. C.C.C., "Forward March," *Woman Citizen* 1 (September 22, 1917): 305–306; "A Bourgeois Movement, *Woman Citizen* 1 (July 7, 1917): 99.

54. C.C.C., "Our Outlook," *Woman Voter* 2 (January 1911): 2–3.

NOTES TO CHAPTER 6

1. C.C.C., "Party Clean ups Are the Crying Need," *Woman Citizen* 16 (April 1931): 15 and 30; C.C.C., "The Direct Primary Under Fire," *Woman Citizen* 5 (May 7, 1921): 1210 and 1218; C.C.C., "Longer and Calmer Terms," *Woman Citizen* 9 (June 28, 1924): 14; C.C.C., speech, "One Growing Menace" (1925), LC 12; C.C.C., "Shall the People Amend?" *Woman Citizen* 9 (December 27, 1924): 16; "N.E. Suffrage Festival," *Woman's Journal* 30 (June 10, 1899): 177–178; C.C.C., "Wanted: A New Department," *Woman Citizen* 5 (January 8, 1921): 861–862.

2. C.C.C., "Baccalaureate Address" (July 16, 1921), LC 10.

3. C.C.C., "A Million New York Women Want To Vote," *Woman Voter* 6 (November 1915): 8; C.C.C., "A Cincinnati 'Research Magnificent,' " *Woman Citizen* 2 (March 16, 1918): 313; Peck, *Carrie Chapman Catt*, p. 120; Buhle and Buhle, *Concise History*, pp. 32–33.

4. Graham, *Great Campaigns*, p. 157.

5. C.C.C., speech (1904), LC 10; C.C.C., editorials, *Woman Citizen* 5 (January 8, 1921; January 15, 1921; and January 29, 1921); C.C.C., "New York's Victory Convention," *Woman Citizen* 1 (December 1, 1917): 12; Harper, *History*, vol. 5, pp. 698–699; "Mrs. Catt Makes Stirring Speech," *Woman's Journal* 44 (May 24, 1913): 161 and 163; C.C.C., "Citizenship" (1920), LC 10.

6. "Mrs. Catt's Course at $200,000,000 A Year," *Woman Patriot* 5 (January 22, 1921): 9.

7. The best discussion is by Lawrence Cremin, *The Transformation of the School: Progressivism in American Education 1876–1957* (New York: Knopf, 1961).

8. Ibid., chapters 2–5.

9. Ida Clyde Clarke, *American Women and the World War* (New York: D. Appleton, 1918), chapter 9.

10. For example, Hugh S. Magill to C.C.C. (April 28, 1920), Catt Collection, Box 4, folder 38, SSL.

11. C.C.C., "Address for a Better America" (early 1920s), Catt Collection, Box 1, folder 15, SSL.

12. See the complete "Citizenship Course," Catt Collection, Box 2, folders 20–21, SSL.

13. "The 'Diabolical Trickery' of a Professional Woman Politician," *Woman Patriot* 2 (March 15, 1919): 2–3 and 5.

14. C.C.C., "The Bookshelf," *Woman Citizen* 7 (September 23, 1922): 28; C.C.C. to Mary G. Peck (December 13, 1911), LC 7.

15. C.C.C., "On the Inside," *Woman Citizen* 4 (March 6, 1920): 945–948; C.C.C., "Citizenship" (1920), LC 10.

16. J. Stanley Lemons, "The New Woman in the New Era: The Woman Movement from the Great War to the Great Depression" (Ph.D. dissertation, University of Missouri, 1967), p. 174; Mary G. Peck to Mrs. Halsey Wilson (October 29, 1940), LCN 24; C.C.C., speech (February 14, 1920), LC 10.

17. C.C.C. to Harriot S. Blatch (August 16, 1924), LC 4; C.C.C. to Mary G. Peck (October 15, 1918), LC 7; C.C.C., "Woodrow Wilson," *Woman Citizen* 8 (February 9, 1924): 14.

18. C.C.C., "Warren G. Harding," *Woman Citizen* 8 (August 11, 1923): 14; Katz, "Carrie Chapman Catt and the Struggle for Peace," pp. 91–99.

19. For the Wadsworth story, see Martin L. Fausold, *James W. Wadsworth, Jr.: The Gentleman from New York* (Syracuse, N.Y.: Syracuse University Press, 1975), especially chapters 7 and 8, and pp. 141–142; also see, for extensive literature on the anti-Wadsworth campaigns, "Suffrage: U.S." Collection, Box 15, folder 224, SSL.

20. C.C.C., radio speech (November 2, 1932), LC 10.

21. Mary G. Peck to Mrs. Halsey Wilson (October 29, 1940), LCN 24; see "President Called Greatest of Men," *New York Times* 84 (January 8, 1935): 19.

22. C.C.C., speech (January 10, 1944), LC 10.

23. C.C.C., speech, Chi Omega Award (May 16, 1941), LC 11.

24. C.C.C., speech (March 26, 1930), LC 10.

25. Alec Barbrook and Christine Bolt, *Power and Protest in American Life* (New York: St. Martin's, 1980), p. 207.

26. For example, C.C.C. to Chairs of Ratification Committees (April 24, 1919), Margaret Roberts Collection, Box 1, folder 7, RL.

27. See the 1920 N.A.W.S.A. Convention Program, "Suffrage: U.S." Collection, Box 6, folder 104, SSL.

28. Maud Wood Park, "National League of Women Voters — First Year," Dillon Collection, Box 24, folder 596, RL.

29. Peck, *Carrie Chapman Catt*, p. 326; Park, "National League of Women Voters — First Year"; Clara Hyde to Mary G. Peck (February 20, 1920), LCN 24.

30. C.C.C., speech, "The Nation Calls," *Woman Citizen* 3 (March 29, 1919): 917–921; "Board of the National League of Woman Voters," *Woman Citizen* 4 (February 28, 1920): 919; Maud Wood Park, "National League of Women Voters — Second Year, Third Year, Fourth Year," Dillon Collection, Box 24, folder 596, RL; McHenry, *Liberty's Women*, p. 314.

31. "The Suffrage Sex Party," *Woman Patriot* 3 (May 3, 1919): 6; "The Case Against the League of Women Voters," *Woman Patriot* 6 (February 15, 1922): 4–6.

32. C.C.C., speech, "The Nation Calls," *Woman Citizen* 3 (March 29, 1919): 917–921; C.C.C., speech (February 14, 1920), LC 10; C.C.C., "The Hope of the Founders" (1930), LC 10; C.C.C., speech (March 26, 1930), LC 10; Lem-

ons, "New Woman," pp. 84, 141, 189, 203, and 205; C.C.C., "Whose Government Is This?" *Woman Citizen* 6 (July 30, 1921): 8 and 16; C.C.C., "The League of Women Voters," *Woman's Home Companion* 47 (May 1920): 4 and 152.

33. Catt's absence from most League activities is obvious in L.W.V. materials from that era; see Dillon Collection, Box 24, folder 596, RL.

34. Lemons, "New Woman," pp. 249–253 and 181, and chapter 6.

35. Maud Wood Park, speech (ca. 1927), Dillon Collection, Box 24, folder 600, RL.

36. C.C.C., statement (April 10, 1919), LCN 84.

37. C.C.C., speech, "On the Inside" (February 14, 1920), LC 10; Peck, *Carrie Chapman Catt*, p. 325; C.C.C., "Partisans or Non-Partisans" (January 28, 1921), LC 10; C.C.C. to Edna Gellhorn (January 6, 1920), Gellhorn Collection, folder 7, RL.

38. Lemons, "New Woman," pp. 154 and 139; C.C.C., "Women Voters at the Crossroads" (1919), LC 10.

39. Anne Martin, "Feminists and Future Political Action," *Nation* 120 (February 18, 1925): 185–186; Lemons, "New Woman," pp. 83–84 and 152–153.

40. C.C.C., "Who's Scared," *Woman Citizen* 6 (January 28, 1922): 12–13.

NOTES TO CHAPTER 7

1. Wiebe, *Search for Order*, pp. 145–151 and 123; for other full-scale treatments of the organizational dynamic at work then, see Weinstein, *Corporate Ideal in the Liberal State;* James Gilbert, *Designing the Industrial State* (Chicago: Quadrangle, 1972); Martin Schiesl, *The Politics of Efficiency: Municipal Administration and Reform in America* (Berkeley: University of California Press, 1977).

2. Anne Firor Scott, "On Seeing and Not Seeing," p. 9.

3. See Karen J. Blair, *The Clubwoman as Feminist: True Womanhood Redefined: 1868–1914* (New York: Holmes and Meier, 1980), p. 15 and chapters 2 and 6; Paulson, *Women's Suffrage and Prohibition;* Epstein, *Politics of Domesticity;* Bordin, *Woman and Temperance.*

4. Kraditor, *Ideas*, p. 13.

5. Anthony and Harper, *History*, vol. 4, pp. 248–249.

6. C.C.C. to Rachel B. Ezekiel, LCN 39.

7. C.C.C., "The Crisis," *Woman's Journal* 47 (September 16, 1916): 301; "Mrs. Catt's Counsel," *Woman's Journal* 47 (January 1, 1916): 4; "Mrs. Catt on the National Campaign," *Woman's Journal* 47 (March 11, 1916): 86; Sinclair, *Better Half*, p. xxiv; "The Atlanta Convention," *Woman's Journal* 26 (February 9, 1895): 41; Alice Stone Blackwell, notes on 1915, LCB 36.

8. Catt and Shuler, *Woman Suffrage and Politics*, p. 109; Anthony and Harper, *History*, vol. 4, pp. 256–257; Morgan, *Suffragists and Democrats*, p. 98; Barbrook and Bolt, *Power and Protest*, chapter 5.

9. C.C.C., "Organizational Committee Report," *Woman Journal* 27 (February 1, 1896): 40.

10. Peck, *Carrie Chapman Catt,* p. 129; C.C.C. and Shuler, *Woman Suffrage and Politics* develops this theme throughout.

11. See "Proceedings," 1895 Convention, especially pp. 21–28, "Suffrage: U.S." Collection, folder 110, SSL; "Proceedings," 1896 Convention, pp. 39–51, "Suffrage: U.S." Collection, folder 111, SSL; "Proceedings," 1897 Convention, pp. 37–41, "Suffrage: U.S." Collection, folder 112, SSL; "Proceedings," 1898 Convention, pp. 30–34, "Suffrage: U.S." Collection, folder 113, SSL.

12. Most illuminating are Catt's Oklahoma reports: "Contributions to Oklahoma work #1" (October 15, 1898), "#2" (November 4, 1898), and "#3" (December 7, 1898), Collection AC 368, RL. State-by-state material relevant to the broader effort before as well as during Catt's era in the N.A.W.S.A. may be found in the "Suffrage: U.S." Collection, SSL, and alphabetically arranged in LCN.

13. C.C.C., "Proceedings," 1900 Convention, "Suffrage: U.S." Collection, folder 115, SSL.

14. On previous effort, see, for example, "Annual Report of the New York State Woman Suffrage Association" (1898), LCN 21; on the Woman Suffrage Party, see Elinor Lerner, "Working-class and Immigrant Involvement in the New York Woman Suffrage Movement" (Paper delivered to Mid-South Sociological Association, 1980), "Suffrage: U.S." Collection, Box 15, folder 221, SSL; Ronald Schaffer, "The New York City Woman Suffrage Party," *New York History* 43 (July 1862): 270.

15. On the Empire State Campaign Committee and New York State Woman Suffrage Party, see: "Annual Report of the New York State Woman Suffrage Association" (1915), especially pp. 14–15, "Suffrage: U.S." Collection, folder 225, SSL; Gertrude Foster Brown, "On Account of Sex" (c. 1956), "Suffrage: U.S." Collection, Box 10, SSL; Schaffer, "New York City Woman Suffrage Party," p. 280; generally, see "New York State Suffrage Associations," LCN 21.

16. Mary G. Peck, "Changing the Mind of a Nation: The Story of Carrie Chapman Catt," *World Tomorrow* 13 (September 1930): 360.

17. The Catt–Helen Owens collection gives a good view of this level; see especially C.C.C. to Helen Owens (March 3, 1914, September 23, 1914, and April 22, 1915), Helen B. Owens Collection, Box 2, RL; Helen B. Owens to C.C.C. (April 13, 1914), Helen B. Owens Collection, Box 2, RL; C.C.C. to Helen B. Owens (November 6, 1913), Helen B. Owens Collection, Box 1, RL; also see Maud Wood Park, "Remember the Ladies," chapter 5, Dillon Collection, Box 24, folder 592, RL.

18. Tax, *Rising of the Women,* pp. 170–176; Lerner, "Working-class and Immigrant Involvement," pp. 4 and 9; Brown, "On Account of Sex," chapters 7 and 9; Schaffer, "New York City Woman Suffrage Party," pp. 274–275.

19. A good example is in the Marjorie Shuler to C.C.C. letters on Oklahoma in 1918, Catt Collection, Box 4, folder 41, SSL; also see state-by-state files in "Suffrage: U.S." Collection, Boxes 12–16, SSL.

20. There are many relevant letters here. Among the most valuable are: C.C.C. to Maud Wood Park (March 20, 1918; June 20, 1918; July 2, 1918; July 9, 1918; October 24, 1918), Catt Collection, Box 4, folder 33, SSL; Maud Wood Park to C.C.C. (October 25, 1918 and November 21, 1918),

Catt Collection, Box 4, folder 33, SSL; C.C.C. to Mabel Willard (August 1, 1918 and August 19, 1918), Catt Collection, Box 4, folder 29, SSL; C.C.C. to Maud Wood Park (ca. 1918), LCN 23.

21. Catt's famous "Plan" for her second presidency: C.C.C., "Report: Campaign and Survey Committee" (1916), LCN 82; also see Maud Wood Park to Inez Haynes Irwin (March 1933), Dillon Collection, folder 588, RL; Maud Wood Park, "Congressional Work for Nineteenth Amendment," Dillon Collection, folder 588, RL; Maud Wood Park, speech (January 9, 1939), Dillon Collection, Box 24, folder 586, RL; also Alice Stone Blackwell (Executive Committee notes, 1915), LCB 36.

22. C.C.C. to Alice Stone Blackwell (September 15, 1920), LC 4.

23. C.C.C. and Shuler, *Woman Suffrage and Politics*, pp. 130–131.

24. See, for instance, Alice Stone Blackwell's diaries, which report on these committee meetings — for example, LCB 1 for the June 10, 1902, meeting. For Catt's second presidency, see C.C.C., "Report: Campaign and Survey Committee" ("The Plan") (1916), LCN 82, it makes clear her goal of centralization.

25. C.C.C., "National Organizational Report," *Woman's Journal* 28 (February 6, 1897): 42; C.C.C. to Maud Wood Park (April 13, 1917), LC 7; C.C.C., speech, Woman's Centennial Congress (November 25, 1940), LC P80-5456; Harper, *History*, vol. 6, p. 470; C.C.C., "How to Win: Plan of the 1917 Campaign," *Woman Voter* 5 (November 1914): 12–13; Park, *Front Door Lobby*, p. 105; C.C.C. and Shuler, *Woman Suffrage and Politics*, p. 343, Catt's "ratification notebook," LC P80-5466; for a good illustration of Catt at work in a late campaign, see Reed, *Woman Suffrage Movement in South Dakota*, p. 106ff.; also see Alice Stone Blackwell's notes on National Executive Committee (1915), LCB 36.

26. Park, "Remember the Ladies," Dillon Collection, Box 24, folder 586, RL.

27. For her emphasis on organizers in plans for Catt's second presidency, see Marjorie B. Shuler to C.C.C. (November 13, 1916), LCN 27.

28. Annie Dougherty, "The National Suffrage School," *Woman Voter* 8 (May 1917): 17; K. R. Fisher, "Mrs. Catt's Suffrage School," *Woman's Journal* 44 (October 4, 1913); 318; C.C.C., "School for Suffrage Workers," *Woman Voter* 4 (September 1913): 8–9; see chapter 6 for a more extensive discussion of Suffrage Schools and their successors, the Citizenship Schools.

29. Wiebe, *Search for Order*, p. 149; Hays, *Response to Industrialism*, chapter 3.

30. On paid employees, see C.C.C., speech, "The Inheritance of the Woman Movement" (April 14, 1938), pp. 3 and 30, Catt Collection, Box 1, folder 14, SSL; also see discussion in LCN 36.

31. See Epstein, *Politics of Domesticity*, and Bordin, *Woman and Temperance*.

32. Gerda Lerner, *The Majority Finds Its Past: Placing Women in History* (New York: Oxford University Press, 1979), pp. 147 and 149–158.

33. Brown, "On Account of Sex," chapter 7, p. 9.

34. C.C.C., speech, "Be Joyful Today" (February 13, 1920), LC 10.

35. Oreola Williams Haskell, *Banner Bearers: Tales of the Suffrage Campaign* (Geneva, N.Y.: W. F. Humphrey, 1920), p. 3.

36. Kraditor, *Ideas,* p. 8; one recent state-level study is Carole Nichols, *Votes and More for Women: Suffrage and After in Connecticut* (New York: Haworth, 1983).

37. C.C.C., statement (May 21, 1915), LC P80-5459; C.C.C. and Shuler, *Woman Suffrage and Politics,* pp. 266 and 296; C.C.C. to Mary G. Peck (December 15, 1910), LC 7; C.C.C., speech (1920), LC 10; C.C.C., *How to Work for Suffrage in an Election District or Voting Precinct* (New York: National American Woman Suffrage Publishing, 1917), pp. 1 and 10–13; C.C.C., "The New York Party," *Woman's Journal* 41 (February 19, 1910): 30–31; C.C.C., "Organize Yourself," *Woman Citizen* 7 (December 16, 1922): 14.

38. "National Conference of Business Women," *Woman Citizen* 1 (July 21, 1917): 139; Clevenger, "Invention and Arrangement," p. 142.

39. Reed, *Woman Suffrage Movement in South Dakota,* p. 43; also see A. Elizabeth Taylor, *The Woman Suffrage Movement in Tennessee* (New York: Bookman, 1957), p. 108.

40. "Letter from Mrs. Catt," *Woman's Journal* 32 (March 16, 1901): 82.

41. Burnett, *Five for Freedom,* pp. 286–287.

42. Catt's ability to generate publicity is recorded in numerous newspaper articles on her appearances; see Catt Collection, Box 1, folder 6, SSL.

43. C.C.C. and Shuler, *Woman Suffrage and Politics,* p. 131; for example, C.C.C. to Alice Moreau (September 13, 1920), LC 7.

44. For many of Rose Young's press releases, see LCN 84; C.C.C. to Millicent G. Fawcett (October 19, 1909), LC 5; Rose Young to C.C.C. (November 14, 1916), LCN 36. On the need for someone to do publicity, see, for instance, C.C.C. to National Board of Directors (April 11, 1916), LCN 22.

45. See 1917 Catalogue, "Suffrage: U.S." Collection, Box 7, folder 119, SSL; many leaflets and flyers are also in Box 7, folder 122; Box 7 also has a good number of the N.A.W.S.A. pamphlets.

46. A couple of examples of her involvement in this side of organization: C.C.C. to Business Committee (March 20, 1901), Dillon Collection, Box 9, folder 235, RL; C.C.C. to Margaret Roberts (March 20, 1918), Margaret Roberts Collection, Box 1, folder 6, RL.

47. The Alice Stone Blackwell papers make this clear, as do her diaries; see, for example, LCB 2.

48. Some of the relevant correspondence: Alice Stone Blackwell to National Board (April 11, 1910); Alice Stone Blackwell to Catharine W. McCulloch (September 29, 1912; November 9, 1912; July 21, 1912); Alice Stone Blackwell to "Dear Friends" (May 1912) — all in Dillon Collection, Box 8, folder 231, RL; Anna Howard Shaw to C.C.C. (November 29, 1915), LCN 27.

49. Alice Stone Blackwell notes Catt's approval regarding the *Woman's Journal* in her notes on the 1916 Convention, LCB 36; Blackwell comments on the *Woman Citizen* and her association with it in LCB 2; Brown, "On Account of Sex," chapter 19, p. 5; Clara Hyde to Mary G. Peck (April 26, 1917), LCN 24, reflects the mood of those who celebrated getting the *Woman's Journal* out of Blackwell's firm grip.

50. C.C.C., "Christmas Shopping Exchange," *Woman's Journal* 26 (November 9, 1895): 354; C.C.C., "Beautiful Woman Suffrage Calendars," *Woman's Journal* 27 (December 19, 1896): 401.

51. For example, C.C.C. to Catharine W. McCulloch (August 25, 1899), Dillon Collection, Box 9, folder 235, RL; C.C.C. to Organization Committee, Collection AC 368, RL.

52. C.C.C. to Business Committee (July 19, 1900), Dillon Collection, Box 9, folder 235, RL; C.C.C. to Harriot Stanton Blatch (February 22, 1898), LC 4; C.C.C. to Mary G. Peck (October 7, 1914), LC 7; C.C.C. and Shuler, *Woman Suffrage and Politics,* p. 107; Gertrude Foster Brown, "A Decisive Victory Won," in *Victory,* p. 112.

53. C.C.C. to Margaret Roberts (February 13, 1919), Margaret Roberts Collection, Box 1, folder 7, RL.

54. Mary G. Peck to Caroline Slade (January 15, 1950), LCN 27.

55. References to her giving, for example, are in Harper, *History,* vol. 6, pp. 46 and 682.

56. For the fight over the Leslie bequest, see LCN 58 and 59; for the will, see Harper, *History,* vol. 5, p. 755.

57. "A Serious Accusation," *Woman Patriot* 3 (April 26, 1919): 6; "Mrs. Catt Compromises Leslie Fund," *Woman Patriot* 5 (January 29, 1921): 7.

58. "Leslie Woman Suffrage Commission — Statement of Receipts and Disbursements," Collection A113, folder 11, RL.

59. Rose Young, *The Record of the Leslie Woman Suffrage Commission, Inc.* (New York: Leslie Woman Suffrage Commission, Inc., 1929), makes this clear.

60. C.C.C., "Proceedings," 1900 Convention, p. 4, "Suffrage: U.S." Collection, Box 6, folder 115, SSL.

61. C.C.C., speech, "The Inheritance of the Woman Movement," pp. 42–43, Catt Collection, Box 1, folder 14, SSL.

NOTES TO CHAPTER 8

1. C.C.C. to Millicent G. Fawcett (June 18, 1912), LC 5.

2. Anthony and Harper, *History,* vol. 4, p. 249.

3. As she told Alice Paul, for instance; see Amelia R. Fry, interviewer, *Conversations with Alice Paul: Woman Suffrage and the Equal Rights Amendment* (Berkeley: University of California Press, 1976), p. 77.

4. C.C.C., speech (June 12, 1921), LC 10.

5. C.C.C., "Organizational Committee Report," *Woman's Journal* 29 (March 12, 1898): 82.

6. Anthony and Harper, *History,* vol. 4, p. 289; a typical 1917 report on Catt's optimism is in Alice Stone Blackwell, LCB 36.

7. Maud Wood Park, "Remember the Ladies," Dillon Collection, Box 24, folder 586, RL.

8. C.C.C., "If We Win In New York," *Woman's Journal* 6 (October 30, 1915): 345.

9. Mary G. Peck, "Carrie Chapman Catt," WRC, RL; Park, *Front Door Lobby,* p. 14; Noun, *Strong-Minded Women,* pp. 236–237; see Alice Stone Blackwell, LCB 36; for another early example: "National-American Convention," *Woman's Journal* 25 (February 24, 1894): 57–58.

10. See discussion in "Proceedings," 1900, p. 57, "Suffrage: U.S." Collection, Box 6, folder 115, SSL.

11. C.C.C. to Maud Wood Park (January 18, 1916), LCN 23.

12. C.C.C. to Clara Hyde (March 1915), LC 6.

13. Flexner, *Century of Struggle,* pp. 281–282.

14. Herbert Croly, *The Promise of American Life* (New York: Macmillan, 1909), pp. 27–51.

15. For example, C.C.C. to Business Committee (August 3, 1900), Dillon Collection, Box 9, folder 235, RL; C.C.C. "Business Committee Reports" (1900); headquarters newsletters (1915–1917), "Suffrage: U.S." Collection, Box 7, folder 124, SSL.

16. Some quite standard examples: C.C.C. to Maud Wood Park (February 9, 1919), Dillon Collection, Box 24, folder 586, RL; C.C.C. to Maud Wood Park (June 24, 1919), Dillon Collection, Box 24, folder 600, RL; C.C.C. to Assembly district leaders (December 6, 1915), Owens Collection, Box 4, folder 37, RL; C.C.C. to Vira Whitehouse (November 5, 1917), Whitehouse Collection, Box 1, folder 2, RL.

17. C.C.C. to Mary G. Peck (June 10, 1915), LC 7; Clevenger, "Invention and Arrangement," p. 61.

18. C.C.C. to Edna Stantial (August 13, 1917), LC 9; letters from C.C.C. to Ima Clevenger (June 1, 1945; June 25, 1945; and July 19, 1940), in Clevenger, "Invention and Arrangement," pp. 76–77.

19. For Peck's analysis see Mary G. Peck to C.C.C. (December 13, 1911), LC 7.

20. Praise is everywhere; for example, Anthony and Harper, *History,* vol. 4, pp. 187, 213, and 246, and Harper, *History,* vol. 5, p. 583; Clevenger, "Invention and Arrangement," pp. 70–76, and Walker, "Speeches," pp. 4–6.

21. Harper, *History,* vol. 5, p. 522.

22. Walker, "Speeches," pp. 344, 411, and 430 and chapter 6; Clevenger, "Invention and Arrangement," pp. 123, 72, 103, 107, 229, and 324–325.

23. Robert E. Reigel, *American Feminists* (Lawrence: University of Kansas Press, 1963), p. 178; C.C.C., "Journal" (September 27–October 31, 1912), LC 2; Walker, "Speeches," p. 65.

24. Peck, "Carrie Chapman Catt."

25. Ibid.

26. Alice Stone Blackwell quotes Catt (1915), LCB 36.

27. C.C.C., "Are You a Normal?" (1924), LC 12; "Mrs. Catt's Counsel," *Woman's Journal* 47 (January 1, 1916): 4; Marjorie Shuler, "Preserves vs. Politics" (1934), LC P80-5459.

28. Park, "Remember the Ladies," Dillon Collection, Box 24, folder 586, RL.

29. C.C.C. to Mary G. Peck (February 2, 1916), LC 7; "Mrs. Catt's Counsel," *Woman's Journal* 47 (January 1, 1916): 4; C.C.C. to Mary G. Peck (February 5, 1911), LC 7; Shuler, "Preserves vs. Politics" (1934), LC P80-5459; C.C.C., "National Organization Report," *Woman's Journal,* 28 (February 6, 1897): 42–43; C.C.C. to Clara Hyde (February 18, 1911), LC 6.

30. Walker, "Speeches," pp. 406–414; Maud Wood Park, "More 'Rampant Women,' " LC P80-5458; C.C.C., *Then and Now*, p. 21.

31. For example, C.C.C. to Business Committee (January 22, 1901), Dillon Collection, Box 9, folder 235, RL.

32. C.C.C. to Josephine Schain (July 15, 1926), Schain Collection, Box 5, SSL.

33. For example, C.C.C., "National Organization Report," *Woman's Journal* 28 (February 6, 1897): 42–43; C.C.C. to Anna Howard Shaw (March 7, 1916), LC 8; C.C.C. to Anna Howard Shaw (February 1, 1916), LC 8; C.C.C. to Anna Howard Shaw (March 16, 1916), LC 8; Alice Stone Blackwell, diary entry (March 24, 1903), LCB 2; C.C.C. to Abigail Duniway (March 14, 1895), in Moynihan, *Rebel for Rights*, p. 194.

34. The quote is from Mary G. Peck to Edna Stantial (February 28, 1951), LCN 24; also see Clara Hyde to Mary G. Peck (September 26, 1917), LCN 24, and the following entries in Alice Stone Blackwell's diaries: February 16, 1900; September 2, 1900; September 3, 1900; June 2, 1901; and March 23, 1903 — all in LCB 1 and 2; also see chapter 3 for a more detailed discussion of Catt and Hay.

35. See Alice Stone Blackwell notes on Catt in LCB 36.

36. C.C.C. to Catharine W. McCulloch (October 2, 1899), Dillon Collection, Box 9, folder 235, RL.

37. Harper, *History*, vol. 5, p. 569; C.C.C. to Mary G. Peck (September 26, 1921), LC 8; Peck, "Carrie Chapman Catt."

38. C.C.C. to Maud Wood Park (April 18, 1933), LC 7.

39. Reed, *Woman Suffrage Movement in South Dakota*, p. 41.

40. C.C.C. to Mrs. Nicholas Shaw Fraser (January 17, 1916), LC 5.

41. "Miscellaneous Quotations," LC P80-5456.

42. Flexner, *Century of Struggle*, pp. 274–275; Walker, "Speeches," pp. 71–72; C.C.C., speech, Chi Omega Award (May 16, 1941), LC 14; C.C.C. to N.A.W.S.A. Board Members (1941), LC 7; C.C.C. to Maud Wood Park (November 19, 1943), LC 7.

43. Young, *Record of the Leslie Woman Suffrage Commission*, p. 37; C.C.C. to Mary G. Peck (April 26, 1910), LC 7; Park, *Front Door Lobby*, p. 15; "Miscellaneous Quotations," LC P80-5456; C.C.C. to Rosika Schwimmer (October 22, 1921), LC 8.

44. C.C.C. to Anna Howard Shaw (February 2, 1916), Dillon Collection, Box 20, folder 461, RL.

45. Anthony and Harper, *History*, vol. 4, pp. 392–393; "Mrs. Catt Sees Coming Victory," *Woman's Journal* 47 (September 9, 1916): 289; C.C.C., "Preparedness, War and Suffrage," *Woman's Journal* 47 (November 4, 1916): 354; C.C.C., "National Organization Campaign," *Woman's Journal* 26 (April 27, 1895): 132.

46. "Miscellaneous Quotations," LC P80-5456; C.C.C. to Maud Wood Park (April 19, 1943), LC 7; C.C.C. to Elizabeth Hauser (March 11, 1947), LC; C.C.C., "An Experience" (July 11, 1912), LC P80-5455; C.C.C., speech (June 12, 1921), LC 10; Shuler, "Preserves vs. Politics," LC P80-5459.

47. Walker, "Speeches," pp. 57 and 431; Park, "More 'Rampant Women,' " LC P80-5458.

48. Catt, speech (June 6, 1921), LC 10; C.C.C. to Anna Howard Shaw (June 22, 1916), LC 8; Shuler, "Preserves vs. Politics," LC P80-5459.

49. For example, Maud Wood Park, "How I Came to Start My Work for Woman Suffrage," p. 5, Dillon Collection, Box 24, folder 600, RL.

50. Peck, *Carrie Chapman Catt*, p. 96.

51. Ibid.

52. Park, *Front Door Lobby*, p. 277.

53. Flexner, *Century of Struggle*, pp. 273–274; Walker, "Speeches," pp. 66–67.

54. Catt, speech (June 12, 1921), LC 10; C.C.C., speech, Woman's Centennial, Congress (November 25, 1940), LC P80-5456; Mary G. Peck to C.C.C. (February 6, 1929), LC 8.

55. O'Neill, *Everyone Was Brave*, p. 125.

56. C.C.C., "Baccalaureate Address" (1921), LC 28.

57. C.C.C. to Clara Hyde (November 1920), LC 6.

NOTES TO CHAPTER 9

1. C.C.C. to Ethel M. Smith (August 3, 1917), LC 8.

2. C.C.C. in "Proceedings" (1919), p. 418, LCN 84.

3. As they often were. See, for example, Abigail Duniway to Alice Stone Blackwell (December 12, 1913), LCN 10.

4. C.C.C. to Jane Addams (December 14, 1914), LC 4; Zimmerman, "Alice Paul and the National Woman's Party," p. 245.

5. C.C.C. to Jane Addams (November 12, 1915), LC 4.

6. Riegel, *American Women*, p. 290; Marie Louise Degen, *The History of the Woman's Peace Party* (1939; New York: Burt Franklin's Reprints, 1974), pp. 36 and 30; Mercedes M. Randall, *Improper Bostonian: Emily Greene Balch* (New York: Twayne, 1964), pp. 162 and 138; Barbara J. Steinson, *American Women's Activism in World War I* (New York: Garland, 1982), chapters 1 and 3; also see Steinson for "Minutes of the Peace Parade Committee" (August 12, 1914), p. 10; O'Neill, *Everyone Was Brave*, p. 174.

7. "The Flag," *Woman's Protest* 9 (October 1916): 3; "The Suffragist Peace Fiasco," *Woman's Protest* 7 (July 1915): 6–7; "Peace of Politics," *Woman's Protest* 6 (March 1915): 4; "For Woman's Service or Woman Suffrage?" *Woman's Protest* 10 (March 1917): 8; Alice Hill Chittenden, "Our Duty to the State," *Woman's Protest* 10 (April 1917): 3; "Questions for Mrs. Catt To Answer," *Woman's Protest* 11 (September 1917): 16; Grace Goodwin, 'Anti-Suffrage,' p. 142.

8. C.C.C. to Executive Council (February 5, 1917), LCN 82.

9. Harper, *History*, vol. 5, pp. 722–730 and 517; C.C.C., "Organized Womanhood," *Woman Voter* 8 (April 1917): 9; Lemons, "The New Woman," pp. 27–28.

10. Steinson, *American Women's Activism*, pp. 237–240 and 308–312; "Third Liberty Loan Drive," *Woman Citizen* 2 (March 30, 1918): 355; also see Mary Sumner Boyd, "The Menace to War Workers," *Woman Citizen* 1 (June 9, 1917): 31, for a characteristic expression of concern for mobilized women.

11. "Mrs. Catt Urges Big Drive For More Food," *Woman's Journal* 48 (April 14, 1917): 85–86; Lemons, "The New Woman," p. 26; Peck, *Carrie Chapman Catt*, pp. 270–272; Ida Tarbell, *All In The Day's Work* (New York: Macmillan, 1939), pp. 320–327; Katz, "Carrie Chapman Catt and the Struggle for Peace," pp. 41 and 44–45; Steinson, *American Women's Activism*, pp. 313–315.

12. Margaret Robinson, "Woman Suffrage and Pacifism," *Woman Patriot* 1 (April 27, 1918): 3; Margaret Robinson, "Germany's Strongest Allies," *Woman Patriot* 1 (July 6, 1918): 4; "Woman's Suffrage To Please Germans Is Now Urged By Suffrage Leaders," *Woman Patriot* 1 (September 14, 1918): 1; "Is Suffrage Pro-German?" *Woman Patriot* 1 (October 26, 1918): 3; "How Pro-Germans and Pacifists Carried Suffrage In New York," *Woman's Protest* 11 (November 1917): 4–5.

13. "Mrs. Catt and the Schwimmer Peace Plan," *Woman's Protest* 11 (October 1917): 10–11; "Suffragists Have No Part in This War," *Woman Patriot* 1 (July 13, 1918): 4; "Mrs. Catt's Defamation of Her Country," *Woman Patriot* 4 (June 19, 1920): 6; "War Record of Mrs. Carrie Chapman Catt," *Woman Patriot* 1 (November 16, 1918): 3 and 5; "Unscrupulous Suffrage Leaders Playing Politics Without Stint Limit with Council of Defense," *Woman Patriot* 1 (October 12, 1918): 1; "Mrs. Catt Again Attacks the Government," *Woman Patriot* 3 (December 27, 1919): 3.

14. C.C.C. to Maud Wood Park (April 13, 1918), LC P80-5453; Harper, *History*, vol. 5, p. 736; Steinson, *American Women's Activism*, pp. 319–320.

15. C.C.C., speech, "Woman Suffrage As A War Measure" *Woman Citizen* 3 (June 1918), and other speeches on the same theme, see LCN 83.

16. "Suffrage 'As A War Measure,' " *Remonstrance* (October 1917): 7; "Is Suffrage A War Measure?" *Woman Patriot* 1 (September 28, 1918): 4; "Suffrage vs. Patriotism," *Woman's Protest* 11 (May 1917): 5.

17. Hofstadter, *Age of Reform*, p. 275.

18. For example, C.C.C., statement, Committee on Judiciary, House of Representatives (1904), p. 19, Catt Collection, Box 1, folder 13, SSL.

19. "The Plan" was in C.C.C.'s "Report: Campaign and Survey Committee" (1916), LCN 82.

20. Morgan, *Suffragists and Democrats*, chapters 6 and 7.

21. C.C.C., "Report: Campaign and Survey Committee" (1916), p. 32, LCN 82.

22. Ibid., pp. 1–2 and passim; C.C.C., *Woman Suffrage by Federal Constitutional Amendment*, pp. 6–7, 35, and passim; C.C.C., speech, "The Crisis" (September 7, 1916), "Suffrage: U.S." Collection, Box 6, folder 117, SSL.

23. C.C.C., "Report: Campaign and Survey Committee" (1916), pp. 34–35, LCN 82.

24. Morgan, *Suffragists and Democrats*, p. 112; C.C.C. to Ida H. Harper (October 14, 1921), LC 5; Irwin, *Angels and Amazons*, p. 372; Buhle and Buhle, *Concise History*, p. 38; also see Alice Blackwell's report on Catt's calculations in LCB 36.

25. C.C.C., *An Address to the Legislature,* pp. 19–22; C.C.C., *An Address to the Congress,* pp. 8, 17, and 19.

26. See "Handbook" and "Proceedings," 1916 Convention.

27. See, for example, Anna Howard Shaw to C.C.C. (July 1916 [two letters] and September 1916), LCN 27; Anna Howard Shaw to C.C.C. (January 4, 1916), LCN 27.

28. C.C.C. to Sue White (May 16, 1918), Sue White Collection, Box 2, folder 21, RL; Kraditor, *Ideas,* p. 173; Clay went last — see Fuller, *Laura Clay,* chapter 9, and the 1919 N.A.W.S.A. Convention "Proceedings," pp. 13–27, LCN 84; also see Dewey W. Grantham, *Southern Progressivism: The Reconciliation of Progress and Tradition* (Knoxville: University of Tennessee Press, 1983), pp. 200–217.

29. C.C.C., *An Address to the Legislature,* pp. 1–23.

30. Amelia R. Fry, interviewer, *Conversations with Alice Paul: Woman Suffrage and the Equal Rights Amendment* (Berkeley: University of California Press, 1976), section I, RL.

31. Ibid., pp. 96 and 106–107.

32. McHenry, *Liberty's Women,* pp. 28, 37–38, 272, and 319–320; Zimmerman, "Alice Paul and the National Woman's Party," p. 40; Caroline Katzenstein, *Lifting the Curtain* (Philadelphia: Dorrance, 1955), pp. 165–200; Inez Haynes Irwin, *The Story of the Woman's Party* (1921; New York: Harcourt, Brace, 1971), p. 12 and Part 1, chapter 5; Harper, *History,* vol. 5, pp. 380–381; Penelope P. B. Huse, "Appeals to Congress," in *Victory,* p. 103; Anna H. Shaw, "Tells of the Stand of the Union," *Woman's Journal* 45 (February 14, 1914): 54; also see *Woman's Journal* throughout 1913 and 1914 (vols. 44–45) on the Congressional Union; Sinclair, *Better Half,* pp. 300–304; Irwin, *Angels and Amazons,* p. 357; C.C.C. and Shuler, *Woman Suffrage and Politics,* p. 255; Inez H. Irwin to Maud Wood Park (March 14, 1921), LCN 17.

33. Anna Howard Shaw to Harriet Laidlaw (August 16, 1917), Laidlaw Collection, Box 8, folder 137, RL.

34. Ibid.

35. See, for example, Anna H. Shaw to Rosamond Danielson (March 11, 1914) and Anna H. Shaw to C.C.C. (October 14, 1916, and March 12, 1916), all in LCN 27.

36. Alice Stone Blackwell to C.C.C. (September 4, 1929), LCB 12; by the 1930s, however, Blackwell and Alice Paul were corresponding fairly regularly; see LCN 23.

37. Fry, *Conversations with Alice Paul,* pp. 96–98.

38. Zimmerman, "Alice Paul and the National Woman's Party," chapter 3 and p. 65; Sinclair, *Better Half,* pp. 303–304; C.C.C. to Harriet Laidlaw (May 23, 1912), Laidlaw Collection, Box 7, folder 101, RL; Fry, *Conversations with Alice Paul,* p. 324.

39. Anna Howard Shaw to Harriet Laidlaw (June 5, 1915), Laidlaw Collection, Box 7, folder 101, RL.

40. Paul claimed that Catt announced no compromise was possible; Fry, *Conversations with Alice Paul,* pp. 202–203.

41. For example, Sue White to C.C.C. (April 27, 1918; May 9, 1918; and May 16, 1918), Sue White Collection, Box 2, folder 21, RL.

42. C.C.C. to Mrs. Leslie Warner (April 24, 1918), Sue White Collection, Box 2, folder 21, RL; C.C.C. to Maud Wood Park (December 11, 1918), Catt Collection, Box 4, folder 33, RL.

43. C.C.C. to Sue White (July 20, 1918), Sue White Collection, Box 2, folder 21, RL.

44. C.C.C. to Clara Hyde (May 29, 1911), LC 6; Flexner, *Century of Struggle*, p. 287; C.C.C., "Their First Convention" (1920), LC P80-5456; Sinclair, *Better Half*, p. 330.

45. C.C.C. to Sue White (May 6, 1918), Sue White Collection, Box 2, folder 21, RL.

46. Catt, "Report: Campaign and Survey Committee" (1916), p. 30.

47. Rose Young to C.C.C. (August 8, 1916), LCB 36.

48. Susan B. Anthony to Alice Stone Blackwell (June 14, 1872), LCB 9, in which she enunciates the classic position that Catt followed.

49. C.C.C. to Jane Addams (January 4, 1915), LC 4.

50. C.C.C. to Joseph Tumulty (January 19, 1917), LC 9; C.C.C. and Shuler, *Woman Suffrage and Politics*, chapter 11; Harper, *History*, vol. 5, p. 714; C.C.C. to Joseph Tumulty (May 3, 1918), LC 9; C.C.C., statement (May 21, 1915), LC P80-5459; Morgan, *Suffragists and Democrats*, chapters 9 and 10; Grace Sample McClure to Alda Wilson (March 20, 1947), LC 9; Park, *Front Door Lobby*, is the fullest account.

51. C.C.C., "The Suffrage Platform," *Woman's Journal* 46 (June 12, 1915): 184; C.C.C., "If We Win in New York," *Woman's Journal* 46 (October 30, 1915): 345; C.C.C., "Opening of the Convention," *Woman Citizen* 2 (December 15, 1917): 54.

52. C.C.C., "Opening of the Convention," p. 54.

53. C.C.C., "What Every Senator Knows," *Woman Citizen* 2 (March 2, 1918): 263; C.C.C. to Maud Wood Park (April 18, 1933), LC 7; C.C.C. and Shuler, *Woman Suffrage and Politics*, pp. 327–328.

54. Fry, *Conversations with Alice Paul*, pp. 209–241.

55. C.C.C., "Why We Did Not Picket the White House," *Good Housekeeping* 66 (March 1918): 32.

56. C.C.C. to Mary G. Peck (April 20, 1913), quoted in Peck, *Carrie Chapman Catt*, p. 210.

57. C.C.C. to Alice Paul, quoted in Zimmerman, "Alice Paul and the National Woman's Party," pp. 238–239.

58. C.C.C., "Excuses Only," *Woman Citizen* 1 (August 11, 1917): 179.

59. "Militant Methods In Action," *Woman's Protest* 10 (November 1916): 5–6; "Organized Obtrusion for a Campaign of Clamor," *Woman's Protest* 9 (July 1916): 3; "Pickets Determine to Persecute President," *Woman Patriot* 1 (August 3, 1918): 1; "Recent Militant Freaks," *Remonstrance* (October 1913): 1; "More Proof that 'Pickets and Conservative' Suffragists Have a 'Mutual Working Agreement,' " *Woman Patriot* 2 (January 4, 1919): 8; "Do American

Suffragists Favor Militancy?" *Woman's Protest* 4 (December 1913): 12; "Picketing and 'Pestering,' " *Woman Patriot* 1 (August 24, 1918): 8.

60. See, for example, C.C.C., "Pickets Are Behind the Times," *Woman Citizen* 1 (November 1917): 470; Zimmerman, "Alice Paul and the National Woman's Party," p. 243; 50,000 is undoubtedly too high a figure for the Woman's Party; so is two million for the N.A.W.S.A. But the proportions are roughly correct.

61. C.C.C. to Sue White (May 6, 1918), Sue White Collection, Box 2, folder 21, RL.

62. C.C.C. to Millicent G. Fawcett (October 19, 1909), LC 5; C.C.C. to E. Garrison (August 1, 1914), quoted in Riegel, *American Feminists*, p. 178; "Mrs. Catt's International Address," *Woman's Journal* 39 (June 27, 1908): 101–103; C.C.C., "Their First Convention" (1920), LC P80-5456; Blatch and Lutz, *Challenging Years*, pp. 129 and 203.

63. Susan D. Becker, *The Origins of the Equal Rights Amendment: American Feminism Between the Wars* (Westport, Conn.: Greenwood, 1981), p. 89; C.C.C. to Millicent G. Fawcett (October 19, 1909), LC 5; Shaw, "Tells of the Stand of the Union," *Woman's Journal* 45 (February 14, 1914); 54; Zimmerman, "Alice Paul and the National Woman's Party," p. 97.

64. Peck, "Changing the Mind of a Nation: The Story of Carrie Chapman Catt," *World Tomorrow* 13 (September 1930): 358–361.

65. C.C.C. to Eileen Morrissey (March 4, 1933), LC P80-5458; on N.A.W.S.A. borrowings, see, for example, Rheta Childe Dorr, *A Woman of Fifty* (New York: Funk and Wagnalls, 1924), p. 222.

66. Others agree: Morgan, *Suffragists and Democrats*, p. 186; Blatch and Lutz, *Challenging Years*, pp. 131 and 199; Buhle and Buhle, *Concise History*, p. 38; Irwin, *Angels and Amazons*, pp. 392–393; Sinclair, *Better Half*, p. 304.

NOTES TO THE CONCLUSION

1. Discussions that implicitly or explicitly address Catt in this context are: Gerda Lerner, *The Woman in American History* (Menlo Park, Calif.: Addison-Wesley, 1971), p. 172; Riegel, *American Women*, pp. 309–310; Buhle, *Women and American Socialism;* Gail Parker, *The Oven Birds: American Women on Womanhood: 1820–1920* (Garden City, N.Y.: Doubleday, 1972), introduction; Paulson, *Women's Suffrage and Prohibition*, p. 63; also see Kraditor, *Ideas*, p. 249–264. Kraditor does not contend that suffrage was either insignificant or all-important; instead she takes it very seriously on its own terms and sees its symbolic importance for raising serious issues about women and feminism.

2. Alice Stone Blackwell to C.C.C. (September 4, 1929), LCB 12.

3. C.C.C. to Alice Stone Blackwell (September 13, 1943), LC 4.

4. C.C.C. to Margaret Roberts (October 8, 1918), Margaret Roberts Collection, Box 1, folder 4, RL.

5. See Alice Blackwell's report of C.C.C.'s observations (December 31, 1919), LCB 2.

6. C.C.C., "Will of the People," *Forum* 43 (1910): 600.

7. Ibid.

8. C.C.C. to Mrs. Charles Craigie (December 19, 1919), Catt Collection, Box 4, folder 29, SSL; also see C.C.C., radio speech, "War or Peace" (August 26, 1925), Catt Collection, Box 1, folder 12, SSL.

9. C.C.C., radio speech, National Federation of Business and Professional Women's Clubs (July 10, 1939), LC 11; C.C.C., speech, "What Have Women Done With the Suffrage?" (n.d.), LC 10; C.C.C., "The Cave Man Complex vs. Woman Suffrage," *Woman Citizen* 8 (April 5, 1924): 36; C.C.C., "What Women Have Done with the Vote," *Independent* 115 (October 17, 1925): 447–448; Marian M. Benedict, "Carrie Chapman Catt at 80 Looks at Life with Serenity," *New Rochelle Standard-Star* 16 (January 7, 1939), LC P80-5459; C.C.C., radio speech, NBC (June 23, 1939), LC 11; C.C.C., *Then and Now,* p. 21.

10. Those inclined to see Catt as fairly conservative here include Flexner, *Century of Struggle,* p. 219; Riegel, *American Feminists,* p. 178; and Parker, *Oven Birds,* pp. 2–3.

11. C.C.C., "We March On," *Woman Citizen* 5 (April 9, 1921): 1141–1142.

12. C.C.C., "Woman Suffrage Only an Episode in Age-Old Movement," *Current History Magazine* 27 (October 1927): 5–6; C.C.C., "The Old Order Changeth," *Woman's Home Companion* 48 (July 1921): 24.

13. C.C.C. to Maud Wood Park (January 21, 1924), Catt Collection, Box 4, folder 33, SSL.

14. C.C.C., speech, Pan-Hellenic Program, New York World's Fair (July 1939), p. 5.

15. C.C.C. to Caroline Reilly (May 8, 1941), Dillon Collection, Box 17, folder 403, RL.

16. Susan B. Anthony II, "Woman's Next Step: As Women See It," *New York Times Magazine* 90 (January 12, 1941): 11.

17. "Proceedings," Woman's Centennial Congress, p. 227, LC 21.

18. For example, C.C.C., speech, Pan-Hellenic Program, New York World's Fair (July 1939), p. 5.

19. For example, C.C.C., statement, "Equal Pay For Equal Work" (May 7, 1917), LCN 83; C.C.C., "Women Police in Great Britain," *Woman Citizen* 1 (December 29, 1917): 86; C.C.C., "War Service for Women Doctors," *Woman Citizen* 1 (September 8, 1917): 272; C.C.C., "The Nation Calls," *Woman Citizen* 3 (March 29, 1919): 917–921; C.C.C. to Mrs. Ellis Meredith (June 29, 1917), LC 7; C.C.C., "The Further Extension," *Woman Voter* 4 (May 1913): 17 and 20.

20. C.C.C., "An Eight-Hour Day for the Housewife — Why Not?" *Pictorial Review* 30 (November 1928): 1–2; C.C.C., "World Politics and Women Voters," *Woman's Home Companion* 47 (November 1920): 4; C.C.C. to Edna Stantial (November 29, 1943), LC 9; Harper, *History,* vol. 5, pp. 98 and 728.

21. Gerda Lerner, "Women's Rights and American Feminism," *American Scholar* 40 (Spring 1971): 235–248.

22. C.C.C., "Statement on the Proposed Equal Rights Amendment," *Congressional Digest* 22 (April 1943): 118; C.C.C., "Will of the People," *Forum* 43 (1910): 595–602.

23. For a balanced, excellent discussion of the Woman's Party in the 1920s, see Nancy F. Cott, "Feminist Politics in the 1920s: The National Woman's Party," *Journal of American History* 71 (June 1984): 43–68.

24. Alice Kessler-Harris, *Out to Work: A History of Wage-Earning Women in the United States* (New York: Oxford University Press, 1982), p. 205 and chapter 7; Lemons, "The New Woman in the New Era," pp. 273–276; Becker, *Origins of the Equal Rights Amendment,* chapter 6; see also C.C.C., 1939 writing fragments, LC P80-5458.

25. Kessler-Harris, *Out to Work,* p. 204.

26. Ibid., pp. 181 and 212–213.

27. C.C.C., seventy-eighth birthday statement, LC 17.

28. C.C.C., "Old Order Changeth," p. 24; Woman's Centennial Congress documents and reports, LC 21.

29. C.C.C., "Anti-Feminism in South America," *Current History Magazine* 18 (September 1923): 1036.

30. For example, C.C.C. to Rose Powell (June 7, 1938), Rose Powell Collection, Box 2, folder 32, RL.

31. C.C.C., speech, Dedication of Bronze Tablet (for Iowa Suffrage Pioneers) in Capitol Building, Des Moines, Iowa (May 10, 1936), Catt Collection, Box 1, folder 14, SSL.

32. C.C.C., "Survival of Matriarchy," *Harpers* 128 (April 1914): 738–748; C.C.C., "A Corset Problem Too?" (ca. 1925), LC 12; Walker, "Speeches," p. 344.

33. Degler, *At Odds,* p. 359.

34. C.C.C. to Caroline Reilly (May 23, 1919), Catt Collection, Box 4, folder 29, SSL.

35. C.C.C. to Caroline B. LaMonte (March 8, 1930), Catt Collection, Box 4, folder 29, SSL.

36. See Sochen, *New Woman in Greenwich Village;* Sochen, *Movers and Shakers: American Women Thinkers and Activists: 1900–1970* (Chicago: Quadrangle, 1973), chapter 2.

37. C.C.C. to Gertrude Brown (November 1, 1928), Catt Collection, Box 4, folder 30, SSL.

38. C.C.C., "Anti-Feminism in South America," pp. 1032–1033.

39. Majorie Shuler, "Preserves vs. Politics" (1934), LC P80-5459.

40. "Reports of the Commission on Ethical and Religious Values," Woman's Centennial Congress (1940), LC 20.

41. Lerner, "Women's Rights," pp. 242–243 and 239; Madeline Gray, *Margaret Sanger* (New York: Richard Marek, 1979).

42. C.C.C., "Shall the People Amend?" *Woman Citizen* 9 (December 27, 1924): 16; C.C.C., "Watch Your Planks," *Woman Citizen* 9 (August 9, 1924): 14 and 29.

43. C.C.C., *Victory,* foreword.

44. C.C.C. to Mary G. Peck (December 12, 1912), LC 7; C.C.C. to Mary G. Peck (1912), LC 7.

45. See for example, C.C.C., "Woman Suffrage Only an Episode," p. 2.

Bibliography

This bibliography is divided into five categories: books and larger published pamphlets by Catt; journal and periodical articles by Catt; other published primary sources, both signed and unsigned, chiefly periodical articles; and secondary sources. Not included here are the Catt speeches and the numerous letters I read and often used; there are simply too many of them. Most of the unpublished primary material may be found in the original sources located in the principal libraries I visited. Their locations are designated in the notes and the bibliography as specified below.

KEY TO NOTE AND BIBLIOGRAPHIC ABBREVIATIONS

LC   Catt Papers, Library of Congress (shorter numbers refer to LC container numbers, longer numbers refer to University of Wisconsin reclassification of same)

LCB   Blackwell Papers, Library of Congress (container numbers)

LCN   National American Woman Suffrage Association Papers, Library of Congress (container numbers)

SSL   Sophia Smith Library, Smith College

RL   Schlesinger Library, Radcliffe College

BOOKS AND BOOKLETS BY CARRIE CHAPMAN CATT

An Address to the Congress of the United States by Carrie Chapman Catt, President of the National American Woman Suffrage Association New York: National American Woman Suffrage Publishing, 1917.

An Address to the Legislature of the United States by Carrie Chapman Catt, President of the N.A.W.S.A. New York: National American Woman Suffrage Publishing, 1919.

The Home Defense. New York: National American Woman Suffrage Publishing, 1918.

How to Work for Suffrage in an Election District. New York: National American Woman Suffrage Publishing, 1917.

Then and Now. New York: Leslie Woman Suffrage Continuing Committee, 1939.

War Aims. New York: National American Woman Suffrage Association, 1918.

Woman Suffrage and Politics: The Inner Story of the Suffrage Movement (with Shuler, Nettie Rogers). New York: Scribner's 1923.

Woman Suffrage by Federal Constitutional Amendment (editor). New York: National American Woman Suffrage Publishing, 1917.

Women in the Industries and Professions. New York: G. P. Putnam, 1901.

SHORTER PIECES BY CARRIE CHAPMAN CATT

"Afraid of Women." *Woman Citizen* 3 (July 20, 1918): 145.

"Anti-Feminism in South America." *Current History Magazine* 18 (September 1923): 1028–1036.

"An Appeal to All Suffragists." *Woman Citizen* 3 (October 19, 1918): 409.

"Beautiful Woman Suffrage Calendars." *Woman's Journal* 27 (December 19, 1896): 401.

"Be Joyful Today." *Woman Citizen* 4 (February 21, 1920): 885.

"The Bookshelf." *Woman Citizen* 7 (September 23, 1922): 28.

"By Way of a New Beginning." *Woman Citizen* 5 (August 28, 1920): 329.

"A Call to Action." *Woman Citizen* 5 (April 23, 1921): 1184.

"The Cave Man Complex vs. Woman Suffrage." *Woman Citizen* 8 (April 5, 1924): 36.

"Chang Sing, Another True Story." *Woman Voter* 5 (January 1914): 13–14.

"Christmas Shopping Exchange." *Woman's Journal* 26 (November 9, 1895): 354.

"A Cincinnati 'Research Magnificent.' " *Woman Citizen* 2 (March 16, 1918): 313.

"College Women As Citizens." *Arrow* 38 (June 1922): 613–620.

"Conspiracy or Slander." *Woman Citizen* 9 (November 15, 1924): 14–15, 29–30.

"Conspiracy vs. Conspiracy." *Woman Citizen* 9 (November 29, 1924): 13, 26.

"Convention Week in Albany." *Woman Voter* 7 (December 1916): 12.

"The Crisis." *Woman's Journal* 47 (September 16, 1916): 299, 301–303.

"Crisis in Suffrage Movement." *New York Times Magazine* 65 (September 3, 1916): 3.

"The Direct Primary Under Fire." *Woman Citizen* 5 (May 7, 1921): 1210.

"Disarmament." *Missionary Review of the World* 54 (December 1931): 934–936.

"Editorial." *Woman Citizen* 5 (January 15, 1921): 885.

"Editorial." *Woman Citizen* 5 (January 29, 1921): 929.

"An Eight-Hour Day for the Housewife — Why Not?" *Pictorial Review* 30 (November 1928): 2, 68, 70, 73.

"Elements in a Constructive Foreign Policy." *Annals of the American Academy of Political and Social Sciences* 132 (July 1927): 187–189.

"Evolution — Fifty Years Ago: A Reminiscence." *Woman Citizen* 10 (July 11, 1925): 7–8, 29.

"Excuses Only." *Woman Citizen* 1 (August 11, 1917): 179.

"The Fascisti in Italy." *Woman Citizen* 7 (December 16, 1922): 8, 9, 28.

"Forward March." *Woman Citizen* 1 (September 22, 1917): 305–306.

"Friction in International Opinion." *Annals of the American Academy of Political and Social Sciences* 126 (July 1926): 49–50.

"The Further Extension." *Woman Voter* 4 (May 1913): 17, 20.

"A Great American." *Yale Review* 25 (December, 1935): 401–404.

"The Home and the Higher Education." *Woman's Journal* 33 (July 26, 1902): 234–235.

"How To Win: Plan on the 1915 Campaign." *Woman Voter* 5 (November 1914): 12–13.

"How Will She Use the Ballot When Won?" *Woman's Journal* 47 (September 30, 1916): 314.

"If We Win in New York." *Woman's Journal* 46 (October 30, 1915): 345.

"Introduction" to Roosevelt, Eleanor, *This Troubled World*. New York: Kinsey, 1938 (pp. 1–5).

"The League of Women Voters." *Woman Citizen* 3 (April 12, 1919): 955.

"The League of Women Voters." *Woman's Home Companion* 47 (May 1920): 4, 152.

"Let's Talk It Over." *Good Housekeeping* 86 (March 1928): 56.

"Letter from Mrs. Catt." *Woman's Journal* 32 (March 16, 1901): 82.

"The Lie Factory." *Woman Citizen* 9 (September 20, 1924): 10, 24–25.

"Lies-At-Large." *Woman Citizen* 12 (June 1927): 10, 11, 41.

"Liquor and Law." *Woman Citizen* 13 (October 1928): 10–11, 47–48.

"Longer and Calmer Terms." *Woman Citizen* 9 (June 28, 1924): 14.

"Make Victory Certain." *Woman's Journal* 46 (October 16, 1915): 331.

"A Million New York Women Want To Vote." *Woman Voter* 6 (November 1915): 8.

"Missouri Protests." *Woman Citizen* 6 (September 24, 1921): 13.

"More About China." *Woman's Journal* 43 (November 2, 1912): 346–347.

"Mrs. Catt on 'The Convert' " (letter). *Woman's Journal* 38 (November 23, 1907): 186.

"Mrs. Catt On The Election." *New York Times* 70 (November 21, 1920): section 7, p. 2.

"The Nation Calls." *Woman Citizen* 3 (March 29, 1919): 917–921.

"National Organizational Campaign." *Woman's Journal* 16 (April 27, 1895): 132.

"National Organizational Report." *Woman's Journal* 28 (February 6, 1897): 42–43.

"The New China." *Woman's Journal* 43 (October 5, 1912): 314.

"The New York Party." *Woman's Journal* 41 (February 19, 1910): 30–31.

"The Old Order Changeth." *Woman's Home Companion* 48 (July 1921): 24.

"One Thing Mightier Than Kings and Armies." *Woman Citizen* 2 (December 15, 1917): 48–49.

"Opening of the Convention." *Woman Citizen* 2 (December 15, 1917): 54.

"Organization Committee Report." *Woman's Journal* 29 (March 12, 1898): 82.

"Organize Yourself." *Woman Citizen* 7 (December 16, 1922): 14.

"Organized Womanhood." *Woman Voter* 8 (April 1917): 9.

"Our Friends — The Enemy." *Woman Voter* 5 (April 1914): 7–8.

"Our New Responsibilities." *Woman's Journal* 29 (October 1, 1898): 317.

"Our Outlook." *Woman Voter* 2 (January 1911): 2–3.

"Our Prospects in the Empire State." *Woman Voter* 6 (January 1915): 7–8.

"Ours is a battle of principles and not of persons." *Woman's Journal* 32 (March 16, 1901): 138.

"The Outlawry of War." *Annals of the American Academy of Political and Social Sciences* 138 (July 1928): 157–163.

"Party Clean-ups Are the Crying Need." *Woman Citizen* 16 (April 1931): 15, 30.

"Pickets Are Behind the Times." *Woman Citizen* 1 (November 1917): 470–471.

"Polluted Sources." *Woman Citizen* 9 (October 4, 1924): 11, 28.

"Preface" to *Victory: How Women Won It: 1840–1940* (New York: Wilson, 1940).

"Prefers Action Through Congress to State Referenda on Vote." *Woman's Journal* 48 (January 13, 1917): 7–9.

"Preparedness, War and Suffrage." *Woman's Journal* 47 (November 4, 1916): 354.

"The 'Red Menace.' " *Woman Citizen* 9 (November 1, 1924): 11–12, 24–26.

"The Right Side." *Weekly News* (New York League of Women Voters) (October 6, 1931).

"The Sad Plight of the Antis." *Woman Citizen* 3 (January 25, 1919): 708.

"School for Suffrage Workers." *Woman Voter* 4 (September 1913): 8–9.

"Shall the People Amend?" *Woman Citizen* 9 (December 27, 1924): 16.

"Some Suffrage Experiences Abroad." *Woman's Journal* 40 (July 10, 1909): 109.

"Spring Organizational Campaign." *Woman's Journal* 26 (July 13, 1895): 218.

"Statement on the Proposed Equal Rights Amendment." *Congressional Digest* 22 (April 1943): 118.

"The Suffrage Platform." *Woman's Journal* 46 (June 12, 1915): 184.

"Suffragists First." *Woman Citizen* 4 (December 13, 1919): 457.

"Surplus Women." *Woman Citizen* 6 (October 22, 1921): 12.

"Survival of Matriarchy." *Harpers* 128 (April 1914): 738–748.

"Telephone Day Makes New York Jubilant." *Woman's Journal* 46 (August 7, 1915): 247.

"Tells of the Stand of the Union." *Woman's Journal* 45 (February 14, 1914): 54.

"They Shall Not Pass." *Woman Citizen* 3 (January 15, 1919): 774.

"Time to Change Says Mrs. Catt." *Woman's Journal* 47 (February 12, 1916): 50.

"Too Many Rights." *Ladies Home Journal* 39 (November 1922): 31.

"The Traffic in Women." *Woman Voter* 4 (March 1913): 14–15.

"A True Story." *Woman's Journal* 44 (January 25, 1913): 26.

"True Systems." *Woman Citizen* 3 (June 29, 1918): 85.

"The Victory in Denmark." *Woman's Journal* 39 (April 8, 1908): 61.

"Votes For All: A Symposium." *Crisis* (November 1917): 19–21.

"Wanted: A New Department." *Woman Citizen* 5 (January 8, 1921): 861–862.

"War Service for Women Doctors." *Woman Citizen* 1 (September 8, 1917): 272.

"Warren G. Harding." *Woman Citizen* 8 (August 11, 1923): 14.

"Watch Your Planks." *Woman Citizen* 9 (August 9, 1924): 14.

"We March On." *Woman Citizen* 5 (April 9, 1921): 1141–1142.

"What Every Senator Knows." *Woman Citizen* 2 (March 2, 1918): 263.

"What the N.A.W.S.A. Has Done." *Woman Citizen* 3 (November 9, 1918): 487.

"What Women Have Done With the Vote." *Independent* 115 (October 17, 1925): 447–448.

"Who's Scared." *Woman Citizen* 6 (January 28, 1922): 12–13.

"Whose Government Is This?" *Woman Citizen* 6 (July 30, 1921): 8–16.

Why I Have Found Life Worth Living." *Christian Century* 45 (March 29, 1928): 406–408.

"Why New York Women Want to Vote." *Woman Voter* 6 (January 1915): 5.

"Why Not?" *Woman Voter* 6 (March 1915): 7.

"Why We Did Not Picket the White House." *Good Housekeeping* 66 (March 1918): 32.

"Why Women Want to Vote." *Woman's Journal* 46 (January 9, 1915): 11.

"Will of the People." *Forum* 43 (1910): 595–602.

"Woman Suffrage As A War Measure." *Woman Citizen* 3 (June 1918).

"Woman Suffrage: The First Ten Years." *New York Times Magazine* 79 (August 24, 1930): 3.

"Woman Suffrage Only an Episode in Age-Old Movement." *Current History Magazine* 27 (October 1927): 1–6.

"Women Organized for Peace." *Missionary Review of the World* 49 (August 1926): 631–633.

"Women's Place." *New York Herald Tribune* (August 22, 1914).

"Woodrow Wilson." *Woman Citizen* 8 (February 9, 1924): 14.

"Working Our Way Out." *Woman Citizen* 6 (September 24, 1921): 7.

"World Politics and Women Voters." *Woman's Home Companion* 47 (November 1920).

"World Progress of Women." *Woman's Journal* 45 (June 20, 1914): 197.

"A Year of Progress." *Woman Voter* 5 (November 1914): 18–19, 24.

"The Years I Like Best." *Good Housekeeping* 77 (October 1923): 17 and 181–184.

OTHER PRIMARY SOURCES: SIGNED

Adams, Mildred. "Mrs. Catt, at 75, Still Faces Forward." *New York Times Magazine* 83 (January 7, 1934): 3.

Anthony, Susan B., and Harper, Ida Husted. *The History of Woman Suffrage: 1883–1900,* vol. 4. New York: National American Woman Suffrage Association, 1902.

Armstrong, Eliza D. "What are the Very Latest Suffrage Arguments?" *Woman's Protest* 6 (April 1915): 4.

Benedict, Marian M. "Carrie Chapman Catt at 80 Looks at Life with Serenity." *The Standard-Star* (New Rochelle, New York) 16 (January 7, 1939).

Blackwell, Alice Stone. *Lucy Stone: Pioneer of Woman's Rights.* Boston: Little, Brown, 1930.

———. "Mrs. Catt's Counsel." *Woman's Journal* 47 (January 1, 1916): 4.

———. "The National Convention." *Woman's Journal* 47 (September 16, 1916): 300.

———. "Washington Notes." *Woman's Journal* 25 (February 24, 1894).

———. "Washington Notes." *Woman's Journal* 31 (February 24, 1900): 60.

Blatch, Harriot Stanton, and Lutz, Alma. *Challenging Years: The Memoirs of Harriot Stanton Blatch.* New York: Putnams, 1940.

Boyd, Mary Sumner. "The Menace to War Workers." *Woman Citizen* 1 (June 9, 1917): 31.

Bronson, Minnie. "How Suffrage States Compare with Non-Suffrage." *Woman's Protest* 4 (January 1914): 7–9.

Brown, Gertrude Foster. "On Account of Sex." Unpublished manuscript (ca. 1956), SSL.

Chittenden, Alice Hill. "Our Duty to the State." *Woman's Protest* 10 (April 1917): 3.

Dorman, Marjorie. "Suffragists Traitors to Democracy." *Woman's Protest* 8 (December 1915).

Dorr, Rheta Childe. *A Woman of Fifty.* New York: Funk and Wagnalls, 1924.

Dougherty, Annie. "The National Suffrage School." *Woman Voter* 8 (May 1917): 17.

Dyer, Frances J. "A Remonstrance." In *Why Women Do Not Want the Ballot*. Massachusetts Association Opposed to the Further Extension of Suffrage to Women, 1903.

Fisher, K. R. "Mrs. Catt's Suffrage School." *Woman's Journal* 44 (October 4, 1913): 318.

Foster, Mrs. H. A. "Taxation and Representation." In *Why Women Do Not Want The Ballot*. Massachusetts Association Opposed to the Further Extension of Suffrage to Women, 1903.

Fry, Amelia R. *Conversations with Alice Paul: Woman Suffrage and the Equal Rights Amendment*. Berkeley: University of California Press, 1976.

Goodwin, Grace D. *Anti-Suffrage: Ten Good Reasons*. New York: Duffield, 1912.

Guilford, Simeon H. "Woman's 'Emancipation' — From What?" *Woman's Protest* 7 (July 1915): 5.

Harper, Ida Husted. *The History of Woman Suffrage: 1900–1920*, vol. 5. New York: National American Woman Suffrage Association, 1922.

———. *The History of Woman Suffrage: 1900–1920*, vol. 6. New York: National American Woman Suffrage Association, 1922.

Haskell, Oreola Williams. *Banner Bearers: Tales of the Suffrage Campaign*. Geneva, N.Y.: W. F. Humphrey, 1920.

Heron, Mrs. John B. "Feminism a Return to Barbarism." *Woman's Protest* 6 (April 1915): 5–6.

———. "Why Suffragists Prefer to Face Legislatures Rather Than Voters-At-The-Polls." *Woman's Protest* 6 (January 1915): 8–9.

Johnson, Helen Kendrick. "The End of Suffrage: A Social Revolution." *Woman's Protest* 7 (June 1915): 10–11.

Katzenstein, Caroline. *Lifting the Curtain: The State and National Woman Suffrage Campaigns in Pennsylvania as I Saw Them*. Philadelphia: Dorrance, 1955.

Kent, C. H. "Arguments for Suffrage Weighed and Found Wanting in Logic and Justice." *Woman's Protest* 2 (February 1913): 3.

Lamar, Mrs. Walter D. "The Menace of Suffrage in the South." *Woman's Protest:* 5 (July 1914): 5–7.

Leonard, John William. *Women's Who's Who of America*. 1914; Detroit: Gale Research, 1976.

Leonard, Priscilla. "A Help or a Hindrance?" In *Why Women Do Not Want the Ballot*. Massachusetts Association Opposed to the Further Extension of Suffrage to Women, 1903.

Martin, Anne. "Feminists and Future Political Action." *Nation* 120 (February 18, 1925): 185–186.

McCracken, Elizabeth. "The Women of American Woman's Suffrage in Colorado." *Outlook* 75 (November 28, 1903): 737–744.

M'Intire, Mary A. J. "Of What Benefit to Woman?" In *Why Women Do Not Want the Ballot*. Massachusetts Association Opposed to the Further Extension of Suffrage to Women, 1903.

Morris, Paul. "The Feminine Viewpoint." *Woman Patriot* 3 (April 26, 1919): 8.

Park, Maud Wood. *Front Door Lobby*. Boston: Beacon, 1960.

———. "More 'Rampant Women.' " LC P80-5458.

———. "Remember the Ladies." Manuscript, RL.

Peck, Mary G. "Carrie Chapman Catt" (1943). Woman's Rights Collection, Radcliffe College, LC P80-5458.

———. *Carrie Chapman Catt*. New York: Wilson, 1944.

———. "Changing the Mind of a Nation: The Story of Carrie Chapman Catt." *World Tomorrow* 13 (September 1930): 358–361.

Price, Lucy J. "Why Wage Earning Women Oppose Suffrage." *Woman's Protest* 2 (January 1913): 7.

Reynolds, Helen. "How Colorado Was Carried." *Woman's Journal* 24 (November 18, 1893): 361.

Reynolds, Minnie J. "Carrie Chapman Catt." *New Idea Women's Magazine* (November 1909), LC P80-5458.

Robinson, Margaret. "Germany's Strongest Allies." *Woman Patriot* 1 (July 6, 1918): 4.

———. "Woman Suffrage and Pacifism." *Woman Patriot* 1 (April 27, 1918): 3.

Scott, Frances. "Extension of Suffrage to Women." In *Why Women Do Not Want The Ballot*. Massachusetts Association Opposed to the Further Extension of Suffrage to Women, 1903.

Shaw, Anna Howard. *The Story of a Pioneer*. New York: Harper, 1915.

———. "Tells of the Stand of the Union." *Woman's Journal* 45 (February 14, 1914): 54.

Stanton, Elizabeth Cady. *The Woman's Bible*. 1895; New York: Arno, 1972.

Stanton, Theodore, and Blatch, Harriot Stanton. *Elizabeth Cady Stanton as Revealed in Her Letters, Diary and Reminiscences*, 2 vols. New York: Harper, 1922.

Stevens, Doris. *Jailed for Freedom*. New York: Boni and Liveright, 1920.

Taaffe, Lillian E. "Coolidge Will Be Nominated, Says Mrs. Catt." *Minneapolis Tribune* (November 8, 1923).

———. "Men's Superiority Complex Called Bar to Equal Rights." *Minneapolis Tribune* (November 8, 1923).

Tarbell, Ida. *All In The Day's Work*. New York: Macmillan, 1939.

Townsend, Metta Folger. "Good Reasons for Opposition." *Woman's Protest* 3 (June 1913): 3.

Waterman, Mrs. J. T. "Women and War." *Woman's Protest* 5 (September 1914): 5–6.

White, Mrs. George P. "Taxation Without Representation — Misapplied." *Woman's Protest* 6 (February 1915): 8–9.

Young, Rose. *The Record of the Leslie Woman Suffrage Commission, Inc.* New York: Leslie Woman Suffrage Commission, Inc., 1929.

OTHER PRIMARY SOURCES: UNSIGNED

"Another Danger Demonstrated." *Woman's Protest* 10 (November 1916): 8–9.

"The Atlanta Convention." *Woman's Journal* 26 (February 9, 1895): 41.

The Blackwell Family, Carrie Chapman Catt, and the National American Woman Suffrage Association: A Register of Their Papers in the Library of Congress. Washington, D.C.: Library of Congress, 1975.

"Catt on Suffrage Foes." *Woman's Journal* 44 (May 24, 1913): 166.

"Conference With Mrs. Catt." *Woman's Journal* 30 (May 27, 1899): 164.

"Convention." *Woman's Journal* 27 (February 1, 1896): 1.

"Copy of Preamble and Protest." Brooklyn Auxiliary New York State Association Opposed to the Extension of Suffrage to Women. In *Why Women Do not Want the Ballot.* Massachusetts Association Opposed to the Further Extension of Suffrage to Women, 1903.

"D.A.R. Head Makes Reply to Mrs. Catt's Criticisms." *San Francisco Chronicle* (July 22, 1927).

"The 'Diabolical Trickery' of a Professional Woman Politician." *Woman Patriot* 2 (March 15, 1919): 2.

"Do American Suffragists Favor Militancy?" *Woman's Protest* 4 (December 1913): 12.

"Equal Suffrage and Equal Obligation." *Woman's Protest* 1 (July 1912): 4.

"Fight Dictators, Mrs. Catt Pleads." *New York Times* 90 (November 26, 1940): 6.

"The Flag." *Woman's Protest* 9 (October 1916): 3.

"For Woman's Service or Woman Suffrage?" *Woman's Protest* 10 (March 1917): 8.

"For You — If You Were Not There." *Woman Citizen* 4 (February 28, 1920): 914–915.

"God Give Us Men." *Woman Patriot* 4 (April 10, 1920): 3.

"Great Welcome to Mrs. Catt." *Woman's Journal* 43 (November 16, 1912): 361.

"Hearings Before the House Suffrage Committee." *Woman Citizen* 2 (January 12, 1918): 130.

"How Has It Worked Where They Vote?" *Woman's Protest* 7 (May 1915): 9–10.

"How Pro-Germans and Pacifists Carried Suffrage In New York." *Woman's Protest* 11 (November 1917): 4–5.

"International Notes." *Woman's Journal* 39 (January 19, 1907): 5.

"Is Suffrage A War Measure?" *Woman Patriot* 1 (September 28, 1918): 4.

"Is Suffrage Pro-German?" *Woman Patriot* 1 (October 26, 1918): 3.

"John Hay, Mrs. Catt, and Patriotism." *Woman Citizen* 1 (November 10, 1917): 456–457.

"The Latest Suffrage Victory." *Woman's Journal* 40 (January 1, 1909): 1.

"Laws of Suffrage and Non-suffrage States Compared." *Woman's Protest* 1 (June 1912): 3.

"A Long Struggle Nearing Victory." *Warsaw* (New York) *Yorker* (July 2, 1914).

"Men Becoming Effeminate." *Woman Patriot* 3–4 (March 20, 1920): 6.

"Militant Methods In Action." *Woman's Protest* 10 (November 1916): 5–6.

Minutes of the Jubilee Convention. New York: N.A.W.S.A., 1919 (pp. 3–39).

"More About Mrs. Catt in South Africa." *Woman's Journal* 43 (January 13, 1912): 13–14.

"More Proof that 'Pickets and Conservative' Suffragists Have A 'Mutual Working Agreement.' " *Woman Patriot* 2 (January 4, 1919): 8.

"Mrs. C. C. Catt Sees Big Boom for Ford." *Dallas Morning News* (November 24, 1923).

Mrs. Carrie Chapman Catt and Charles City, pp. 1–12, LC 16.

"Mrs. Carrie Chapman Catt — Constructive Decisionist." *Everybody's Magazine* 35 (November 1916): 639–640.

"Mrs. Catt Again Attacks the Government." *Woman Patriot* 3 (December 27, 1919): 3.

"Mrs. Catt and Mrs. Barry." *Woman's Journal* 41 (November 12, 1910): 204.

"Mrs. Catt and the Schwimmer Peace Plan." *Woman's Protest* 11 (October 1917): 10–11.

"Mrs. Catt at the Helm." *Woman Voter* 1 (September 1910): 5.

"Mrs. Catt Believes Women Should Continue in Chosen Career, Although Married." *Wichita Eagle* (November 25, 1923), LC 14.

"Mrs. Catt Compromises Leslie Fund." *Woman Patriot* 5 (January 29, 1921): 7.

"Mrs. Catt Describes New York Opposition." *Woman's Journal* 46 (November 13, 1915): 361.

"Mrs. Catt Doing Well." *Woman's Journal* 41 (June 11, 1910): 95.

"Mrs. Catt Elected National President." *Woman's Journal* 46 (December 25, 1915): 407–408.

"Mrs. Catt Favors Ralston Nation's Next President." *Fort Worth Record* (November 25, 1923).

"Mrs. Catt Gets 1933 American Hebrew Medal." *New York Herald Tribune* 93 (November 24, 1933): 12.

"Mrs. Catt Getting Better." *Woman's Journal* 41 (May 28, 1910): 85.

"Mrs. Catt in Bohemia." *Woman's Journal* 40 (May 1, 1909): 72.

"Mrs. Catt in Burmah." *Woman's Journal* 43 (July 13, 1912): 221.

"Mrs. Catt in Norway." *Woman's Journal* 42 (June 3, 1911): 169.

"Mrs. Catt Makes Stirring Speech." *Woman's Journal* 44 (May 24, 1913): 161.

"Mrs. Catt Much Better." *Woman's Journal* 41 (July 9, 1910): 109.

"Mrs. Catt On League of Nations." *Woman Citizen* 5 (October 16, 1920): 538–541.

"Mrs. Catt on the National Campaign." *Woman's Journal* 47 (March 11, 1916): 86.

"Mrs. Catt on Patriotism." *Woman's Journal* 44 (November 1, 1913): 349.

"Mrs. Catt Puts Straight Query." *Woman's Journal* 45 (May 30, 1914): 169.

"Mrs. Catt Scents State Victory." *Woman's Journal* 47 (September 9, 1916): 289.

"Mrs. Catt Sees Coming Victory." *Woman's Journal* 47 (September 9, 1916): 289.

"Mrs. Catt 76 Years Old." *New York Times* 84 (January 10, 1935): 19.

"Mrs. Catt's Address." *Woman's Journal* 30 (June 10, 1899): 178.

"Mrs. Catt's Address." *Woman's Journal* 34 (April 25, 1903): 133.

"Mrs. Catt's Address." *Woman's Journal* 35 (February 20, 1904): 57.

"Mrs. Catt's Address." *Woman's Journal* 42 (July 15, 1911): 217.

"Mrs. Catt's Course at $200,000,000 A Year." *Woman Patriot* 5 (January 22, 1921): 9.

"Mrs. Catt's Defamation of Her Country." *Woman Patriot* 4 (June 19, 1920): 6.

"Mrs. Catt's International Address." *Woman's Journal* 39 (June 27, 1908): 101–103.

"Mrs. Catt's Norwegian Maid." *Woman's Journal* 38 (June 22, 1907): 98.

"Mrs. Catt's Resignation." *Woman's Journal* 35 (February 6, 1904): 42.

"Mrs. Catt's Speech." *Woman's Journal* 47 (June 17, 1916): 199.

"Mrs. Catt's Suggestion To Aid Starving Chinese." *Woman Citizen* 5 (February 26, 1921): 1014.

"Mrs. Catt Talks of State Tour." *Woman Voter* 6 (February 1915): 57–58.

"Mrs. Catt Tells of Slave Traffic." *Woman's Journal* 44 (January 11, 1913): 16.

"Mrs. Catt Tells of White Slaves." *Woman's Journal* 44 (February 1, 1913): 40.

"Mrs. Catt Tells View on War." *Woman's Journal* 45 (August 15, 1914): 234.

"Mrs. Catt Under Equator." *Woman's Journal* 42 (May 18, 1912): 157.

"Mrs. Catt Urges Big Drive For More Food." *Woman's Journal* 48 (April 14, 1917): 85–86.

"Mrs. Catt vs. Mrs. Meyer." *Woman's Journal* 39 (March 21, 1908): 48.

"N.E. Suffrage Festival." *Woman's Journal* 30 (June 10, 1899): 177–179.

"National-American Annual Meeting." *Woman's Journal* 21 (March 1, 1890): 68.

"National-American Convention." *Woman's Journal* 24 (January 28, 1893): 26.

"National-American Convention." *Woman's Journal* 25 (February 24, 1894): 57–58.

"National Suffrage Mrs. Catt's Theme Before Senate." *Woman's Journal* 48 (April 28, 1917): 97–98.

"The New York Party." *Woman's Journal* 41 (February 19, 1910): 30–31.

"New York's Victory Convention." *Woman Citizen* 2 (December 1, 1917): 12.

"No 'Natural Right' to Vote." *Woman Patriot* 1 (October 26, 1918): 7–8.

"Organization Committee's Report." *Woman's Journal* 27 (February 1, 1896): 37.

"Organizational Obtrusion for a Campaign of Clamor." *Woman's Protest* 9 (July 1916): 3.

"Origin of the Children's Bureau." *Woman Patriot* 5 (August 15, 1921, and September 1, 1921).

"Peace of Politics." *Woman's Protest* 6 (March 1915): 4.

"Petition Against the Child Labor Amendment." *Woman Patriot* 5 (May 15, 1921): 1–5.

"Picketing and 'Pestering.' " *Woman Patriot* 1 (August 24, 1918): 8.

"Pickets Determine to Persecute President." *Woman Patriot* 1 (August 3, 1918): 1.

"President Called Greatest of Men." *New York Times* 84 (January 10, 1935): 19.

"President of International Woman Suffrage Alliance to Be Guest of Dallas Women." *Dallas Morning News* (November 25, 1923).

"Questions for Mrs. Catt to Answer." *Woman's Protest* 11 (September 1917): 16.

"Recent Militant Freaks." *Remonstrance* (October 1913): 1.

"A Referendum To Women." *Woman's Protest* 10 (January 1917): 4.

"A Serious Accusation." *Woman Patriot* 3 (April 26, 1919): 6.

"Suffrage 'As A War Measure.' " *Remonstrance* (October 1917): 7.

"Suffrage vs. Patriotism." *Woman's Protest* 11 (May 1917): 5.

"The Suffragist Peace Fiasco." *Woman's Protest* 7 (July 1915): 6–7.

"The Suffragist's Ideal of Womanhood." *Woman Patriot* 3 (August 23, 1919): 4–5.

"Suffragists Have No Part in This War." *Woman Patriot* 1 (July 13, 1918): 4.

"Their Fundamental Error." *Woman's Protest* 8 (April 1916): 8–9.

"Third Liberty Loan Drive." *Woman Citizen* 2 (March 30, 1918): 355.

"Two Letters and Sunday Senators." *Woman Citizen* 2 (May 4, 1918): 445–446.

" 'Up and at 'em' Mrs. Catt Exhorts Business Women." *New Rochelle Standard-Star* (July 11, 1939).

"Up-to-Date." *Woman Patriot* 1 (May 25, 1918): 4.

"The Vote of 2,000,000 Negro Women." *Woman's Protest* 4 (April 1914): 16.

"War Record of Mrs. Carrie Chapman Catt." *Woman Patriot* 1 (November 16, 1918): 3.

"The Washington Convention." *Woman's Journal* 27 (February 1, 1896): 1.

"The Washington Convention." *Woman's Journal* 31 (March 3, 1900): 66–67.

"The Washington Convention." *Woman's Journal* 33 (March 22, 1902): 91.

"Welcome Home to Mrs. Catt." *Woman Voter* 3 (December 11, 1912): 6.

"Where Black and White Women Vote." *Woman Patriot* 3 (August 16, 1919): 2–3.

"The White Woman's Peril at Washington." *Woman Patriot* 3 (July 12, 1919): 4.

Why Women Do Not Want the Ballot. Massachusetts Association Opposed to the Further Extension of Suffrage to Women, 1903.

"Woman Suffrage, the Enemy of Good Government." *Woman Patriot* 3 (May 10, 1919): 8.

"Woman's Suffrage To Please Germans Is Now Urged By Suffrage Leaders." *Woman Patriot* 1 (September 14, 1918): 1.

"Women Competing With Men." *Women Patriot* 3 (May 31, 1919): 4.

"Women, Great Affairs." *Time* 7 (June 14, 1926): 8–9.

"World Peace Up To Women." *Kansas City Star* (December 2, 1923).

SECONDARY SOURCES

Allen, Devere, ed. *Adventurous Americans*. New York: Farrar & Rinehart, 1932.

Anthony, Katharine. *Susan B. Anthony*. Garden City, N.Y.: Doubleday, 1954.

Anthony, Susan B., II. "Women's Next Step: As Women See It." *New York Times Magazine* 90 (January 12, 1941): 11.

Ascher, Carol, DeSalvo, Louise, and Ruddick, Sara. *Between Women: Biographers, Novelists, Critics, Teachers and Artists Write About Their Work On Women*. Boston: Beacon, 1984.

Banner, Lois. *Elizabeth Cady Stanton: A Radical for Woman's Rights*. Boston: Little, Brown, 1980.

Barbrook, Alec, and Bolt, Christine. *Power and Protest in American Life*. New York: St. Martin's, 1980.

Becker, Susan. "International Feminism between the Wars: The National Woman's Party versus the League of Women Voters." pp 223–242 in Lois Scharf and Joan Jensen, ed., *Decades of Discontent: The Women's Movement: 1920–1940*. Westport, Conn.: Greenwood, 1983.

————. *The Origins of the Equal Rights Amendment: American Feminism Between the Wars*. Westport, Conn.: Greenwood, 1981.

Behnke, Donna. *Religious Issues in Nineteenth Century Feminism*. Troy, N.Y.: Whitston, 1982.

Blair, Karen J. *The Clubwoman as Feminist: True Womanhood Redefined: 1868–1914*. New York: Holmes and Meier, 1980.

Bordin, Ruth. *Woman and Temperance*. Philadelphia: Temple University Press, 1981.

Brownell, Blaine A. "Interpretations of Twentieth Century Urban Progressive Reform." In David R. Colburn and George Pozzetta, ed., *Reform and Reformers in the Progressive Era*. Westport, Conn.: Greenwood, 1983.

Buhle, Mari Jo. *Women and American Socialism, 1870–1920*. Urbana: University of Illinois Press, 1981.

Buhle, Mari Jo, and Buhle, Paul, ed. *The Concise History of Woman Suffrage*. Urbana: University of Illinois Press, 1978.

Burnett, Constance Buel. "Carrie Chapman Catt." *American Girl* 29 (April 1945).

————. *Five for Freedom*. New York: Abelard, 1953.

————. "The Great Feminist: Carrie Chapman Catt." Pp. 181–197 in Anne Stoddard, ed., *Topflight: Famous American Women*. New York: Thomas Nelson, 1946.

Camhi, Jane Jerome. "Women Against Women: American Anti-Suffragism 1880–1920." Ph.D. dissertation, Tufts University, 1973.

Campbell, Barbara Kuhn. *The "Liberated" Woman of 1914: Prominent Women in the Progressive Era.* 1976; Ann Arbor, Mich.: UMI Research, 1979.

Cartwright, William H., and Watson, Richard L., Jr., ed. *The Reinterpretation of American History and Culture.* Washington: National Council for the Social Studies, 1973.

Chevigny, Bell Gail. *The Woman and the Myth: Margaret Fuller's Life and Writings.* Old Westbury, N.Y.: Feminist Press, 1976.

Clarke, Ida Clyde. *American Women and the World War.* New York: D. Appleton, 1918.

Clevenger, Ima Fuchs. "Invention and Arrangement in the Public Address of Carrie Chapman Catt." Ph.D. dissertation, University of Oklahoma, 1955.

Conrad, Charles. "The Transformation of the Old Feminist Movement." *Quarterly Journal of Speech* 67 (1981): 284–297.

Conway, Jill. "Women Reformers and American Culture: 1870–1930." *Journal of Social History* 5 (Winter 1971–1972): 164–177.

Cott, Nancy F. "Feminist Politics in the 1920s: The National Woman's Party." *Journal of American History* 71 (June 1984): 43–68.

Cremin, Lawrence. *The Transformation of the School: Progressivism in American Education: 1876–1957.* New York: Knopf, 1961.

Croly, Herbert. *The Promise of American Life.* New York: Macmillan, 1909.

Crunden, Robert. *Ministers of Reform: The Progressives' Achievement in American Civilization: 1889–1920.* New York: Basic Books, 1982.

Davis, Allen F. *American Heroine: The Life and Legend of Jane Addams.* New York: Oxford University Press, 1973.

Degen, Marie Louise. *The History of the Woman's Peace Party.* 1939; New York: Burt Franklin's Reprints, 1974.

Degler, Carl. *At Odds: Women and the Family in America.* New York: Oxford University Press, 1980.

DuBois, Ellen. *Feminism and Suffrage: The Emergence of an Independent Women's Movement in America: 1849–1869.* Ithaca, N.Y.: Cornell University Press, 1978.

———. "The Radicalism of the Woman Suffrage Movement: Notes Toward the Reconstruction of Nineteenth-Century Feminism." *Feminist Studies* 3 (Fall 1975): 63–71.

Elshtain, Jean. "The New Porn Wars." *New Republic* 190 (June 25, 1984): 15–20.

Epstein, Barbara Leslie. *The Politics of Domesticity: Women, Evangelism, and Temperance in Nineteenth Century America.* Middletown, Conn.: Wesleyan University Press, 1981.

Faderman, Lillian. *Surpassing the Love of Men: Romantic Friendship and Love Between Women from the Renaissance to the Present.* New York: Morrow, 1981.

Falk, Candace. *Love, Anarchy, and Emma Goldman.* New York: Holt, Rinehart & Winston, 1984.

Fausold, Martin L. *James W. Wadsworth, Jr.: The Gentleman From New York.* Syracuse, N.Y.: Syracuse University Press, 1975.

Finch, Edith. *Carey Thomas of Bryn Mawr.* New York: Harper, 1947.

Flexner, Eleanor. *Century of Struggle: The Woman's Rights Movement in the United States.* 1959; New York: Atheneum, 1973.

Fuller, Paul E.. *Laura Clay and the Woman's Rights Movement.* Lexington: University of Kentucky Press, 1975.

George, Margaret. *One Woman's "Situation": A Biography of Mary Wollstonecraft.* Urbana: University of Illinois Press, 1970.

Giele, Janet Zollinger. "Social Change in the Feminine Role: A Comparison of Woman's Suffrage and Woman's Temperance: 1870–1920." Ph.D. dissertation, Harvard University, 1961.

Gilbert, James. *Designing the Industrial State.* Chicago: Quadrangle, 1972.

Gluck, Sherna. *From Parlor to Prison: Five American Suffragists Talk About Their Lives.* New York: Vintage, 1976.

Goldman, Eric. *Rendezvous with Destiny.* 1952; New York: Vintage, 1956.

Gornick, Vivian. *Essays in Feminism.* New York: Harper, 1978.

Graham, Abbie. *Ladies in Revolt.* New York: Woman's Press, 1934.

Graham, Otis L., Jr. *The Great Campaigns: Reform and War in America: 1900–1928.* Englewood Cliffs, N.J.: Prentice-Hall, 1971.

Grantham, Dewey W. *Southern Progressivism: The Reconciliation of Progress and Tradition.* Knoxville: University of Tennessee Press, 1983.

Gray, Madeline. *Margaret Sanger.* New York: Richard Marek, 1979.

Griffith, Elisabeth. *In Her Own Right: The Life of Elizabeth Cady Stanton.* New York: Oxford University Press, 1984.

Gurko, Miriam. *The Ladies of Seneca Falls: The Birth of the Woman's Rights Movement.* New York: Macmillan, 1974.

Hardesty, Nancy A. *Women Called to Witness: Evangelical Feminism in the Nineteenth Century.* Nashville, Tenn.: Abingdon, 1984.

Hays, Elinor Rice. *Morning Star: A Biography of Lucy Stone: 1818–1893.* Harcourt, Brace & World, 1961.

Hays, Samuel P. *The Response to Industrialism: 1885–1914.* Chicago: University of Chicago Press, 1957.

Hofstadter, Richard. *The Age of Reform: From Bryan to F.D.R.* 1955; New York: Vintage, 1960.

Huthmacher, J. Joseph. "Urban Liberalism and the Age of Reform." *Mississippi Valley Historical Review* 49, no. 2 (September 1962): 231–241.

Irwin, Inez Haynes. *Angels and Amazons: A Hundred Years of American Women.* 1933; New York: Arno, 1974.

Janeway, Elizabeth. *Between Myth and Morning: Women Awakening.* New York: Morrow, 1974.

———. *The Story of the Woman's Party.* New York: Harcourt, Brace, 1971.

Jensen, Joan. "All Pink Sisters: The War Department and the Feminist Movement in the 1920s." Pp. 199–222 in Lois Scharf and Joan Jensen, ed.,

Decades of Discontent: The Women's Movement: 1920–1940. Westport, Conn.: Greenwood, 1983.

Katz, David Howard. "Carrie Chapman Catt and the Struggle for Peace." Ph.D. dissertation, Syracuse University, 1973.

Keller, Evelyn Fox. *A Feeling for the Organism: The Life Work of Barbara McClintock*. San Francisco: W. H. Freeman, 1983.

Kennedy, Susan Estabrook. *If All We Did Was To Weep At Home: A History of White Working-Class Women in America*. Bloomington: Indiana University Press, 1979.

Kerber, Linda K., and Mathews, Jane. *Women's America: Refocusing the Past*. New York: Oxford University Press, 1982.

Kessler-Harris, Alice. *Out To Work: A History of Wage-Earning Women in the United States*. New York: Oxford University Press, 1982.

Kirkland, Winfred, and Kirkland, Frances. *Girls Who Became Leaders*. New York: R. Long and Richard R. Smith, 1932.

Kleppner, Paul. *The Third Electoral System: 1853–1892: Parties, Voters, and Political Cultures*. Chapel Hill: University of North Carolina Press, 1979.

Kraditor, Aileen S. *The Ideas of the Woman Suffrage Movement: 1890–1920*. New York: Columbia University Press, 1965.

———. *The Radical Persuasion: 1890–1917*. Baton Rouge: Louisiana State University Press, 1981.

Lasch, Christopher. *The New Radicalism in America: The Intellectual as Social Type*. New York: Knopf, 1965.

Lemons, J. Stanley. "The New Woman in the New Era: The Woman Movement From the Great War to the Great Depression." Ph.D. dissertation, University of Missouri, 1967.

———. *The Woman Citizen: Social Feminism in the 1920s*. Urbana: University of Illinois Press, 1973.

Lerner, Elinor. "Working-class and Immigrant Involvement in the New York Woman Suffrage Movement." Paper delivered to Mid-South Sociological Association, 1980; in "Suffrage: U.S." Collection, Box 15, folder 221, SSL.

Lerner, Gerda. *The Female Experience: An American Documentary*. Indianapolis: Bobbs-Merrill, 1977.

———. *The Grimké Sisters from South Carolina: Rebels Against Slavery*. Boston: Houghton Mifflin, 1967.

———. *The Majority Finds Its Past: Placing Women in History*. New York: Oxford University Press, 1979.

———. *The Woman in American History*. Menlo Park, Calif.: Addison-Wesley, 1971.

———. "Women's Rights and American Feminism." *American Scholar* 40 (Spring 1971): 235–248.

Linkugel, Wil A., and Griffin, Kim. "The Distinguished War Service of Dr. Anna Howard Shaw." *Pennsylvania History* 28 (October 1961): 372–385.

Lutz, Alma. *Created Equal: A Biography of Elizabeth Cady Stanton*. New York: John Day, 1940.

———— *Susan B. Anthony*. Boston: Beacon, 1959.

Mann, Arthur. *Yankee Reformers in the Urban Age*. Cambridge: Harvard University Press, 1954.

Martin, Wendy. *The American Sisterhood: Writings of the Feminist Movement From Colonial Times to the Present*. New York: Harpers, 1972.

McGovern, James R. "Anna Howard Shaw: New Approaches to Feminism." *Journal of Social History* 3 (Winter 1969): 135–153.

McHenry, Robert, ed. *Liberty's Women*. Springfield, Mass.: Merrian, 1980.

Morgan, David. *Suffragists and Democrats: The Politics of Woman Suffrage in America*. East Lansing: Michigan State University Press, 1972.

Mowry, George. *The California Progressives*. Berkeley: University of California Press, 1951.

————. *The Progressive Movement 1900–1920: Recent Ideas and New Literature*. Washington, D.C.: American Historical Association, 1958.

————. *Theodore Roosevelt and the Progressive Movement*. Madison: University of Wisconsin Press, 1946.

Moynihan, Ruth Barnes. *Rebel for Rights: Abigail Scott Duniway*. New Haven: Yale University Press, 1983.

Nichols, Carole. *Votes and More for Women: Suffrage and After in Connecticut*. New York: Haworth, 1983.

Noun, Louise R. *Strong-Minded Women: The Emergence of the Woman-Suffrage Movement in Iowa*. Ames: Iowa State University Press, 1969.

Oakley, Mary Ann B. *Elizabeth Cady Stanton*. Old Westbury, N.Y.: Feminist Press, 1972.

O'Neill, William L. *Everyone Was Brave: The Rise and Fall of Feminism in America*. Chicago: University of Chicago Press, 1969.

————. *The Progressive Years*. New York: Dodd, Mead, 1975.

Parker, Gail. *The Oven Birds: American Women on Womanhood: 1820–1920*. Garden City, N.Y.: Doubleday, 1972.

Parrington, Vernon L. *Main Currents in American Thought*. New York: Harcourt, Brace, 1930.

Paulson, Ross Evans. *Women's Suffrage and Prohibition: A Comparative Study of Equality and Social Control*. Chicago: Scott, Foresman, 1973.

Randall, Mercedes M. *Improper Bostonian: Emily Greene Balch*. New York: Twayne, 1964.

Reed, Dorinda Riessen. *The Woman Suffrage Movement in South Dakota*. Pierre: State University of South Dakota, 1958.

Riegel, Robert F. *American Feminists*. Lawrence: University of Kansas, 1963.

————. *American Women: A Story of Social Change*. Rutherford, N.J.: Fairleigh Dickinson University Press, 1970.

Ryan, Mary P. *Womanhood in America*. New York: New Viewpoints, 1975.

Schaffer, Ronald. "The New York City Woman Suffrage Party." *New York History* 43 (July 1962): 269–287.

Scharf, Lois, and Jensen, Joan, ed. *Decades of Discontent: The Women's Movement: 1920–1940*. Westport, Conn.: Greenwood, 1983.

Schiesl, Martin. *The Politics of Efficiency: Municipal Administration and Reform in America*. Berkeley: University of California Press, 1977.

Schramm, Sarah Slavin. *Plow Women Rather Than Reapers: An Intellectual History of Feminism in the United States*. Metuchen, N.J.: Scarecrow, 1979.

Scott, Anne Firor. *Making the Invisible Woman Visible*. Urbana: University of Illinois Press, 1984.

————. *Women in American Life: Selected Readings*. Boston: Houghton Mifflin, 1970.

Scott, Anne Firor, and Scott, Andrew. *One Half the People: The Fight for Woman Suffrage*. Philadelphia: Lippincott, 1975.

Sinclair, Andrew. *The Better Half: The Emancipation of the American Woman*. New York: Harper & Row, 1965.

Sochen, June. *Movers and Shakers: American Women Thinkers and Activists 1900–1970*. Chicago: Quadrangle, 1973.

————. *The New Woman in Greenwich Village: 1910–1920*. Chicago: Quadrangle, 1972.

Steinson, Barbara J. *American Women's Activism in World War I*. New York: Garland, 1982.

Strom, Sharon Hartman. "Leadership and Tactics in the American Woman Suffrage Movement: A New Perspective from Massachusetts." In Jean E. Friedman and William G. Shade, ed., *Our American Sisters: Women in American Life and Thought*. Boston: Allyn & Bacon, 1976.

Tax, Meredith. *The Rising of the Women: Feminist Solidarity and Class Conflict: 1880–1917*. New York: Monthly Review Press, 1980.

Taylor, A. Elizabeth. *The Woman Suffrage Movement in Tennessee*. New York: Bookman, 1957.

Terborg-Penn, Rosalyn. "Discontented Black Feminists: Prelude and Postscript to the Passage of the Nineteenth Amendment." Pp. 261–278 in Lois Scharf and Joan Jensen, ed., *Decades of Discontent: The Women's Movement: 1920–1940*. Westport, Conn.: Greenwood, 1983.

Thelen, David P. *The New Citizenship: Origins of Progressivism in Wisconsin, 1885–1900*. Columbia: University of Missouri Press, 1972.

Walker, Lola Carolyn. "The Speeches and Speaking of Carrie Chapman Catt." Ph.D. dissertation, Northwestern University, 1950.

Weinstein, James. *The Corporate Ideal in the Liberal State: 1900–1918*. Boston: Beacon, 1968.

Wexler, Alice. *Emma Goldman: An Intimate Life*. New York: Pantheon, 1984.

Wiebe, Robert H. *The Search for Order: 1877–1920*. New York: Hill and Wang, 1967.

Zimmerman, Loretta E. "Alice Paul and the National Woman's Party: 1912–1920." Ph.D. dissertation, Tulane University, 1964.

Index